Reaching Out to

SPECIAL
PEOPLE

**A Resource for Ministry With Persons
Who Have Disabilities**

Reaching Out to

SPECIAL
PEOPLE

A Resource for Ministry With Persons Who Have Disabilities

Jim Pierson and Robert E. Korth, Editors

STANDARD PUBLISHING
Cincinnati, Ohio   29-03139

Library of Congress Cataloging-in-Publication Data

Reaching out to special people : a resource for ministry with
persons who have disabilities / edited by Jim Pierson and
Robert E. Korth.
    p. cm.
   Bibliography: p.
   Includes index
   ISBN 0-87403-569-4
  1. Church work with the mentally handicapped.
2. Church work with the handicapped.   I. Pierson, Jim.
II. Korth, Robert E.
BV4461.R4   1989
259'.4 – dc20   89-4560
                                       CIP

Expressing the views of their own hearts, the authors may express views
not entirely consistent with those of the publisher.

Unless otherwise indicated, all Scripture quotations are from the *Holy
Bible, New International Version,* copyright © 1973, 1978, 1984 by the
International Bible Society. Used by permission of Zondervan Bible Pub-
lishers and the International Bible Society.

The chapter "Overcoming Barriers" is copyright © 1989 by Harold H.
Wilke.

Contributors

B.D. Briese is Senior Pastor of the Ipswich Baptist Church, Queensland, Australia. He has taught religious education and special education at the Brisbane College of Advanced Education. He also lectures and contributes to journals on the subject of religious education for mentally retarded persons.

Jerry L. Borton is the founder and director of Power Ministries, Clarksville, Indiana. Power Ministries assists churches in becoming aware of the needs and abilities of persons with disabilities and developing programs for them. Mr. Borton was born with cerebral palsy and is a 1983 graduate of Cincinnati Bible College.

Duane King is founder and director of Deaf Missions, Council Bluffs, Iowa. Deaf Missions prepares and distributes Bible visuals for deaf people and trains workers for deaf ministries. Mr. King has also served as a minister, singer, and a worker with the National Missionary Convention and the North American Christian Convention.

Marsha B. Uselton is a vision specialist with Knox County (Tennessee) schools, where she teaches visually impaired children

5

educated in regular classes. She has taught special education students for eighteen years, and has written and illustrated for education journals and other publications.

Sue Abegglen is Associate Professor of Education at Culver-Stockton College in Canton, Missouri. She teaches methods courses to elementary and special education teachers. She has taught people with learning disabilities in public and private school, in Bible school, and as a tutor.

Linda King is Associate Professor of Health and Physical Education at Milligan College, where she teaches motor learning. She taught a class of children with learning disabilities for several years at a church in Springfield, Ohio.

Carol Carrington teaches children with learning disabilities in the Crawfordsville, Indiana public schools, and helps with the special education Bible school class in her church. She has also taught those with emotional disturbance in the Children's Christian Home in Ladoga, Indiana.

Robert O. Fife is a minister and teacher. He taught at Milligan College for 21 years. He is co-founder of the Westwood Christian Foundation. He has taught at Pepperdine University, Fuller Theological Seminary, and Johnson Bible College, and is presently on the faculty of Emanuel School of Religion.

Harold H. Wilke is founder and director of The Healing Community, an organization that helps congregations become accessible to persons with disabilities. He has taught at the Menninger Foundation School of Psychiatry and at Union Theological Seminary, New York, and is a consultant to government and rehabilitation agencies. He is the author of four books, including *Creating the Caring Congregation* (Abingdon).

Shirley L. Leutton is the mother of four adult children, including a daughter with mental retardation. She is a full-time worker with Crossroads Fellowship with Handicapped Persons, Queensland, Australia.

Laura Knoop Burton has supervised various types of residential facilities for persons with mental retardation and other handicaps. She has taught daily living, social, and work skills for the Hamilton County (Ohio) Board of Mental Retardation.

Deborah Shell is a music teacher and therapist with Knox County (Tennessee) schools, where she teaches children with multiple handicaps, and a children's choir director. She has a Masters of Music Education from the University of Georgia.

Don Crooker is founder and executive director of Christian Berets, Modesto, California. Christian Berets ministers to handicapped people throughout northern California in many ways, but mainly through its program of summer camps.

Bonnie G. Wheeler is the mother of several children with disabilities, some adopted. She is also the author of several books, including *Challenged Parenting* (Regal) and *Meet the Overcomers* (Moody Press), and a popular speaker at conferences and retreats.

Marie B. Latta is a disabilities and special needs consultant. She has taught children with behavior disorders for the Atlanta school systems. She is also Director of the Ministry to Handicapped Children at Mt. Carmel Christian Church, Atlanta, Georgia.

Gloria Fife Lacy has a major in English and a minor in Special Education, and teaches the fundamental English class at Farragut High School in Knoxville, Tennessee. She has worked in many Bible-school special education programs. Her lessons were written as a result of work done at Johnson Bible College.

Contents

Close Enough to Notice

I first learned about Dorothy when she applied to become a resident at the Riverwood Christian Community (a residential facility for adults with mental retardation). At first my knowledge was through letters from her parents and a couple from her.

When the Admissions Committee interviewed prospective residents in April of 1986, I met her. The benign tumors of von Recklinghausen's disease had disfigured her outward appearance. She had lived with the deformities most of her life. Having to deal with stares, unkind comments, and rejection had given her a special dignity. She walked with pride. An interviewer asked her if her home state, Michigan, was not a long way from Tennessee. Yes, it was, she replied. She would miss her parents (and cat) and she would be homesick, but here she would have friends.

Her loneliness was deep. I felt for her.

At lunch time Dorothy was waiting in line. I approached her to let her know that I saw *her*, not the tumors. A three-quarter length sleeve made it easy to deliberately touch the tumors on her hands and arms. Looking her in the eye, I remarked, "Dorothy, you are one of the most beautiful people I have ever seen."

"Thank you, Mr. Pierson," she said. "Most people don't get close enough to notice."

People need people. It is easy to care for people who look like us, think like us, talk like us, walk like us, and yell for the same football team we do. But if they don't, we put up barriers that block the caring. People with disabilities are frequently omitted from our caring. This book is meant to help remove the barriers by describing who they are, what their needs are, and how we can help. It's about being close enough to notice the needs of people with disabilities – especially the spiritual needs.

The focus of our concern is persons with mental retardation. The Lord told His followers that His gospel was for everyone. No one should be denied the right to know the Good News. Many persons with mental retardation achieve a mental age of 9 to 13 years, the age at which many people become Christians. The church has a responsibility to them. Those who do not achieve this mental age need to learn as much about Jesus and His teachings as their cognitive skills will permit. Every person, no matter what his mental ability, needs to know that he is cared about. That ministry can be done without a word. A look, a touch, an act of acceptance – gifts invaluable to people who need them.

Persons with other handicaps need to be taught as well. In my introduction to a 1977 book, I noted: "The barriers that prevent the blind and the orthopedically handicapped from being taught in church are mainly physical and do not relate to learning per se." But I've learned a lesson since then. While this statement is accurate, persons with other handicaps are often kept from the Christian education programs of the church because attitudinal barriers prevent acceptance and inclusion in the life of the congregation. In short, they need to be present before they can be taught. The co-editor of this book, Robert E. Korth, shared a startling statistic he learned at a conference on ministry to persons with disabilities: Only five percent of the congregations in the United States have formal programs for persons with disabilities!

While we want congregations to use this book to start ministries, we also want individuals to be involved with individuals who have disabilities. It is a rewarding experience. The chapter by Shirley Leutton gives some excellent help. My life is richer not just because I have worked with people having disabilities, but also because they have ministered to me.

Recently I attended a worship service for a large group of persons with disabilities. During the prayer time the leader requested prayer for my safety in travel – I would have to drive 300 miles that afternoon. Another man requested prayer for his mother, who would have surgery the next day. A lady asked for prayer for a family whose father had died. There were others, but I remember those three. I bowed my head and soon became aware that hands were touching my shoulders, arms, and hands. Looking up, I saw members of the group also surrounding the man and the lady and the others who had requested prayer. They wanted us to know they supported us. The experience was moving. I received ministry! To this day, I work to make my prayers for people personal.

The language in this book reflects our attitude toward people and our adherence to current usage. People with disabilities are first and foremost people. They love, care, think, hope, dream, cry, forget, get angry, sneeze, and do everything else people do. In order to communicate who we are talking about, we have said "people" or "persons" followed by "with mental retardation" or "with learning disabilities," or whatever disability. Sometimes, for the ease of construction, we have used the participle – "retarded adults." As individual chapters develop, you will notice the use of "people" and "persons" without a prepositional phrase or a participle. The reference to a specific disability is clear by then, and using it repeatedly serves no real purpose.

Because some of our writers work with children, they naturally used the words "child" and "children" in their writing. In editing, we left their original language; perhaps "child" was changed to "person." The principles being discussed can be used with children or adults.

Eighteen individuals contribute to the work. By experience and heart they are "close enough to notice." Each one of them does what they tell you to do. They minister *with* people, not just to them.

Two contributors are Australians. Brian Briese taught special education teachers at the college level. Shirley Leutton works with Crossroads, an organization that provides travel experience for people with handicaps by enlisting people without handicaps to travel with them as companions. They travel all over the world. It is a great experience. My wife, daughters, and I traveled for ten days in the Outback with a Crossroads tour.

Two of the contributors have written books that are widely

known. Bonnie Wheeler's *Challenged Parenting* and Harold Wilke's *Creating the Caring Congregation* have made excellent contributions to parents and to congregations.

When I reviewed Debbie Shell's and Marsha Uselton's chapters, I wished that we could add a videotape to each chapter so you could see them with their students. Debbie is a music therapist and Marsha is a vision specialist. I've watched them work. They are superior!

The co-editor of this book is a writer, a good one. He knows his craft. For six years he has worked with people with mental retardation as a volunteer in a group home and at church. He and his wife Dawn arranged their wedding so their friends from the group home could attend. The Korths made their friends their special guests. I was delighted when he volunteered to help with this book.

Each of the contributors to this book, like Bob, has experience and the heart to contribute. Enjoy the fruits of their ministries.

After you have read this book, we trust that the results will be a new Bible-school class, a person mainstreamed into a regular class, a renewed interest in an existing special education class, a commitment to a one-to-one ministry, or just a more caring attitude toward people—especially people with disabilities.

Your willingness to read and use the ideas in this book expands the ministries of each contributor. You will teach and nurture people we will never know. So, sincerely, thank you for being close enough to notice.

Jim Pierson
Knoxville, Tennessee
March, 1989

PART ONE

Persons With Mental Retardation

This first section looks in detail at persons with mental retardation:

- what they are like
- how they learn
- what learning deficiencies they have
- what techniques will help overcome these deficiencies
- how to set up a curriculum for teaching
- how a classroom can best be managed

But before you read about learning characteristics and lesson plans, you may just want to know what it's like teaching a Bible-school class of, and becoming friends with, a group of mentally retarded adults.

CHAPTER 1

Your Special Friends

*Misconceptions, temptations, and surprises
in ministry with adults
having mental retardation*

by Robert E. Korth

If you are reading this, you're probably a church leader or teacher who is in one of two situations. You're trying to decide whether to start a ministry to people with mental retardation, or some other disability, at your church. Or you're a veteran of such a ministry who knows someone, perhaps someone you're recruiting, trying to make the decision to join such a ministry. You (or your friend) are contemplating a kind of leap into the unknown, a strange new way of serving God and others. This chapter is meant for you.

I teach a Bible-school class of adults with mental retardation, and I have become friends with most of them. Perhaps hearing about my own mistakes and misconceptions, and what I've learned, will make you more comfortable about beginning a ministry with these people.

I have worked with thirty or forty people who have a wide range of ages, backgrounds, and abilities. My youngest was 13, my oldest about 58. Some came from Christian families and had Christian teaching; most did not. Some were abused in their home situations; some grew up in institutions because there was no place else for them to live. Most of my friends were "trainable," having an IQ below 50. A few were not able to communicate verbally. A few others were close to normal intelligence, able to

19

read and write, hold regular jobs, and live more or less independently.

Misconceptions

They Would Be All Alike

I thought that their mental disabilities would reduce them all to the same level, minimizing the natural differences that occur among people. They would act alike, think alike, talk alike. This was, you might have guessed, the silliest misconception of any, but I did think it. I couldn't have been more wrong! Their handicaps *accentuate* their differences rather than minimizing them.

Lori has a volatile personality. She is red-faced with tension even at her calmest, and it shows in her voice, too – she's never far from an explosion. But for Lori, singing is just as important a means of communicating as talking. She knows all the "oldies" from the fifties, commercial jingles, movie and show songs, and quite a few hymns and carols. Before I met her, I would have been too embarrassed to sit and sing a song with someone in the middle of a crowd of people. But often something you say reminds Lori of a song – from *Take Me Out to the Ball Game* to *The Old Rugged Cross*. She also loves birds and animals, rhymes, puns, and tongue-twisters – anything that makes or has to do with sound.

Dale is a scientist. He's rare in that he can understand some abstract principles. He can point to where he is on a map, and where his sister lives. He can talk about time travel in a movie he saw ("They went long, long ago, and then they came back"). He can look at a picture of Noah building the ark and tell me most of the story of Noah. But for all his smarts, Dale does not know the names of half the people at his group home – people he's been living with the past two years!

A year or two ago, Elizabeth could crack jokes and make conversation as well as anyone. She could also cook a meal for twenty people. She recently celebrated her 43rd birthday, but she has Alzheimer's disease moving into its advanced stages. "I'm still a spring chicken," she'll tell you, but soon she'll be unable to do or remember even the simplest function.

Bill's current fad is exercise. He gets anxious if he can't do his daily routine to his Richard Simmons tape. I'm convinced that Bill believes that the people he sees on TV and on tape are really talking to him. A friendly "You're doing great!" from Richard Simmons is apparently as real to him as a compliment from me. Usually when I see Bill, we sit down and write a letter to someone. Bill can read and write. He can spell even difficult words like September, Christmas, and Exercise, but he cannot put the words together into sentences. We used to write to TV personalities until I realized what he was doing; now I insist it must be "real" people he knows.

Angela has a pouting voice like Shirley Temple, but she's surprisingly tough and strong for her tiny stature. At 22, she's the "baby" of her group home. She's learning to do her laundry, which for her includes standing there all the while the washing machine runs. When she first came to the group home, she used to hide behind the curtains, avoiding other people, watching the cars and trucks on the highway outside and waiting for her mother to come in one of them. But now she is growing up. When I come in the door she shouts, "Bobby! Bobby!" and toddles up to me with arms open, crashes into me, and pounds me on the back.

I hope you're beginning to get the idea. You can't even communicate with two people exactly the same way. You have to learn what to do and say to each one individually.

They Would Be Not Quite Human

Wrong again. I can't explain what exactly I meant by this, besides the thought there would be something missing in them. But brain power doesn't make you human. My friends possess a complete range of emotions, reactions, aches, pains, joys, and fears, good and bad. In fact, often they illustrate for me in a simple way things that would be difficult to see in non-retarded people. You see, we do all the same things they do, but we are much more skillful at rationalizing or hiding it.

Carolyn was "the best" at her group home for a long time, and she was conscious of being the best, too. Last year she got to be an extra in the movie *Rain Man,* filmed partly in Cincinnati. When she found out she had been picked to go and take part in the filming, she started telling others about it. "I'm going to be in the movies. You can't go, David.... I get to go downtown and meet Dustin Hoffman, Bill. You don't." There wasn't much Bill and David could do. "I know," they said, over and over. I was disappointed in her attitude until I realized that many of us do this very thing, only we're just more skillful at it.

For weeks I taught my class about giving to the church, and they all seemed agreeable. But one morning they realized that I was talking about giving *their own money* to the church. They were horrified! "We have to buy clothes!" they protested. "We have to save money for our vacation!" They had been taught to be responsible with their money, and not to waste it on soda pop and cookies at the vending machines at work. It must have seemed to them that I was telling them to be irresponsible. But how many church leaders have heard comments just like these during a stewardship campaign?

One Sunday at camp a group of them woke me too early in the morning with their noisy behavior. I was still disgruntled during my "sermon" that morning. "Some of you act like a bunch of babies!" I said. No one had much of a reaction, except for Carolyn, who started to protest and then burst into tears. I had to go back on what I said. Here was the most responsible person in the group, the one who least needed to hear my accusation, and yet she was the one who took it to heart. What preacher hasn't had this experience?

Intellectual abilities aside, their other abilities—intuition, feeling, senses, their ability to appreciate visual beauty or music or humor, their capacity to feel pleasure or pain—is often as great as anyone's.

They Would Be Innocent Angels

I did not have this particular misconception myself, but some people do. The general idea is that most of these people lead blissfully ignorant lives, sheltered from the cares of the world, the traffic jams, taxes, and deadlines.

My friends may not have to face all the trials that we do, but they face trials and responsibilities that are equivalent for them. They do know right from wrong—not as abstract principles, but in terms of concrete actions and rules they abide by at home or at their group home, rules they need in order to live together well. A large part of our teaching at church is to show them that we and God uphold these rules: doing your chores, cleaning up after yourself, not stealing, telling a parent or staff member when you go out, and appealing to the staff instead of retaliating in a fight.

I have learned the importance of such rules and responsibilities by observing the lives of some people who have grown up without them. The people who had to learn and obey rules grew up; they could feed and dress and care for themselves and contribute to their community. Some loving parents, with the best of intentions, try to shelter their children, but such parental "grace" only makes their children more dependent and less capable of growing as persons. They need "law," too.

They Would Have Normal Health

I thought that for most of them, mental retardation was their only disability, and that physically they were completely healthy. But most of my friends have some physical problems as well; some have emotional problems. Down syndrome, for example, includes retardation but also the possibility of heart defects, the characteristic facial appearance, eye and ear problems, susceptibility to Alzheimer's disease, and other physical problems.

You will need to be careful of their diets, especially when you have a large class. Some can't have sugar, some can't have salt, some must have sugar because they cannot have artificial sweetener. Unsupervised at a potluck dinner, some will eat at full tilt until you physically remove the food from them (or them from it). Others insist on dieting and turn down snacks, at least as a gesture of willpower—the way some people might eat four slices of pizza but drink a diet soda pop.

I Would Need Formal Training

At first I thought I would need formal training in special education to be able to teach them. It helps, of course. Any training you can get will certainly benefit you. But the best training is to get to know the people personally—learn how to communicate with them, when to stand up to them, when to let things go, when to have fun, when to be serious, how to keep their interest, how to help them feel they belong. The best experience, for them as well as you, is to gain the kind of experience friends have with each other. Even if you have no formal training, you can contribute greatly to a special friend.

Your friendship and the relationships that you build are more important than your formal teaching. Granted, your role in their lives as a teacher helps to form the foundation for building a friendship.

Fears

There was no foundation for the misconceptions listed above, but there actually was some foundation for my fears. I had to face each one and deal with it, and in some cases, like the first one, it continues to take work. But in every case the fear turned out to be manageable, and usually not a serious problem at all.

I Would Not Be Able to Communicate

This was my greatest fear. About half of my friends have some difficulty with speech. From the start it actually was hard for me to understand some of them.

One thing you must not do is pretend you understand what someone is saying when you really don't. Chances are the other person will realize what you're doing. It's better just to admit you didn't understand, ask him to repeat himself, or ask for help from someone around you. Once during class I could not understand someone even after four or five attempts at speech and various gestures that looked like we were playing charades. Finally I gave up and asked the class, "Does anyone know what he's saying?" Sure enough, one of them interpreted for me.

Some of my friends have different kinds of communication problems. Many lack the language skills necessary for talking about complex feelings. They have trouble expressing themselves in a proper way when they are hurt, angry, or upset. Rather than tell what the problem is, they might withdraw, abuse themselves, or express anger in some unrelated way. Even if you cannot communicate with them in an instance like this, time spent with them will be seen as caring.

This too has its counterpart with non-retarded people – they are the kind of people who "don't do conflict well," who pretend everything is all right and go on hurting inside, who go home after a bad day and yell at the kids.

They Would Not Be Able to Learn

They can learn, but the process is slow. Often you will have to repeat a whole lesson for an idea or task similar to one you have just taught, because it is difficult for them to draw a general conclusion from a series of ideas or events. For many of my friends, the theoretical does not exist. Theology does not exist. What we call "doctrine" does not exist. If they cannot see something, then it is not there.

Once I sat with the class while someone else taught. "We all know that Jesus is here with us," the teacher began.

I could hear David objecting in the front row: "No, He isn't."

The teacher tried to calm him – "Oh, yes, Jesus is here with us, isn't He?" – but she was unsuccessful.

David's objections got louder, and he stood up. "Where is Jesus? He is *not* here! I don't see Him." I could hardly blame him. Like some of my other friends, David forgets to wash his hair on the back of his head because he cannot see it when he looks in the mirror. If he can't see it, it's not there.

In my class the students' abilities vary widely, and almost nothing you can do is going to keep the interest of all of them at once. I have taught classes in which I went around the room and spoke to each one in turn. The others would lose interest when it wasn't their turn, but at least I could have some contact with everyone.

They can learn, but each individual learns in unique ways. The more different kinds of learning experiences you can give them, the more likely you will be getting through to all of them.

They Might Get Violent

Yes, I admit it, they might. But as the father of one of my special students will tell you, "Then again, *I* might get violent." We have had incidents of pinching and hair-pulling, and these had to be disciplined. We have never had an instance where a person has been out of control, though it has happened to one of our friends once when we weren't around.

Most of the violence I see them commit is directed at *themselves*—several of my friends have the tendency to self-abuse when they are upset or they are in an unpleasant situation. One friend had a problem at home the weekend before, and he would not talk about it. Instead he went off by himself and scratched his arms until they bled. When I saw him, his arms were covered with band-aids, but he would not tell me what was bothering him. It makes me wonder again about us non-retarded people. Do we just have more subtle ways of doing the same kind of self-destructive things?

I Could Not Help in an Emergency

I was worried at first that one of them would get upset or sick, or have a seizure—and I would not know what to do.

One of the earliest things I had to learn was what to do in case one of them had a seizure. You lie the person down on his side, listen to make sure he can breathe properly, support his head, and keep him still. The seizure should last up to a couple minutes. Time how long it takes, record the incident, and report it to those caring for him—his family or group home staff. If it takes longer than three minutes, and keeps persisting, or if there are repeated seizures, call an ambulance. Afterward the person may need to void or act disoriented or want to sleep.

We have had seizures occur several times during Bible-school class, but have never had to call an ambulance.

Temptations

To Think of Them as Children

"How are your kids?" most of my non-retarded friends ask me, and I no longer correct them as I used to. I no longer correct them because I know they realize as well as I do that my friends are not children. But some people, myself included, resort to that word for shorthand.

They are not children. Some of my friends go to night clubs and dance. They have dating relationships. None have married yet, but marriage is a possibility for some of them. Some of them talk about going to live in their own apartments. Independence is a goal that we encourage if it seems within their reach.

Adults do not, as a rule, like lessons that talk down to them as if they were children, or pictures or crafts that are obviously made for children. Sometimes they will tolerate these for the sake of the others among them not as advanced.

To Do Everything for Them

The same temptation exists, say, for a church leader and a new assistant, a teacher and a student, or a parent and child. If you can do a task better and faster, you are tempted to do it for them rather than allowing them or teaching them to do it for themselves. But you do this at your peril. Some of them are fiercely independent and want to do their own work, however imperfect it is, and will get angry with you. Worse yet, some of them will learn dependence on you and *let* you do everything for them.

You have to get to know each person individually and learn what they are capable of and incapable of. Then you can judge how to help and when not to help. Even then, I usually make it a practice to ask permission whenever proposing to help one of my friends. A simple, "Would you like me to help you do that?" will often get you a quick, direct answer one way or the other and avoid misunderstandings.

To Get Discouraged

It can be easy to think, after a while, that you really are not having any effect on them and that they do not appreciate what you do for them. You see little change in them, even after years of work. You can get to feel that you're doing very little good and that they don't particularly care about you.

We sit in the worship service once each month, trying hard to keep quiet and yet stay awake. We recognize some of the hymns, and sing along with those. Our minds tend to wander during a long sermon, especially if it isn't funny or colorful. We understand that the Lord's Supper is something very important and very special, but we really don't understand what it all means. And finally when it is time to leave, our minds start going back immediately to the events of home and what we're supposed to be doing the rest of the day.

Now if that last paragraph sounds a little like you and me, it was supposed to. It may be a negative way of making the point, but how much change do you see in non-retarded people? It's almost as easy to get discouraged with them.

To Overestimate Them

I suppose it's a greater temptation to underestimate them, but this one exists too. I overestimate my friends' ability to do certain logical processes, simple ones, that I take for granted. Finding patterns in thought and making comparisons is natural for me, and I thought they could do simple ones. They can, but only after much training on a specific operation. As a rule, my friends cannot generalize; they cannot draw a principle of thinking from a series of concrete operations.

Surprises

They Will Participate

The point is made elsewhere in this book that it is better to have a ministry *with* persons having disabilities than a ministry *to* them. I found this to be true even for my class. They will participate in what you plan. They will respond better if you can show them how they can be involved. You do not have to do everything for them. At camp, they volunteer to help clean up the dishes after eating. During Bible-school class certain everyday chores are looked forward to by the people who help with them – passing the offering box, setting up chairs and tables, collecting the trash, passing out napkins or craft supplies.

Once or twice a year, we have our own formal worship service in class. The week before we discuss the service and all the jobs that need to be done – announcements, prayer, song leading, passing the offering box, and serving the Lord's Supper. We ask for volunteers for these jobs. On our first try, no less than five people volunteered to stand up and bring special music for the whole group. We heard them all.

They're Fun

I had hoped to find this a fulfilling ministry, but I didn't expect it to be as much fun as it is. My friends are often hilarious. They still say and do things I don't expect, and they are just plain fun to be around and to do things with. Usually I come away in a better mood from having been with them, like I would from seeing any group of friends—even those times I hadn't been looking forward to seeing them.

"What did you do today?" Elizabeth asked my wife one night.

"Oh, I just cleaned house," she said. "The kitchen and the living room and the bedroom. Everything except Bob's desk."

"Yeah," said Elizabeth, I'm sure with that familiar tone of sympathy, "he should learn to do that for himself."

Another conversation took place with JoAnne. "Do you get much exercise?" she asked.

"No, I work in an office. I sit at a desk all day."

"You can exercise your butt that way," JoAnne said, with perfect seriousness.

We go bowling together about once a year. We occupy three lanes at the far end of the alley, jammed solid with people needing shoes tied and bowling balls selected. We take an hour and a half to bowl one game each. In general we make a complete spectacle of ourselves, the entire group cheering and applauding whenever someone makes a strike (in some cases, if they knock down any pins at all).

When I visit the group home on summer evenings, a bunch of us go out and throw a softball around. Kenny hardly ever says anything, but he is an exuberant ball player. He cries out with joy whenever that ball hits his glove, and his face sags with disappointment when it's time to go in.

You Can Form Lasting Friendships

When Dorothy was nine, she was placed in a state institution. There were family problems and she had some slight birth defects, but there was nowhere else for her to go. She could have lived a near normal life but as it turned out, she lived at the institution for forty years until it closed. While there she made friends she still has to this day, people who went to different group homes in the area after the institution closed down.

I know more about Dorothy, from what she told me herself, than I know about many friends. I have visited her in the hospital, had her to my house Christmas day, joked with her ("Santa's bringing you a switch with a ribbon on it," she told me), discussed Communion ("It tasted sweet. It won't hurt you"), and showed her samples of the books I have edited ("How do you get all those words in there so neat, all in rows like that?").

I've been with my friends to camp, to Special Olympics, at my own wedding, on vacation, at graduation from school, and just doing nothing.

They Understand More Than They Show

Just because they don't communicate it back to you, it does not mean they haven't understood. Jimmy is about 30 and has Down syndrome. He seldom said more than a word at a time, and only after coaxing. I had assumed he had a very low level of understanding. But driving him home one day, I found he understood perfectly what I was talking about. He rolled up his window when I mentioned it and pointed out his house for me as we approached. At a restaurant once I watched as Jimmy sang "Happy Birthday" to some lady at a neighboring table, after the waitress brought them a cake.

Virginia is another one. She does not speak at all, and her face is not very expressive. Rarely she will express anger or delight at something, but it happens. We made a paper plane for her one night and started flying it back and forth to her, and she obviously enjoyed that. Another time I sat and watched her blowing soap bubbles at camp. She was all alone. She raised up her hand and blew a bubble, then lowered her hand and watched it float away, colors dancing on its surface, and fall slowly, brush the grass, and vanish. Then she raised her hand again, blew another bubble, and stood and watched.

There's a lot going on inside even the most unresponsive person. They understand much more than you suppose.

How They Learn

*Learning characteristics of persons
having mental retardation*

by B. D. Briese

The first step in learning how to teach learners with mental retardation is to understand what the term means. It is not a disease, though diseases may cause it or accompany it. The following definitions are made not to limit our concept of mental retardation or people who have it, but to give us a common basis for further discussion.

Some Definitions

Mentally retarded and intellectually normal people are more alike than different. In many areas a child with mental retardation functions as a normal child, but as a normal child at a younger age—especially if he suffers from no specific syndrome and has an IQ over 50. Some differ from non-retarded people only in their slow rate and lower level of cognitive development. They pass through the cognitive development stages in the same order but at a slower rate, and they may stop growing at a lower level. Others, because of a specific syndrome and the resulting physical appearance, may stand out from the rest of the population.

Some children may develop normally in one area of learning, be well behind in others, and miss some areas altogether. Nothing can be taken for granted.

Mental Retardation

The term has been defined in a variety of ways over the years. The 1983 AAMR (American Association on Mental Retardation) definition is the most commonly accepted.

Mental retardation refers to significantly subaverage general intellectual functioning resulting in or associated with concurrent impairments in adaptive behavior and manifested during the developmental period.

To be classified as "mentally retarded," a person must be well below average in both *intellectual functioning* and *adaptive behavior* while passing through the *developmental period.* These three concepts are explained below.

Intellectual Functioning. For the purpose of placement in programs, persons with mental retardation are classified in groups. Among organizations like the AAMR and the NARC (National Association for Retarded Citizens), the most common classification system was as follows:

Level	IQ
mild	55-69
moderate	40-54
severe	25-39
profound	24 and below

The educational system divides the same population into three groups:

Level	IQ
Educable (EMR)	50-75 or 80
Trainable (TMR)	25-50
Dependent (DMR)	below 25

Adaptive behavior is more important than IQ in determining a person's level of capability. Adaptive behavior refers to how well he adjusts to the natural and social demands of his environment and age. The same child who scores low on an intelligence test may be "streetwise" when it comes to taking care of himself, riding the bus, or communicating with his peers.

Adaptive behavior changes with age. It moves to higher levels as a child grows. In early childhood, social skills, self-help, sensory-motor, and communication skills are important. In childhood and early adolescence, academic skills in daily living activities, mastering the environment, and interpersonal skills are more highly valued. In late adolescence and adulthood, job skills and social responsibilities become predominant.

Developmental period. This usually refers to the time between conception and eighteen years of age, during which a person's intellectual, physical, educational, emotional, social, and moral development occurs.

Mental Age

Mental age (M.A.) is a measure of all the person's abilities according to a formula that does not take into account variations in ability in different kinds of learning. (C.A. is chronological age.)

$$\text{M.A.} = \frac{(\text{C.A.}) \times (\text{IQ})}{100}$$

According to the formula, for example, a person 25 years old having an IQ of 40 would have a mental age of 10.

People having the same mental ages might be similar in some ways, but an older person with a lower IQ would have much more experience to draw from. Adaptive behavior levels could also be different even though mental ages were identical. Mental age, then, is a poor variable for grouping purposes, and a doubtful predicter of learning ability, except in young EMR children.

Characteristics of the Learners

All mentally retarded persons have potential for growth and learning, but they are slow and inefficient learners. Their development parallels that of non-retarded people, but at a slower rate. Not every mentally retarded person has all the following learning characteristics, but all of these can be found within any large group of them. Their behavior varies widely, and each one must be considered as a separate and unique person.

After each characteristic is discussed, there will follow a short list of techniques the teacher can use to facilitate learning in this area.

Reduced Ability to Learn

Compared to their chronological-age peers, they are deficient in some areas of learning ability. More time to learn is also needed.

- Be patient, unhurried and calm.
- Discover the learning pace and interest of each student and instruct him in that pace.
- Let the student know you expect him to succeed.

Failure and Negative Self-Image

When people fail they lose faith in themselves and develop a negative self-image. Many mentally retarded people experience repeated failure. They have come to expect failure and disappointment. Their approach to learning problems is one filled with apprehension and misgivings. Each student wants to succeed and secure the approval of teachers or parents, but if they have a history of failure, they tend to put their energy into *avoiding failure* rather than striving for success.

Students respond to failure in one or more of the following ways:

- Learn to expect failure.
- React passively and make stereotyped responses.
- Avoid situations they perceive as having potential for failure.

- Become defensive and make excuses for avoiding these situations.
- Accept a low level of success.
- Act out aggressively in response to a situation perceived as threatening failure.
- Respond impulsively and not expect success.

As negative self-image and learned helplessness grow, people tend to look outside of themselves for approval and support. They are seen as unwilling to spend the time and effort to master learning tasks, while at the same time they depend on parents or teachers for direction. They also have difficulty monitoring their own behavior. Since research suggests that mentally retarded people have more energy than their non-retarded peers, they will have problems channeling their energy into worthwhile learning pursuits.

Only *repeated success* (through practice and overlearning) can enhance students' feelings about themselves and motivate them to learn. This is the teacher's most important role and the test of all his teaching strategies and techniques.

- Help each student to perceive a need to learn.
- Plan for success. Never let the student fail. Successful experiences create a desire to learn. Build a success-oriented classroom atmosphere.
- Use familiar events and materials in classroom activities.
- Allow students to participate in developing rules that govern the class.
- Encourage social interaction by having class members praise each other for efforts at success.
- Provide opportunities for the students to demonstrate their particular areas of competence such as art, music, dance, physical education, crafts, etc.

Attention Difficulties

Students with mental retardation are highly distractable, lacking the ability to pay attention. The concept of attention is a complex one. Attention can be broken down into three distinct components:

- attention span—the length of time a person can concentrate on a task
- attention focus—the result of ignoring or preventing distractions
- selective attention—choosing the important characteristics of a task and paying attention to those alone

Your students have poor attention spans. They have difficulty screening out distractions so they can focus on the task and in choosing the most important features to concentrate on. Studies have shown, though, that *once attention was gained,* learning took place at about the same rate as non-retarded children. They generally take longer to learn a task, but they do as well as non-retarded children once they "catch on" to the correct solution.

- Seat students away from doors and windows where they could look out.
- Use pictures and objects that have clear and obvious dimensions.
- Only selected stimuli should be present. Put all other pictures and equipment away so they do not distract.
- Combine as many senses as possible in the learning task.

Memory Deficits

Memory may be the most heavily studied learning characteristic of mentally retarded persons. It is an area in which they have long been regarded as deficient. Some of the most consistent findings relate to short-term memory (STM) and long-term memory (LTM).

Retarded children do poorly on exercises requiring recall from STM. Once they have learned the material, they do just as well as their non-retarded peers in recall from LTM. Most people, in order to remember a grocery list or a telephone number, *rehearse* the information aloud or inaudibly in order to keep the details "alive" in their STM long enough to be acted upon. Retarded persons do not usually rehearse in these situations. They lose a great deal of information they are capable of remembering.

Rehearsal plays a crucial role in memory. Without it material may be quickly lost from STM. In most normal children this strategy is clearly evidenced by third grade.

Rehearsal over carefully spaced periods of time facilitates the "planting" of material in LTM. This process is called *overlearning* when it goes beyond the point of initial mastery.

- Use meaningful material out of the person's experience.
- Provide repetition, drill, and review to aid long-term memory.
- Provide incentives for remembering.
- Move from simple to more complex situations.
- Provide an opportunity for the learner to practice skills in many different contexts using his different senses.

Concept Formation Problems

Forming concepts is a way of organizing information from the environment around us so we can make sense out of the many thousands of "messages" we receive through the senses every day. Concepts allow us to sort and categorize information so that we don't have to learn something all over again every time the brain receives a similar piece of information.

Understanding the *sameness* and *differences* of objects is a crucial first step toward concept formation. *Association* is a second. Similar objects or events are first of all loosely associated as precepts. These associations are later enlarged and strengthened through abstraction and generalization to form concepts. Concept formation is closely linked to problem solving.

Retarded people form concepts the same way as their non-retarded peers, but at a slower rate. Concept formation is more closely associated with mental age than chronological age, though experience plays a significant role.

Concept attainment is not easy for retarded children. Even with instruction they are still easily confused. To compensate, routines should be established in instruction. Care must be taken to avoid "concept leaps"—large steps in sequential learning—and to match instruction to the child's cognitive level.

- Look for likenesses and differences among objects. Group for likenesses and differences.

- Look for sequence in story cards; events that precede other events.
- Develop lessons that allow the learner to *do* rather than to see and listen.

Problem Solving Inabilities

Attention to detail and memory are essential for problem solving. Retarded people have deficits in both these areas. Another aspect of problem solving relates to asking questions intended to secure information.

Questions that refer to more than one alternative are *constraint-seeking;* questions that refer to an individual item are *hypothesis-testing.* Retarded people tend to perform poorly on problem-solving tasks because they ask random hypothesis-testing questions. They also tend to be impulsive in answering questions, giving quick, frequently incorrect answers. The more reflective learners respond more slowly and accurately.

Retarded people find it difficult to adapt objects or ideas that have been used repeatedly in one type of situation for novel use in another context—for example, using the heel of a shoe to hammer a tack if a hammer is not available.

- Encourage the student to design a simple plan of action in separate steps.
- Reward students for reflective responses.

Deficient Learning Set

The terms *learning set* and *transfer set* refer to the ability of a person to learn how to solve additional problems because of previous experience with similar situations. This ability has sometimes been called "learning to learn." The ability to establish a learning set seems to be directly related to mental age; it is tied to concept formation and problem solving. When retarded persons are given an opportunity to solve and master easy problems before being exposed to more difficult problems, the learning set is established more rapidly. Generally, retarded people form learning sets and transfer sets more slowly than do normal people.

The reverse type of *learning set* or *transfer set* is called *failure* set. Retarded people experience much failure in their everyday lives.

- Present easier material first and gradually increase the difficulty.
- Assist the student in developing rules and generalizations to transfer learned information to new experiences.
- Present many examples.
- Provide language for the student that describes what he has learned.

Imaginative Play Deficits

Play is a natural setting for social skills training and is closely linked to imitation (observational learning) and incidental learning. Through play children improve strength and coordination. They also adopt various roles and emotionally prepare themselves for older or adult behaviors. They also test their competence and capacity to control the world.

Mentally retarded children generally do not initiate play. When they do, it is at a stage below that of chronological age peers. In some instances a child may isolate himself from other children and refuse to interact. Such a condition of withdrawal may require expert help by way of play therapy. It is not unusual to see mentally retarded children playing with younger children. This is natural for them, because interest is closely tied to mental age.

Perspective-taking (seeing something from the other person's point of view) is also slower to emerge; the egocentric (self-centered) stage of development persists longer than it does in normal children. Cooperative play and sharing also come later. Imagination, resourcefulness, and innovation are lacking in most play situations.

Learning through play is not so much trial-and-error and role-playing as with non-retarded children, but it depends heavily upon imitating other children at play. Because of attention and STM deficits, mentally retarded children may not stay at any one activity for very long.

For certain levels of retardation, even in adulthood, it may be necessary to provide specific instruction in play and recreational activities. Meeting "adult-infant" play needs of dependent adults poses particular problems, if their chronological age is 40 but their mental age is 5.

- Plan play periods so that specific social skills are learned.
- Use drama, puppets, pictograph, etc. to involve the students in gaining and keeping knowledge or skills.
- Establish a warm, friendly atmosphere at play. Try not to overdirect or dampen enthusiasm or initiative.
- Use the names of the students in "Hello" songs. Name use is critical for the development of self-image.

Socialization and Moral Development

Learning associated with socialization, self-care, making of friends and moral judgment is closely linked to imaginative play. A person's social and self-help skills are closely related to mental age, but they also depend upon training and social learning through experience. The same may be said about values development and moral awareness.

It cannot be taken for granted that retarded children will learn *incidentally* from experience. Even with careful instruction using small steps (task analysis), progress is often slow.

- Friendship-making and moral awareness can be increased by the use of role-play strategies.

Inability to Express Ideas

Ideas can be expressed vocally, by gestures, in writing, or through key pressing in computer programs.

Mentally retarded children tend to be poor in all these areas. The situation is probably due to production deficiency, lack of early stimulation, poor models in the home, and inability to learn incidentally.

Carrying on a conversation entails responding to a speaker within a certain time, turn-taking, and catching on to what he is talking about. Retarded people are slow in reaction time, and it is further reduced by attention problems. Impulsiveness – the tendency to rush into action without considering the consequences, answering without thought or interrupting, may also tend to terminate a conversation. This is characteristic of mentally retarded and learning disabled children when they become interested in what is being done. Normal children tend to be more reflective and are better problem solvers.

Slow reaction time and impulsiveness may appear in the same person given changing circumstances. In addition, mentally retarded children have a reduced ability to use language.

What is true in conversations is also true of the expression of ideas by gesture, writing, or computer. Poor fine motor coordination, short-term menory, and attention problems all add up to poor expression, even though an idea may be in the retarded person's mind.

- Acting out a favorite story, or re-enacting a Bible story while telling it, aids in language development.
- Students should feel that their efforts are not heavily evaluated or criticized.
- Have "show and tell" sessions in which students bring something and talk about it.
- Show a picture and have pupils tell about it. Have them guess what may have happened before and after.

Physical Characteristics and Depressed Learning Ability

Most EMR children are similar to normal children in height, weight, and motor coordination. A small number are inferior in health and in coordination. Many TMR and DMR children, because of organic causes, are physically inferior and have poor coordination. Other handicaps – vision, hearing, and cerebral palsy – often accompany mental retardation. Because of depressed academic learning ability, sensory experience and physical motion appeal to him more than verbalization.

- Plan concrete experiences to facilitate learning.
- Readiness activities suitable for non-retarded kindergarten children are useful, but keep in mind that your learners are older chronologically and may have had different experiences.

Productive Thinking Inability

It cannot be assumed that retarded children can "think for themselves." They generally lack creativity of thought and are poor in spontaneous productive thinking but possess potential for being trained. Productive thinking should be encouraged through carefully structured problem-solving strategies.

- Play a game of "What would happen if..." and list the alternatives the students offer. Evaluate these in terms of the problem.

Behavior Problems

There are more behavior problems and slightly more delinquency among retarded persons than among people of average intelligence. Such problems interfere with learning.

A major cause is the discrepancy between what is expected of him and his capacity to perform. Another is his need for recognition, which leads to attention-getting behavior. A third is his low frustration tolerance.

Control over conduct disorders is necessary for successful teaching to take place. The teacher can maintain control through enhancing the learners' self-image, using peer pressure, developing interpersonal skills, and satisfying their need for love and attention.

- Give short, clear directions.
- Plan carefully to avoid boredom. Be aware of attention span and interest level. Have work planned for those who finish a task early.
- Avoid the use of sarcasm or derogatory remarks. Use voice and eye to help keep control.
- Reinforce correct responses immediately.
- Provide a good model in your dress, speech, manners, and relationships with others.
- Check if the student is taking medication, and see what its effects are.
- Try to discover what "sets him off."
- Find out if the student is undergoing therapy and what your expected role within that plan is.

Specific Learning Deficits

Mentally retarded persons have deficits in each of the six following learning areas:

Incidental Learning

Incidental (informal) learning does not typically occur without conscious or concentrated effort. People who are non-retarded tend to be aware of and absorb much peripheral information from the environment as they go through their daily activities of dressing, eating, traveling, working, and relaxing. In almost any kind of environment, much learning is haphazard and unplanned. Such learning is often the foundation for more learning and depends upon incidental memory.

Independent functioning and independent study are related to incidental learning. Though they are more structured, they rely upon self-direction, attention to detail, and memory. All of these are weak in retarded persons.

- Give opportunities to experience a great number of events.
- Take the children on meaningful field trips, giving attention to careful preparation and follow-up as an important part of the experience.

Initial Learning

Mentally retarded students do poorly when first faced with new learning situations. This is partly due to their low cognitive ability, expectancy of failure and poor short-term memory. Given success experiences and opportunity for practice, some of the slow start is overcome. If a student is given practice on easier material first, he has a greater chance of initial learning success.

- Impress on the students the personal significance of the material to be learned.
- Relate all new learning to past experiences.
- Give the students opportunity to explain the new concepts in their own words.

Discrimination Learning

Learning to tell sameness and difference is basic to concept formation. Discrimination in hearing, vision, touch, and movement form the basis for most learning processes. Because of minimal brain damage or limited cognitive ability associated with certain syndromes, mentally retarded people have deficits in all these areas. Before they can make a choice or identify what is the same or different, they must carefully pay attention to all the features of the object or event. The attentional problems of mentally retarded children further complicate the issue.

- Be certain the student knows exactly what is required of him.
- Don't talk too much. Give the student a chance to think.
- Keep the anxiety level low. Too high an anxiety level interferes with choice.
- Attach labels to objects as an aid to making discriminations.

Observational Learning

Observational learning is imitative learning—patterning behavior after that of an observed model. It depends heavily upon attention to the model, retention of what is seen, reproduction, and motivation. Imitative learning is a pervasive part of learning throughout life; children have always learned this way, since it is an activity method.

Generally speaking, retarded children are poor at observational learning because of problems associated with attention, short-term memory retention, discrimination, production, and motivation. Yet, given the right modeling conditions and good teaching techniques, it is one of the most powerful methods available to the teacher. Providing appropriate models (including visual aids) for imitation is an important part of the teacher's task.

- Break the task down into clear, definite steps.
- Model the task for the students more than once, so they can rehearse it in their memory.
- Have the students imitate your actions and give them feedback on how they are doing.

- Practice the behavior or task to reinforce it in their
  long-term memory.

Paired-Associate Learning (PAL)

Learning in this area involves being able to associate pairs such as words and objects, names and places, and dates and events. The use of PAL is closely related to success in school-type learning. It is a powerful technique for teaching many familiar tasks, such as vocabulary learning, attaching names to faces and generally forming associations or connections among items. It depends heavily upon the use of language and the process of making associations. Retarded children are generally poor with language and are poor at forming associations. This makes them inefficient learners.

They can use paired-associate learning to help them memorize, but do not think to do so. The teacher's task is to present, for example, a picture until meaning is clear, then present the words to express this meaning. The child can then transfer meaning from the picture of the word associated with the picture.

- Guide the students in explaining cause-and-effect
  situations.
- Provide pictures to facilitate learning of words and
  concepts (this is a way of teaching beginning reading).

Operant Learning

Operant learning (stimulus-response-consequence) is also called behavior modification. It follows the pattern, stimulus-response-consequence. For example, a child is shown a picture of a duck in a language lesson. If he says "duck," he is immediately rewarded (reinforced) as a consequence of his correct answer. If the teacher can discover what consequence the child will value and work for (a token, food, star, praise, special privileges, or the removal of something unpleasant), almost any material (stimulus) can be taught and learned (response) by the child as he tries to gain the reward (consequence).

Since they find learning difficult and have developed failure-sets, *operant learning is the most powerful tool in the hands of any teacher of retarded children.* Your task as teacher is to sequence learning material in small steps (task analysis) so that success is assured and can be reinforced immediately.

- Select material within the grasp of the student to be taught.
- Present the material in a sequenced manner.
- Provide the student something he values as a reward for learning. Depending on the student's level, the reward can be tangible (a gold star) or intangible (praise).
- Do not give out punishment or take away privileges unless your efforts at positively reinforcing correct behavior have failed.
- Where possible, ignore inappropriate behavior (interruptions, for example) rather than rewarding it with your attention.

A basic knowledge of learning characteristics, and of the teaching techniques designed to compensate for learning deficiencies, will help you successfully teach your special learners about Christ. If teaching these people is new to you and you can't remember everything you need to do, you can refer back to this chapter for specific help with the learning problems you will encounter.

A Teaching Program

Building a curriculum for persons having mental retardation

by Jim Pierson

Persons with mental retardation need to know about God, Jesus, the Holy Spirit, the church, the Bible, and Christian living. Their depressed IQ does not make their need of the soul any less. They have spiritual needs, and their souls need to be exposed to the teachings of Jesus and nurtured in His love. However, it must be remembered that the retarded person can never progress as far as the normal one. Realistically, he can be guided to the peak of his own capabilities.

Discover Their Abilities

The first step with any new class is to spend time with them. Help them get to know you, the rest of the teaching staff, each other, and the building you're meeting in. Your first lessons should be general ones. Use the time during your first unit of teaching to assess each student's abilities and awareness. The knowledge you gain at this stage will be crucial in planning future lessons and goals.

The following guidelines show three levels of mental retardation and the general characteristics of each level.

Educable Mentally Retarded (EMR)

• They must have special help to prepare for adulthood.
• They can learn to manage their own affairs.
• They may be physically smaller than their peers.
• Their peak mental ages will be from 9 to 13 years (50-80 IQ).
• They will have more than their share of behavioral problems—rebellion is common; withdrawal is frequent.
• They will have trouble with abstract ideas and generalizations.
• They can read.
• Their chief problem will be depressed mental abilities.

Trainable Mentally Retarded (TMR)

• Their IQ is 30-50.
• They can learn to talk, walk, and do activities of daily living.
• They will have limited ideas.
• They will seldom exceed the second grade academically.
• They will use language and speech poorly.
• They can be taught to read directive signs.
• They will lack good coordination.
• They can be taught a trade, but they will need supervision to perform.

Dependent Mentally Retarded (DMR)

• They will never be able to care for their basic needs.
• They may not walk or talk.
• They may be bed-bound.
• They often reside in an institution.
• Their IQ is below 30.

Most lists of characteristics are negative commentaries. The good teacher will be aware of such characteristics and not let them interfere with creative teaching. A good teaching program recognizes a person's abilities and builds on them. It is important to see the mentally retarded person in terms of what he *can* do, not what he *cannot* do.

Testing

It can be difficult to determine what children know about religious matters and what their learning capabilities are. One tool that will help you do this is a test developed by my college students to determine basic Christian concepts of children who are retarded. The test begins on page 305. It is designed for young trainable retarded children and for Bible-school teachers without formal special education training.

In addition to general concepts, the test is meant to elicit a child's awareness of God, Jesus, the Bible, the church, and Christian activities. Re-evaluation should be done regularly to chart the child's progress.

Suggestions:

- Give the test in several sittings.
- Mount the suggested pictures on heavy cardboard and keep them with copies of the test for future use.
- A good way to determine the child's awareness of his surroundings is to ask him the items in the Basic Information section. Get full information from his family.
- Record any information that indicates the child's understanding of the Bible or related religious knowledge. Mark "X" if the child does not respond.
- Make the test fun. Praise the child's correct responses.
- Add additional concepts if the child shows advanced awareness. You can adapt the test for older children and adults.
- Study the comments and record concepts the child needs to learn. For example, "She needs to learn that prayer is talking to God." Or, "He needs to learn that God and Jesus are Father and Son."
- Repeat the test to determine progress.

Develop Your Curriculum

"Where can I get materials to use in my class for retarded youngsters?" the frustrated teacher asks. You can get lesson materials from three sources.

Obtain Materials

You can buy curriculum materials specially prepared for people with mental retardation. Often these are written for older children and adults, like the *Friendship* series. For a list of publishers of curriculum materials, see the Resource Section, page 280. The advantage of using these materials is that you may not have to assemble pictures, take-home materials, and craft ideas to coordinate with the lesson. These are usually provided. Some excellent materials are available, but you must keep in mind that you will probably have to do some work adapting even these specially prepared materials.

You can adapt curriculum materials written for children who are the same mental age as your students. Such materials will reflect accurately the learning characteristics of your students and employ the most effective teaching techniques. There are some drawbacks to this method of building a curriculum, though. The lessons may not deal with the kind of subject matter you have determined that your students need to work on at this time. Another drawback is that your students, especially if they are adults or teens, might object to the pictures, stories, or activities if they are obviously meant for very young children.

Ask these questions when adapting materials:

- Does it meet the needs of your students?
- Is it written in simple language?
- Is it communicating Christ in a concrete way?
- Will the activities interest the student?
- Are the pictures simple?
- Does it suggest the additional resources you will need?
- Does it give the teacher ample instruction?
- Are the songs meaningful?
- Can the parent or staff member carry over the lesson at home?

The third source is to prepare your own materials. The obvious drawback to this method is the greater amount of work involved. But if you can build up a list of creative teaching techniques and the resources to go with them, and learn to use a variety of learning channels when teaching, this method could give you a better chance of reaching the specific learning goals that you can see your students need.

Carefully study the teacher's manual and pupil's workbooks prepared for the normal child whose mental age corresponds to your students. For example, if one of your students is a ten-year-old child who functions at half his age level, study a lesson publisher's materials for the normal five-year-old in order to provide some basics for curriculum development. Note themes, language level, and concepts.

Set Learning Goals

Both short- and long-range goals are important. The teacher will best know the need. If the class is new, some short-range goals could be to teach how to act in church, what Sunday school is, or just how to sit quietly. An established class might be ready to learn how to pray, how to relate to others, Bible stories, lessons about what God is like, or accepting Jesus.

The lessons you plan and the goals you set can be based on the needs you discovered in getting to know the students and testing their knowledge. If the class has had no previous religious teaching, you can teach according to the following general outline:

Unit 1: Getting to Know Each Other
Unit 2: God
Unit 3: Jesus
Unit 4: The Holy Spirit (especially the fruit of the Spirit)
Unit 5: The Church
Unit 6: Christian Living

General goals for the class might include the following:
1. Develop a concept of God.
2. Live a full life.
3. Respect God's house.
4. Learn Bible stories.
5. Learn religious songs.
6. Learn to pray.
7. Feel God's love.
8. Learn to relate to others.
9. Learn social graces.
10. Accept Jesus.

Every lesson needs to have a specific goal that leads to the accomplishment of a general goal. For example, if your general goal for the quarter is to develop a concept of God, the specific purpose for a lesson might be "to learn that God made animals."

Use Appropriate Teaching Methods

Never forget that your special student learns slowly. That is the key to helping overcome his learning problems. Information must be presented to him slowly and in terms that he understands. The teacher must know common learning characteristics of the mentally retarded person and practice teaching principles that recognize these characteristics. Here in brief is a list of teaching techniques for mentally retarded people. For more detail, read Chapter 2.

Teach in steps. Sequential learning is essential to educational progress. Tasks should be simple and uncomplicated. Each new task should have the fewest possible parts to it, and most of the parts should be things the student already knows.

A brief task or activity will focus their attention on the purpose of the lesson. Plan for many brief activities or parts within each total lesson. Build one new skill or concept on what was learned before. Nothing succeeds like success.

Individualize the lesson. Apply the lesson to the student's environment and his experience. Apply the concepts you are teaching to the type of lifestyle your special learner leads. If he can't apply it to his everyday living, what you say isn't very important. There is no reason, for example, to stress being a foreign missionary if the pupil spends most of his time in a sheltered workshop.

Repeat the facts. Repetition is a necessary ingredient for an effective curriculum. "Overlearning" is necessary to retain what has been learned. Don't become overanxious or discouraged over the amount of repetition needed. The most creative teacher can repeat and present the same concepts in dozens of different ways.

Vary the approach. It is not always easy to know how the student is learning. Learning occurs by reading and writing, listen-

Suggested Schedule

This sample schedule for a two-hour period may be adapted to a Bible-school or worship hour.

Opening Exercise
Use background music to relax the class.
Share with and love the pupils.
Recognize birthdays.
Let the group share happenings.
Pray.
Pledge the flags and the Bible.

Singing Period
Sing with gusto.
Sing several times.
Use visuals to illustrate.
Use songs that are concrete.

Roll Call
Use a physical answer (pasting bird seals on a chart, for example).
Stress the purpose of attendance.

Bible Story
Tell it, don't read it.
Use lots of visuals.
Tell on the pupil's vocabulary level.
Talk slowly.
Decide the point to stress.
Use voice variation.
Exaggerate emphasis.
Use movement.
Apply the lesson of the story.

Refreshment Period
Say a prayer of thanks.
Be sure a pupil is not allergic to a certain food.
Correlate with the lesson.

Handwork
Carry over the purpose of the lesson.
Don't just make this a keep-busy time.

Worship
Song time
Bible time
Prayer time
Offering time
Sing an offering song.
Let a pupil collect.
Let a pupil pray.
Stress the purpose of giving.
Sermon (object lesson)

Closing
Sing a song.
Say a prayer.
Say good-bye.

ing, talking, seeing, touching, moving, smelling, and tasting. The alert teacher will select those techniques that stimulate the most learning styles.

Some regular educational techniques and materials can be effective learning aids.

Interest centers	Motion pictures
Music (rhythm band)	Cutting, pasting
Stories	Finger paint, clay
Conversation	Games
Pictures and objects	Drama

The more ways the idea is presented, the better the learning.

Stress the sensory and the physical. Just as normal children have different learning channels, so do your students. The alert teacher will select those techniques that stimulate the most learning styles. Allow the child to touch, taste, see, hear, and smell.

Study the "learning channel" wheel on the next page and apply it to any technique. Let's consider puppets as an example. Puppets make use of learning channels 2 (listening), 3 (talking), 4 (seeing), and 6 (moving). Other channels such as 1 (reading and writing), 7 (smelling), and 8 (tasting) could be worked into the puppet activity.

Be flexible. No curriculum is better than a flexible teacher who can alter the plan if the class is not ready for the next unit.

Use a lot of praise. Failure only makes learning more difficult. Plan each lesson so that your special person can do what you ask him to do. Practice telling your students when they are doing a good job. To have a successful class experience, plan well.

Once you know your students, this can be easy and fun. The younger the group, the more structure, or planning for small details you will need to do. Starting your class may demand more planning than what you are used to doing ... but this task will get easier and less time-consuming with time.

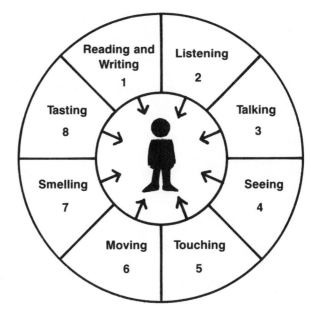

Learning Channels

Here is a summary of teaching tips for your class:

- Teach in steps.
- Make each lesson apply to the present.
- Avoid the general and abstract.
- Be routine to a degree.
- Repeat!
- Motivate.
- Stay away from symbols.
- Don't direct too much.
- Be clear in direction giving.
- Be consistent.
- Praise a student for the slightest accomplishment.
- Teacher independence
- Keep your vocabulary simple, but not childish.

Use Planning Worksheets

To build a curriculum, use five worksheets. The worksheet for the year simply gives the overall theme for the year and each quarter. Take advantage of the emphasis given to holidays—Christmas and Easter. Learning at these times will be high.

Worksheet #1

Worksheet for the Year

Theme _____

FIRST QUARTER

    General purpose _____

    Special days _____

SECOND QUARTER

    General purpose _____

    Special days _____

THIRD QUARTER

    General purpose _____

    Special days _____

FOURTH QUARTER

    General purpose _____

    Special days _____

After the teacher(s) has completed the form for the year, work on one quarter. When complete, record on the sheet the sources of songs and materials. Be specific in noting the needs of individual children: "Billy doesn't understand sharing. Stress it."

Worksheet #2

Quarterly Worksheet

Theme _____

General Purpose _____

_____

	Specific Purpose	Possible Materials & Techniques	Needs of Individual Children	Songs to be Taught
Lesson				
1				
2				
3				
4				
5				
6				
7				
8				
9				
10				
11				
12				
13				

The next level is the individual lesson plan.

Worksheet #3   Date _____

Lesson Plan

Purpose _____

Bible Reference _____

Songs _____

Story (list points to stress) _____

_____

_____

Application _____

Activity _____

Refreshments _____

Bible Words (memory verse)* _____

*If class has good recall, use; if not, talk about the meaning.

After each lesson has been taught, analyze the results. This exercise will greatly benefit continued curriculum development. After some time, monthly analysis may be adequate.

The lesson that lingers is one that the parents can help with at home. In planning, provide for lesson materials that can be sent home for parents to use to help enforce the learning in Bible school.

Worksheet #4

Evaluation Form

Results
    Positive:
    Negative:

Materials
    Worked: Why?
    Did not work: Why?

Individual Children's Responses

Child's Name   Response

1. _____

2. _____

3. _____

4. _____

5. _____

6. _____

Finally, maintain a progress sheet on each child. Such a system makes for easier curriculum planning, charts the child's responses, and rates the teacher's effectiveness.

Worksheet #5

Progress Sheet

Child's Name _____ Age _____

Parents _____ Birthday _____

Address _____

Phone _____

Date entered class _____

When he entered the class,
what did he know about:

God

Jesus

Holy Spirit

Church

Bible

Christian Activities
  Prayer
  Singing
  Sharing

Enjoy the Rewards

Everyone needs to know about Jesus. Your student can best be guided to that knowledge by a teacher who cares about him, wants him to know more, and is willing to do some creative curriculum planning to accomplish it.

For several months I observed a twenty-four-year-old lady with trainable mental retardation being taught stories about the life of Jesus. Every Sunday the teacher constructed a new visual to illustrate the lesson. Discouraged by the lack of response, the teacher wondered if she should continue her lessons. On the next Sunday she taught a lesson based on Jesus' healing of Peter's mother-in-law. She dramatized the lesson with clothespins that represented the people involved.

After the lesson I asked my friend what the lesson was about. She laid the clothespin representing Peter's mother-in-law on the table. Slowly, she walked Jesus over to the mother-in-law. She leaned Jesus toward the mother-in-law until the clothespins touched. Popping her lips to indicate that Jesus had kissed her, the eager learner stood the mother-in-law upright. When I asked her who made the mother-in-law well, she responded verbally (a rarity for her), "Jesus." I assured the teacher that her lessons were getting through.

A thirty-five-year-old lady with athetoid cerebral palsy had been given individualized Bible instruction for many weeks. The teacher developed a set of lessons on baptism designed to overcome her learning problems. The lessons hit a responsive chord— she asked to be baptized!

Mentally retarded people can grasp as much about the Bible as their mental abilities will allow. I doubt seriously that my trainable friend will ever progress to the point that she can understand what accepting Christ is all about. On the other hand, my other friend's teacher guided her in lessons on Christian growth. Regularly, she encourages her friends at the sheltered workshop she attends to come to Bible school with her and learn about her Lord. Physically, she has difficulty in talking. Spiritually, she witnesses and leads her friends to the Lord.

A trainable mentally retarded lady in her twenties was watching a puppet show in the worship service of her special Bible-school program. The story concerned a little girl who could not go to the ball game until after she had raked the leaves. Her friend said he would ask her mother, who said no. However, when the puppet told the audience that he would tell his friend that her mother said she could go, the retarded lady—essentially nonverbal—shouted "No!" Hours of instruction had not been wasted.

CHAPTER 4

Classroom Management

Creating an effective learning environment
for students with mental retardation

by B. D. Briese

Effective teaching of mentally retarded learners depends upon the following:

- the competence of the teacher in using specific techniques of teaching
- an appropriate environment for learning
- methods that lead the learners to make progress without reacting negatively to instruction.

The Classroom Environment

Next to the learners themselves, an effective teacher is the most important factor in a learning environment for persons with mental retardation. However, because they are easily distracted and have other learning difficulties, a cluttered and disorganized room will interfere with the learning process, lead to frustration and confusion, and create negative attitudes toward the teacher and the lesson material. The classroom environment must assist the teacher in instruction.

A room is not always necessary. Children learn best in real-life situations in which they can use all senses of seeing, hearing, touching, smelling, and tasting. Emphasize *doing* rather than seeing or being told.

The Classroom

Where a room is used for instruction, keep in mind the following factors:

The room should be self-contained. All facilities – storage areas, quiet room, sink, drinking fountain, restrooms – should be part of the room or nearby.

The room should be large enough. Persons having mental retardation usually require more space than those who do not. Some cannot sit still for long and need a change of activity. Some are sensitive to crowding and may become aggressive if closely packed. Allow 25 to 30 square feet of floor space per child. If children have physical handicaps requiring wheelchairs, this space should be increased.

The room should be functionally and aesthetically arranged. Children are easily distracted. Keep materials not in use in closed cupboards or in storage areas. The room must be free of clutter. The only materials visible, other than furniture, should be those being used for that day's lesson or theme. Bulletin boards and displays should be changed frequently; left in disuse they become a source of distraction. The focus should be centered entirely on the immediate objective.

Two or three supervised teaching areas will result in meaningful learning. Put out only what is essential for the current lesson. Such areas may each accommodate three to five students at a time. You should be able to supervise the work of each person in the group.

"Learning centers" may also be set up for partly supervised work. These may include a quiet area for looking at books, an area for art activities, an area for puzzles or games, and a place where music may be heard through earphones. Learning centers are limited only by your imagination.

A time-out area should be planned. There should be a large

carpeted area free of furniture where whole-group activities, such as drama or storytelling, can take place.

Your students find change stressful and routine reassuring. They are generally more comfortable and secure in an environment where furniture and station functions remain the same from week to week. Think out the room plan carefully, arrange it, and then leave it that way.

Ideas for Learning Centers

Redecorating, buying new furniture, and rearranging can usually be done only on a limited basis. However, the teacher of the class can plan activity centers. Planning as many centers as there are adults working with the class will insure usefulness. One center each month to enforce the theme will be sufficient. The students' ages, abilities, and needs should be considerations in planning the activity centers. You should relate the activity centers to the lesson being taught. The centers will benefit the student's poor muscular coordination, build speech and language skills, increase limited attention span, encourage creativity, and provide an outlet for excess energy.

Block Center. Collect blocks of all kinds and sizes—corrugated cardboard, plastic, wood. Allow the children to build objects for their creation.

Favorite Things Center. Parents may bring favorite objects, toys, and clothing. Discussing the objects can be helpful in learning about the child as well as helping him communicate.

Transportation Center. Assemble toy cars, planes, boats, tricycles, and trucks. The children can role play daddy going to work, mother going shopping.

Housekeeping Center. This old reliable lends itself to encouraging the children to be good helpers.

Sense Centers. Provide one for smell, one for touch, one for sight, one for hearing, one for taste. The activities should increase sensory abilities while stressing God's creative powers and love for us.

"Do It" Center. Assemble finger paint, crayons, glue, clay, play dough, blunt scissors, and plenty of paper; then let the class be creative!   *(J.P.)*

The room should have appropriate equipment and materials. Specialized equipment is rarely needed unless some of your students have additional handicaps. Most regular equipment can be modified to allow for children in wheelchairs.

Tables and chairs, one of each per student, should be provided, matched for height and size according to the student. Since there is likely to be a great variety in sizes among students, several different sizes of tables and chairs will be required in the room.

Have two bulletin boards, each about six feet by three feet, and mounted at an appropriate height for your students. Reserve one for a display board for the current lesson theme and the other for the students' art work. A rail to support pictures for storytelling can be mounted at the bottom of a bulletin board.

Other equipment might include several study tables for highly distractable students, an overhead projector, filmstrip projector, tape recorder, record player, a piano or other source of music for singing and drama, and supplies of pictures, paper, pencils, crayons, puzzles, games, books, and so on. Because equipment can break down, have a second teaching plan in mind that does not include equipment use.

The room should be pleasant to work in. There should be adequate soft lighting, good ventilation, and non-glare paint on walls and ceiling. Windows should be screened or curtained so that children are not easily distracted by what is happening outside. The room should be away from any annoying noise or traffic.

Classroom Rules

Rules should be few in number—three to five major rules are adequate. They should be worded positively. "Stay in your seat unless you ask permission to leave" is positive; "Do not leave your seat" is negative. They should be adhered to and supported consistently. They may be added to, deleted, or changed. Students should be encouraged to take part in formulating rules.

Since disruptive behavior interferes with learning, rules help to keep structure, organization and routine in the classroom while clearly outlining responsibilities of cooperation.

Discipline

Where do you go when you need help keeping order in your classroom? It can be just as frustrating for the learners as it is for the leaders when standards of behavior are not upheld.

The leader alone can never affect proper discipline. The special learner himself must exert some of his own control. The learner exerts internal control (self-discipline) and the teacher gives external control. The following are some principles for effective discipline:

- Discipline must be a team effort between teacher and student.
- It requires *do's* as well as *don'ts*.
- Examine the purpose for discipline before enacting it.
- Deal with the behavior problem with the individual, not with the group.
- Avoid anger and remain calm.
- Reinforce your student's good behavior.
- Make your rules realistic.
- Make your rules clear and easily understood.
- Be consistent; mean what you say and say what you mean.
- Try to correct any causes of poor discipline (environment, learner involvement, etc.).
- Be a "name dropper;" when a person hears his name, his attention will turn back to you.
- A gentle touch can also help keep someone's attention on what you're saying.
- Get to know each of your learners; pray for them and spend time with them. *(J.P.)*

Motivation and Management

In the classroom *motivation* means creating a desire in students to work for valued consequences while increasing their knowledge or skills. *Management* means decreasing certain behaviors so that learning can take place. The following are some principles of successful motivation and management:

- Get to know each child personally. Discover his interests and needs. Meet his parents and involve them in the child's

program. Suit instruction to personal abilities.
- Plan and prepare carefully. There is no substitute for good preparation. Prepare more work than you need so you have some options.
- Have all materials and test equipment ready before instruction begins.
- Keep to a regular schedule, but add variety by weaving interesting, exciting, and enjoyable (as well as educationally profitable) activities into each day's work.
- Keep the objectives for each day's work clearly in mind. There is more than one way to reach a goal. Be flexible.
- Meet regularly with aides or helpers. Clearly define their tasks so they too can prepare in advance and help achieve the same objectives.
- Try to anticipate any problems or difficult questions.
- Look well ahead in planning a unit of work so that the overall goals of the unit are achieved. Some supplies or equipment must be ordered well in advance.
- Have a visitor to talk about a particular subject or to demonstrate a skill. Give your guest plenty of advance notice and information.
- Remember personal events, such as birthdays, and celebrate them in class.
- Your students learn by structured imitation. Present a good model of bearing, speech, attitude, caring, and behavior.
- In managing any classroom be firm but friendly. Your students will respect a mixture of strength of character tempered with love but despise weakness and unfairness. Be a composite of teacher, friend, counselor, and workshop foreman.
- Use as many senses as possible in any lesson. Some people are visual learners; others learn by ear, some by touch, some by movement. Generally, people learn best by doing—by imitating or shadowing—rather than by listening and seeing alone. Singing and playing often aid learning because they employ most learning channels.
- Don't forget to clean up afterwards. Tidiness and order are more "caught" than taught. Have an eye for the aesthetic.

Other Teaching Environments

Special events or visits will necessitate teaching in places other than the classroom. Your students learn best in daily-living, real-life situations. Motivation and management procedures for the classroom can be followed, but some additional ones must be mentioned:

- Make sure you have parents' permission if the space is outside of the school or church grounds.
- Safety aspects are always important; outside the regular classroom they become paramount. Your duty of care increases with their level of retardation. It also increases when the regular location is changed.
- Increase the number of helpers so that there is as close to a one-to-one ratio as possible.
- Make sure of departure and arrival times and any special transportation arrangements.
- Plan well ahead. Visit the location yourself in advance. Anticipate any problems.
- Make sure of any arrangements about equipment, food, etc.
- Give a written schedule to each helper. Carefully outline the responsibilities of each.
- Check often to make sure every child is present and safe.

PART TWO

Persons With Other Disabilities

This section looks at what the church can do for persons having specific disabilities other than mental retardation:

- physical disabilities involving mobility impairment
- hearing impairments
- visual impairments
- learning disabilities
- behavioral disorders

Dreams Come True

Ministry with persons having
physical disabilities

by Jerry L. Borton

The term "physical disability" can refer to any condition not related to intelligence or mental ability. This definition can mean blindness, deafness, mobility impairment, health impairment, and many other physical conditions. For this chapter we will narrow that definition to mean *mobility impairment,* but most of the principles discussed here have relevance to other types of disabilities.

This chapter will introduce you to some of the challenges faced by persons with physical disabilities and to some avenues of ministry on a day-to-day basis as well as in the typical church program.

Needs of Physically Disabled Persons

The Recovery of Dreams

Every parent has a dream for his child. The child will become the President of the United States or Miss America—perhaps both! Whether a person's disability happens at birth, through illness, or through injury, one of the first difficulties his family must face is the death of that dream. If the disability occurs later in life, the individual's own dreams of education, career advancement, choice of spouse, or family may also seem to be destroyed.

In responding to this crisis, the family may lash out in anger seeking to place blame for the disability on the doctor, another family member, themselves, or God. The Christian should not feel the need to defend God in this situation, but to help the family be honest with their feelings toward God.

After the anger and frustration that accompany their grief process have subsided, they can be reminded that God is still in control. He is the Master who can take seemingly impossible circumstances and mold them into a dream come true for His glory.

In the Psalms, David shows a wide range of emotions in his relationship with God. Joseph must have wondered about his dreams of greatness when he was sold into slavery and later thrown into an Egyptian prison. Yet God used these very circumstances to make his dreams a reality. Joseph did not choose the circumstances he was in, but he did choose to react to them in a way that would honor God.

A disability may alter our dreams, but it need not destroy them.

The Value of Life

Another crisis the family may face at the onset of a disability is the attitude of the doctor. A doctor might place a higher value on the life of some individuals than others, especially in the case of an unborn child. He might advise against certain medical procedures because the individual's "quality of life" would not live up to his standards. The doctor may also have difficulty in facing disability because of his inability to cure it.

The family may have no idea what effect the disability will have on their family member or themselves. They may have no idea what the individual's potential is or isn't. They believe that the doctor should know what he is talking about, and they are not in a position to evaluate the doctor's attitude.

The church must step in and remind the family of God's attitude about the sanctity of every human life. The church may also need to assist the family in finding a doctor who will be willing to give needed medical treatment. I am not saying that heroic measures should be taken in every instance, but medical treatment should not be withheld from an individual solely because the individual is disabled.

The Demands of Rehabilitation

The treatment and rehabilitation process may take months or years; in many instances it will be a lifelong process which will take its toll on the entire family. The individual and his parents or spouse may spend many hours going from doctor to doctor to various evaluations and therapy sessions. Most families find it virtually impossible to fit in all the work, school, and church activities and still care for the disabled family member. There may be no time at all for cooking, cleaning, and normal household chores. In some families one spouse is responsible to care for the needs of the disabled family member while the other is responsible for keeping the rest of the family together. Four out of five families that include a disabled member end in divorce.

The goal of today's rehabilitation process is to bring the individual back as close as possible to his former lifestyle. Many devices and techniques are available to help compensate for lost physical abilities. The role of the church in this process is to support the family and eliminate as many barriers as possible that keep the person from being involved in the life of the church body.

Ways to Help

Should the church body step in and offer its assistance, or wait until asked? Most people with disabilities have heard someone offer, "If you ever need anything, let me know." This offer goes unaccepted many times because we don't want to be a burden on others. We aren't sure the offer is truly genuine. Maybe we can't really think of anything important enough to bother somebody else with.

Church members need to step in with specific offers of help. The list of ways you can help is limited only by your imagination. Offer to do the laundry, clean house, do the shopping, provide meals, provide transportation, help with therapy, or help with any other need that you see that you can meet comfortably and consistently (see Chapter 16).

Respite Care

This is perhaps one of the biggest needs of families with disabled members. The term means time away from each other. It is not unusual to hear of parents who have not been away from their child for seven years, twelve years, nineteen years or longer. Nor is it unusual to hear of a spouse who spends all his time taking care of his disabled spouse and has no time for socializing or activities that he enjoys. The disabled individual also needs time away from the day-to-day routine and an opportunity to meet new people and experience new things.

The thought of providing respite care may at first seem scary. The first step in providing respite care is to take the time to spend with the family and get to know the needs of the individual. Watch the routines and techniques that are used in transferring, dressing, toileting, and feeding. Take note of the use of any special adaptive equipment he may have. Note any activities he particularly likes or doesn't like. Listen as the individual or family member explains various needs that may arise and the ways to meet those needs. Don't be afraid to ask questions.

Next, ask if you may assist in the caregiving routines. After you and the family become more comfortable, allow the family members to leave for short periods of time. You can gradually extend the length of the respite caregiving to longer periods of time, possibly overnight or a weekend. Make sure you have phone numbers where the family members can be reached in an emergency and of any specialist who may be needed, as well as the normal emergency numbers.

Friendship

It is possible to spend so much effort in caregiving that the *person* becomes lost. Remember that a disabled individual is first of all a person and is in need of your friendship as well as your care. You develop such a friendship in much the same way as you would an individual who is not disabled. Start by finding a common interest.

I have cerebral palsy and use a wheelchair. When I was in junior high and high school one of my favorite activities was playing a game called Strat-O-Matic Baseball. It's a board game based on the statistics of real life ballplayers. My minister would come once a week and play the game with me. As we played we would also talk about whatever was happening at that time in my life. Through this process I was drawn into a more active role in the life of the church.

Encourage your new friend to be as independent as possible. Allow him to be what he is able to be himself. Avoid the temptation to do something for him simply because it would be faster or easier for you to do.

Help your friend set realistic goals, and at the same time allow him the freedom to fail. Don't be too quick to decide what is "realistic" and what isn't. Many of the things that, by God's grace, I have been able to accomplish have been termed unrealistic by "those who should know about such things."

All goals start as a dream. God can use dreams that are unrealistic. One of the dreams I had while growing up was that of becoming a professional baseball player. It didn't take long in the backyard with my friends to realize that this dream was unrealistic. I decided that if I couldn't play, I could coach or be a sportswriter. While coaching Little League I realized that although I may not be another Sparky Anderson, I did enjoy working with kids. This led to the dream or goal of becoming a youth minister. While studying at Bible college, I came to realize there is a great need for churches to understand the need for ministry to and with persons who are disabled. This led to the founding of an organization called Power Ministries.

This process was possible because my parents, family, and friends allowed me the freedom to fail. They helped me determine some of the obstacles that might prevent my reaching my goals. They forced me to create ways to overcome those obstacles. They gave me their advice, but in the end, the decision and the responsibility to live with the consequences of that decision was mine. For some, it may become easy to be dependent on overprotective family and friends and government assistance programs. Persons with disabilities must take responsibility for their lives.

Your friend faces the same challenges and problems that you face: the first day in a new school, adjusting to a new job, making friends, dating, looking for a job, deciding on a career. In dealing with these issues he will face some of the stereotypes and prejudices of society. He will also face the temptation to blame all of his problems on his disability.

You will have the opportunity to help your friend through the painful task of sorting through prejudice and facing the growth areas for which he is responsible. Sometimes people, because of fear of rejection, their own prejudices, or lack of experience, can be their own worst enemies. Help your friend develop people skills. For some, because of the effort necessary to maintain their day-to-day existence, it becomes easy for them to become absorbed in their own problems.

Spiritual Needs

At some point in your relationship, two important questions may arise. The first is, "Why? Since God is an all-powerful, all-loving God, why are there disabilities?" There seem to be two possible answers. First, God determines that some individuals will have a disability for purposes only He can know. Second, God does not cause the disability but He allows it to occur.

In John, the ninth chapter, Jesus' disciples asked Him this question when they encountered a man who was born blind. Jesus answered that this man was born blind to show the power of God at work in him. The real question may not be, "Why are there disabled people?" but, "How will we react to a disability?"

Two people seek to be glorified by a disability. The first is Satan. He is glorified when we act as if God has cheated us or believe that God does not remember or care about us. God is glorified when we allow Him to work through our disability, like Paul with his thorn in the flesh (2 Corinthians 12).

The second question to be dealt with is "What about healing?" Without discussing the method of miraculous healing used by the apostles in the first century, I believe that in most cases the issue behind this question is self-esteem. The individual is really asking, "Am I OK?" The answer is yes! God created you and counted you worthy enough to send His Son to die for your sins. Although our physical appearance may not live up to the world's standard, it is helpful to remember what the Lord said to Samuel: "Do not consider his appearance or his height, for I have rejected him. The

Lord does not look at the things man looks at. Man looks at the outward appearance, but the Lord looks at the heart" (1 Samuel 16:7).

Christians need to develop the disciplines of daily prayer and time in the Word. Bible pages may be difficult to turn and may be replaced by tapes, or better yet, by reading the Scriptures with someone else. Prayer lists and journals, instead of being written into notebooks, may be typed into computer memory or dictated onto cassette tape.

The growing Christian also needs the opportunity to minister to others. The disabilities of some people allow for much time that could be used in prayer for others. Some would serve well as pen pals. Is it possible that one who understands what it means to be imprisoned in their own body would understand the feelings of someone who is imprisoned in a jail cell? Many persons with disabilities can be teachers, youth sponsors, committee members, elders, deacons, or assume some other leadership position in the church.

Less than 14% of the disabled population claim to be Christians. In order to reach this vast mission field, some Christians who have disabilities need to be challenged to attend Bible college and assume ministry positions, including those of pulpit minister and youth minister. In order to help a disabled individual through the Bible college experience, a committee made up of the dean of students, dean of men or women, a faculty advisor, and a dorm parent, along with the student himself, could meet to determine how his special needs could be best met.

A friend of mine who has spina bifida is fulfilling his dream of being a youth minister. Not only is he meeting the spiritual needs of his youth group, but by his example he is breaking down some of their fears and prejudices.

Organizing for Service

Congregational Awareness

You can help your fellow church members become more comfortable around your friend by providing them with information about various handicapping conditions. One way this can be done is through a "Disability Awareness" resource center in your church library. The resource center would include books, tapes, and magazines on various age levels. It would also include files on organizations that deal with different types of handicaps. The librarian or other volunteer can obtain a list of national organizations that help disabled people, or you can begin with the resource section of this book. Each organization on the list should be sent a letter asking for general information about the organization's purpose, resources available from the organization, a listing of state and local chapters and how they may be contacted, and a request to be put on the organization's mailing list.

Another way to raise the congregation's awareness level is to invite representatives from area chapters of organizations to present their work to the congregation. Brochures about working with disabled individuals can be used as bulletin stuffers. The National Easter Seal Society has a catalog of brochures that would be helpful in this area (see the Resource Section for a listing of materials for congregational awareness).

If there seemingly are no disabled individuals in your congregation, you can develop a pool of prospects. First ask the members of your congregation to write on the back of roll call cards the names of any disabled individuals they know. You may be surprised at the number of responses. You can volunteer with area organizations that work with disabled people. You can allow these organizations to use your church building. By doing this, you will accomplish several goals: You will show these organizations that you care about disabled people, you will help your church members to become more comfortable with them, and you will give yourself the opportunity to become aware of needs that the church can fill, thus opening the door to share the gospel.

A Plan for Continuing Ministry

Many churches are used to providing services in a crisis situation, but most crisis situations are short-term. A disability is a long-term condition, possibly lifelong. As the days turn into weeks and the weeks into years, many individuals find that the level of caregiving by their local fellowship dwindles.

There needs to be a system to guarantee that caregiving will remain at the necessary level. Let me suggest that we borrow and modify an idea from special education. In the special education system today, every person has his own individualized education program, called an IEP for short. The IEP file on an individual includes a detailed description of his disability, a list of skills he needs to work on, medical treatments and therapy that may be necessary during the school day, and other useful information. The church can put together an individualized evangelism program for each disabled person.

The persons meeting to put together such a program could include

- the parents
- a special education teacher (or regular teacher) in the congregation
- the Sunday-school teachers and youth sponsors working with the individual
- the previous year's teachers and youth sponsors
- the individual himself, if old enough
- the minister or other church leader responsible for the shepherding of the person
- the individual responsible for coordinating the special needs caregiving.

The parents of a disabled child should be encouraged to share information from their child's special education IEP with the church. If the individual is an adult, previous IEPs may be available, or the individual may be able to give permission to receive information from a local vocational rehabilitation caseworker. The church's IEP may also include information such as:

- In what ways does the individual learn best?
- What teaching methods should be used?
- Should the individual be mainstreamed into a regular classroom situation?
- What assistance would the individual need in a regular classroom?
- What discipline procedures will be followed?
- Is transportation assistance needed?
- What other caregiving services (such as laundry, cleaning, cooking, shopping, or respite care) are needed?

If special caregiving services are needed, an individual outside the person's family should be assigned the responsibility of coordinating volunteers to provide the needed services. For example, if it is determined that providing an evening meal twice a week would be a help to the family, a group of volunteers would be recruited and assigned certain dates to provide the meals. Another group of volunteers may be recruited to provide weekly housecleaning chores.

Another area of opportunity for ministry is that of financial support. Many people require surgeries and adaptive equipment such as wheelchairs, braces, or computers that cost thousands of dollars above what may be covered by insurance. College students may also need financial assistance, especially those who choose a Bible college education.

The church's IEP should be evaluated at least once a year, sooner if one of the individuals that helped write the program is not meeting current needs adequately. The church IEP has several benefits. It helps assure that the needs of an individual will not be lost in the crowd of a busy church's activities. It helps volunteer caregivers understand the limits and abilities of an individual and their own responsibilities. It also gives the disabled individual and his family a written record to remind them that someone cares.

Accessibility

Let's now take a look at the parking lot and church building. There should be at least one handicapped parking space for every fifty parking spaces. It should be 12 to 14 feet wide, to accommodate transfers and wheelchair lifts. The space should be marked with the international access symbol painted on the pavement and it should also be marked with a sign in case of snow. The congregation should be taught that these spaces are reserved only for those individuals with handicapped parking plates or window stickers. Even a very short stay in a handicapped parking space may give a message that you do not intend to give.

If your church has steps, you have three options: installing a chair lift, elevator, or ramp. A chair lift is limited to those who are mobile but cannot climb steps, or those who can transfer from their wheelchair onto the chair lift. An elevator gives you the most flexibility – access to all your floors – but it is also the most expensive. A ramp gives you access to one level, usually the sanctuary.

Before deciding which option to choose, take a look at the individuals requiring the access. Which option would give the most access to the most people? Does your church have most of its Bible-school classes on an upper level? Does your church have a fellowship hall in the basement? What financial resources are available for the project? When determining the location for an elevator or ramp, the location should be near the parking area, and if possible, the location should be one of the main entrances. A ramp at the front of the church building sends the message that people with mobility impairments are welcome.

When installing a ramp, elevator, or any other piece of adaptive equipment, seek professional help. Make sure you are working with a contractor who knows the state and local building codes. For best results seek a contractor who has experience in barrier-free design. An improperly built ramp may be more hazardous than steps. You need to make sure that the ramp has the correct slope, the correct number of rest areas, the proper railings, and a non-skid surface.

A fourth option for churches that have steps is to carry a wheelchair. Some people feel that this lowers their dignity and will not allow it. If done improperly, carrying a wheelchair can be hazardous to both the person being carried and the people carrying him. Never try to carry a wheelchair alone. Have the individual show you the correct procedure for carrying his chair.

Seating areas should be allowed for wheelchair users in the sanctuary and other areas. Sometimes this is done by providing a wheelchair parking area for all wheelchairs in the front or the back of the room. The problem with this method is that it does not allow the wheelchair user to sit with the people he came with. It is better that the seating areas be spread throughout the room. There should be one wheelchair seating space for every fifty people. The seating area for a wheelchair is level and at least 36 inches wide by 52 inches long facing the front. A deacon, usher, or other individual should be assigned to each individual with a mobility impairment to assure a safe exit in the event of an emergency.

Several other areas should be made accessible, such as water fountains, public telephones, and restrooms. An extensive accessibility audit is available from the United Methodist Church (see page 298 of the Resource Section).

If your church is accessible, advertise! Use the phone book and newspaper ads; send brochures to area organizations that serve persons with disabilities. Let people know.

Staffing

The potential for burnout needs to be briefly noted. In order to provide the necessary caregiving services over the long term, you will need to set time limits. Many workers will respond to a crisis situation by committing themselves to provide a service as long as it is required, even if it means forever. Forever is a long time. Such a commitment may be sincere and God-honoring, but it is also unrealistic.

Many church's programs coincide with the local school system. A volunteer may make a commitment for a semester, for a full school year, or for the summer. Even the person who wishes to make an indefinite commitment should be given a specific length of time for his commitment. The finite period of time gives all parties involved an out if individual circumstances change, or the level of care is not up to required standards, or if a rest is needed. The time limit also eases one of the biggest fears that occurs in the beginning of a ministry to disabled people: the feeling that, "If I help this person I will be committed for the rest of my life."

There will likely be more needs than resources to meet them. Boldly meet the needs that you can and trust God to take care of the rest. Recruit, rest, and replace workers often.

Ministry to persons with physical disabilities can be tiring and time consuming and worth every bit of the effort. To do this ministry we need not have degrees in special education, rehabilitation counseling, physical therapy, or occupational therapy. If persons with these backgrounds are available in your congregation, use them in this ministry. However, it is not the degree on the wall that matters as much as the degree we allow Christ to abide in our hearts and work through our lives.

A Separate Culture

*Ministry with persons
having hearing impairments*

by Duane King

The worst handicap of all is not to be deaf, blind, emotionally disturbed, or confined to a wheelchair–nor even to have all of these handicaps at once. The worst handicap of all is to meet God on judgment day without Jesus as your Savior. That handicap cannot be overcome. It is eternally devastating. For this reason more than any other, people who are deaf need the ministry of the church.

Many deaf people don't consider themselves handicapped at all. They generally manage with the things of the world so well that hearing people may hardly recognize deafness as a problem. In fact, some deaf people manage so well that they can miss the whole purpose of their existence. They may live without knowing why and die without knowing Jesus.

Hundreds of thousands of prelingually deaf people (people who became deaf before learning a language) live in the United States, with millions more in other countries. These people cannot hear a sermon or lesson. Many of them, though intelligent, cannot read a sermon or lesson in English and understand it well. If a person cannot hear or read the Word of God, that person is likely to have the worst handicap of all, because speech and the printed page are the methods most often used to spread the Word.

Deaf Culture

Deaf people, like all people, are God's children who need to know their Father. On the average, they are warm, friendly, and intelligent. They use two different languages (sign language and English) almost every day. They are usually good workers. They are not subhuman (nor superhuman, as is sometimes thought). They have all the normal human strengths and weaknesses.

Deaf people laugh and cry. They have opinions and express them. They love, marry, and parent children. They buy groceries, drive cars, go to school and play ball. They are simply people— people who can't hear.

Most prelingually deaf people are part of a separate culture because communication with hearing people is usually difficult; normal communication (from their point of view) is easy when they are together. Whatever your language, it is more natural and pleasurable to socialize or go to church with people who use your language than those who don't.

Prelingually deaf people comprise a separate and distinct culture, probably in every nation around the world. The typical list of "people groups" to reach for Jesus should be doubled in number to include the deaf population in each people group. Truly we are engaging in cross-cultural evangelism. Don't let this fact scare you away; many Christians have served well without understanding the cultural differences. But you can gain many advantages by being aware of the culture, and even more by becoming part of it.

Deaf people vary tremendously within that culture. (Are all Spanish people the same, or all city people?) They vary in personality, education, language skills, speech/lipreading skills, religious background, and in all the other ways that hearing people differ. Some are sorry about their deafness ("But in Heaven I will be able to hear"), while others are glad to be deaf ("Heaven won't be Heaven unless everybody uses sign language"). Some passively accept what they consider to be the natural consequences of being deaf (low-paying jobs, no understanding at church). Others militantly fight for what they consider to be their rights (a deaf president of Gallaudet College, an interpreter).

Some deaf people seem unusually emotional when they talk. Their sign language requires inflection to be seen, while hearing a person's spoken language requires inflection to be heard. Some deaf people, especially those who become deaf *after* learning a spoken language, are themselves not part of the deaf culture. Being physically deaf does not make one culturally deaf. Some communicate orally, by speaking and speechreading, with varying degrees of success. Some communicate with forms of sign language that are not American Sign Language, particularly in classrooms that use special sign systems to more nearly match with English. But whether they are part of the hearing culture or not, they all need to be reached for Jesus.

Language

Sign language, as prelingually deaf people generally use it, is a separate and distinct language. It is not "English on the hands," "bad English," or "English with shortcuts." In its pure form, it is not English at all. In fact, the roots of ASL are said to be in France.

People are best educated when taught in their native language. Amazing as it may seem, deaf people almost never enjoy this luxury, not even with Christian education. At best, their education comes bilingually, combining some form of sign language with the native language of the local hearing culture. Almost no reading materials are presented in sign language. Most materials for deaf people are written in simplified English (or some other language of hearing people) and presented in printed form. Sign language is best read person-to-person, or by way of movies and video—but certainly not in printed form.

It is astounding that a prelingually deaf person learns any English at all. Imagine trying to learn a new language—Japanese, for instance—being taught to you by a person who does not know English. Then place a soundproof glass wall between the two of you. Now, learn Japanese!

Even so, deaf students in the United States graduate from high school with an average of a fourth-grade reading level in English. A fourth-grade level may seem poor, but it is wonderful considering that English is a hearing person's language—even in its printed form. The average deaf person has a twelfth-grade reading level in his native language (ASL) and a fourth-grade reading level in his second language (English). Their reading ability is superior to most hearing people in the USA, who know only one language!

Christian Education
in the Deaf Culture

The traditional Christian education methods, *listening* to the preacher or teacher and *reading* your Bible and the lesson, are unsuited for sharing God's message with deaf people. Not hearing the teacher, and not understanding the Bible or lesson, they usually don't even attend church meetings.

What often makes the situation even more confusing is that deaf people don't look handicapped. Theirs is sometimes called the "hidden handicap." The casual observer expects them to hear the preacher or teacher. Since they have normal vision, they are expected to be able to read the Bible or the lesson. But the sense of sight does not automatically give a person language any more than the sense of taste gives a person food!

Throughout history, Christian people have usually led the way in making critical breakthroughs and innovations for educating deaf people. Christians must now accomplish two major goals: First, we must invent new and better ways to present God's message, using modern psychology and technology, while not forgetting the old standards of Christian love and chalkboards, and second, we must more effectively use what we have and know now.

Two major problems hinder Christians from sharing the Good News with deaf people. The first is a feeling of inadequacy ("I don't know sign language well enough," or "I don't understand the deaf culture"). The second is a feeling of superiority ("I know sign language better than you," or "I must do what I can for those poor, helpless deaf people"). The first problem hinders you from sharing the gospel. The second problem psychologically hinders people from wanting to receive the gospel from you. Neither problem should exist—at least not for long.

The feeling of inadequacy can be overcome by training in sign language, followed by practicing the language with deaf people. As with any other language, you cannot really learn sign language until you use it in practical, everyday situations. It is desirable to know the culture, even to be part of it. But if only those Christians who already belonged to the deaf culture ministered among deaf people, their Christian education would be set back a century!

Enrolling in a good interpreter training program can offer help to overcome feelings of inadequacy with both the language and the culture. If you do enroll, be careful of discouragement. Some well-meaning teacher may bombard you with details of the language and culture, then lead you to believe that you can't really help a person until you are immersed in the culture and expert with the language. Depend upon God, His people, and your own hard work and good sense to overcome feelings of inadequacy.

The feelings of superiority can be overcome by realizing that deaf people are not helpless. They are, in fact, very helpful when given opportunities—and we need to give them those opportunities. They can become some of the most loyal and hard-working members of your congregation.

People are not to be pitied or looked down upon because of deafness. They don't need your condescending attitude, though a few may take advantage of you and permit you to become their servant. In that case, you should teach those few to become whole people and let them earn self-respect while you share Jesus with them. In general, deaf people prefer someone who respects them over someone who simply signs skillfully. Try for both—respect deaf people *and* sign skillfully.

When it comes to "I know sign language better than you," just remember that no one (including every deaf person and yourself) knows any language completely. Even if you are the best around, others are needed, and must be encouraged by you to use their skills. The woods would be silent if only the best birds sang.

Individual Service

We are not to become servants of deaf people so much as servants *with* them. They need to become servants of God while they, themselves, learn to serve others. This is best accomplished in the spirit of Galatians 5:13, "Serve one another in love." In so doing, we all serve God. If hearing people only minister *to* deaf people, then at best, only the hearing people are serving God—and that not very effectively.

Start With the Right Qualities

Be a Christian. This seems obvious, but it must be mentioned. You must also be committed to souls. Many Christians, particularly those who have been believers for several years, seem to have lost this commitment. Put first things first.

Become informed. Ask questions. Write to established organizations and get on their mailing lists. Go to workshops. Visit area ministries to the deaf. Helpful books, college majors, and seminars are available for churches and persons who are serious about serving with persons who are deaf.

Be motivated. Catch the vision. Thrill to the excitement. Share it with others and receive it from others. Exercise influence on church leaders. If you are a church leader, you have an advantage. If you are not, you will need to find some way to influence church leaders. You will need to have their commitment to your ministry.

Become goal-oriented. Someone must set goals and mobilize people and resources to reach these goals. If you will not be that person, then likely it won't happen. You are needed. Of course, just setting goals never accomplishes them—begin to fulfill the goals.

Get to Know Deaf People

Practice the language. The language is the key to the culture. You can only learn about the culture until you learn the language; then you have the key to actually enter the culture. Sign language is only truly learned by practice. Classroom work is valuable, but no amount of classroom work can substitute for practice—especially among deaf people.

Don't be discouraged if you make slow progress with the language. Language skills come to the student by "jumps," not by a gradual learning curve. The next "jump" may be just around the corner—your next lesson or your next contact with deaf people. Keep learning, practicing, and applying the language.

Visiting with deaf people is not only the best way to learning sign language, but it also builds your confidence in yourself. Deaf people will come to respect you more as they see you progressing. You will gain new friends, some of whom will surely be prospects for your top priority – winning souls to Jesus.

You can find deaf people anywhere, but look particularly at vocational rehabilitation centers, in special public school classes, at state schools for deaf people, at hearing aid dealers, and as subscribers to services from gas companies and electric companies. Ask people you know who work in these places. Often when you find one person, he will lead you to others – if you build a trust and friendship.

Become a friend. A deaf person may not call it a "cultural difference," but he may be well aware of the difference between your two cultures. He may be reluctant to invite you into his home until friendship and trust have been established.

Start with one person. Go out with your friend to parties, events at school, and so on – maintain your Christian standards, but do not be upset if his standards are different. Become a friend of his hearing family members, too. A hearing child of deaf parents stated, "My mother and father always asked me what I thought of anyone from the 'hearing world.' If I liked the person, fine. If I distrusted or disliked the person, my parents wouldn't have anything to do with him."

Include your deaf friends in events and in planning for events. You will need to consciously think of when and how to include them. Include them in your conversations – it is so easy to leave them out! Sign for them, even the seemingly unimportant words. Let them tell you if you give them too much information. Of course, if they are bored and don't want to pay attention, don't try to force their attention. To make it easier for everyone, it would be good if some of your other hearing friends learned sign language – then both they and your deaf friends will feel better about being together.

Find Your Own Place

Become a teacher. It doesn't have to be on a grand scale in the church auditorium. Host deaf people in your home. Let them see how you live and who you are, how a Christian family does things, and how you relate with each other. Be sure what they learn is good! You could teach incidentally (as they see it, anyway), when you mention Jesus at a ball game or while you respond to a death, an accident, or a windfall of money.

You may want some teacher training. Learning sign language does not make you a good teacher of deaf people any more than learning English made you a good teacher of the hearing!

By this time your deaf friends have been in your home and you've been in theirs. They've seen you improving in their language and they know you care about them. You have subtly taught them about Jesus and your love for Him and His Word. Now it's time to invite them to attend church with you. Be sure your congregation is prepared, or your deaf friends may be turned away by ignorant or prejudiced Christians. Be sure your deaf friends are not left out of conversations and that they receive the content of sermons and lessons. You will realize that you're probably still not the skilled interpreter that you plan and hope to be. But the deaf people know you. They know you respect them. They've watched you and helped you learn. They've seen you improve, and they will help you continue to improve as long as they see that you are also helping yourself.

Entire books have been written on interpreting. In the Resource Section, organizations are listed from which you may receive more in-depth information. There will always be a need for interpreting, even if your congregation chooses to have separate services for deaf people.

Win souls to Jesus. This goal is the ultimate joy on earth— exceeded only by the joy of greeting these souls in Heaven. Not all your deaf friends will become Christians. Jesus and His disciples had some of the same disappointments. But the joy will come. Our job is to present the gospel so that it is at least possible for people to become Christians and to grow in Christ. The Spirit does the work of convicting and converting through the Word; our work is to make the Word available in a form that communicates.

Edify the deaf Christians. We need to help these new Christians become an integral part of the church. They need the church, and the church needs them. Help them find their spiritual gifts. Teach them to become dependable parts of the church and to depend upon others.

A hundred stalks of corn that are dead from lack of nutrients and water are not as valuable as one stalk of corn that is strong and healthy because it was nurtured well. From the healthy stalk, more seed will finally come. Develop a fair balance between nurturing new Christians and seeking to win more souls.

Be careful of burnout. It can be easy for you to get so involved in ministry that you forget your own family. Or you may be nearly killing yourself in your effort to remember your family and all of these other steps, too. Too much work could result in burnout—being so overloaded that you just give up. Quitting is not the answer. It leaves you with guilt feelings and fails to accomplish what needs to be done.

The answer lies in being sure that the local congregation is doing its work. If the congregation is not yet involved enough to offer you some help and new recruits, then you should review and once again approach your church leaders for help. Explain to them that they made a commitment, and now that commitment can be fulfilled only if you receive help.

Develop deaf leaders. Don't expect deaf people to flock to your meetings unless deaf people are in charge, or unless they can clearly see that you are working toward that goal. Deaf Christians must be trained. They must practice, serve, and learn by their own mistakes. (Be sure the mistakes they make aren't the kind that will lead them astray from God.) This step is commonly accepted when missionaries seek to evangelize other cultures. The deaf culture is no different—it is best reached by deaf people.

Revive the congregation of deaf people. Often a respected outsider can come for a series of revival meetings or for just a one night banquet meeting.

Shepherd the deaf Christians. By now, deaf elders should be shepherding their own flock. But if you have to do it yourself, do it—even if evangelistic efforts must be curtailed. Both hearing and deaf people should be in training—hearing people in deaf culture and sign language; deaf people in Christian leadership; both in the Word.

Support missions. Hopefully, even before this time, the deaf people have decided to reach out to others—by personal contact, prayer, and financial support. If so, expand upon it. If not, then lead them to missions now.

Find your own place. By now you could be complacent, tired, and discouraged as you see others surpass you in skill. Maybe your place isn't where it used to be, but don't just back out of it all. Those who respect you for what you have done will accept a change in your role, but not a termination of your love and care.

Take time to improve yourself. Perhaps it will be your place to start a new congregation of deaf people. If you don't do it, be sure someone does. Or you could become an ASL signer/reader. When you achieve this, not only will you have the admiration of deaf people; you will have many opportunities to enter deeply into their culture and affect their lives for Jesus.

A Churchwide Ministry

Prerequisites

Be Bible-based. You don't have the reason for a Christian ministry to deaf people unless your reason is found in the Bible.

Be evangelistic. If you are satisfied with the way things are, you won't reach deaf people. One elder stated, "I guess we don't need a ministry to deaf people, since we don't have any coming." Obviously he is not evangelistic.

Be benevolent. Some of the needs of deaf people may be physical needs—food, clothing, shelter, job, money, etc. True, any person's greatest need is for Jesus, but benevolence often opens a way to meet that greatest need.

Be prayerful. Every church should be prayerful, but its evidence doesn't always show! It should.

Be mission-minded. Definitions of missions vary, but reaching deaf people for Jesus is cross-cultural, can be foreign as well as local, and often includes the task of opening new fields for harvest. This is missions.

Be growth-oriented. It can be discouraging for Christian workers to labor in an environment that is not enthusiastic about growing.

Preparation

Become aware of deaf people, their needs, and their strengths. A "deaf awareness" program might be brought to your church by one of the organizations listed in the Resource Section or by someone local.

Be sure the leadership commits itself to an ongoing ministry. Without this commitment, the program will work only a few years if at all. The leadership will provide the personnel and material needs of any other ministry of your church. The deaf ministry should have equal consideration. Deaf people don't need "flash in the pan" ministries that end when the prime motivator leaves or quits.

Select a leader. Without one, a hodgepodge of misdirection is possible. Worse yet, a jealousy or pride problem is more likely to develop without clear-cut leadership. Selecting a leader also establishes the authority where it belongs—with the eldership of the church who selected the leader. Later, the eldership can sponsor the deaf believers as an entirely new congregation with its own eldership.

Plan well. Even if you don't know how to plan, try. Surely someone in the church is a good planner, even if he knows nothing about deaf people. Set goals and establish a timetable.

Early in your planning you will need to survey the deaf people who have contact with your congregation. How many are there? Where are they? What ages are they? Where do they work? What is their primary mode of communication?

Another important survey is a survey of Christian ministries available to the deaf in your area. Where are they? What denominations sponsor them? Are they effective? How many attend? Are they integrated (deaf meeting with hearing) or segregated (deaf meeting separately)? Do mostly children or mostly adults attend? Can you work *with* the existing ministries instead of competing?

The results of your surveys will make a difference as you build your ministry.

Recruit and train. Potential workers can be many different ages, experienced and inexperienced. Sometimes a skilled signer is already a member of the congregation, but has not revealed his talent. It is usually more difficult to enlist men than women, but some men should be involved. A few workers are needed for publicity, operating video equipment, transportation, etc. Let them know it is hoped that someday a deaf person will be doing each worker's job.

Not all workers need to become highly skilled with sign language, though that would be ideal. Minimal skills should be expected. If training is not available to you, look for help from one of the organizations in the Resource Section.

Involve the whole congregation. Mention the goals of your ministry with deaf people from the pulpit, in the bulletin and midweek paper, at prayer times, casually in conversation, and in leadership meetings. You may teach a sign each week during worship. Sometimes sign the special music (do it all the time, of course, if deaf people are already integrated into your services).

Visit among the deaf (see page 88f). A natural outgrowth of your ministry will be the friendships formed between your workers and deaf people. These can help bring in new prospects, start home Bible studies, and expand your ministry.

Determine the style of your ministry. Will the deaf people be integrated with hearing people or segregated for their own culturally-oriented lessons and worship? Some churches try to have some of each—a segregated Bible lesson time and an integrated worship time, for example. Do not assume that culturally deaf people should always be integrated with hearing people, or that you *must* start with an integrated approach, then change to a segregated one. This topic should be considered with input from the deaf people and others experienced in this field of ministry.

Locate facilities. Where will this ministry meet—for lessons, worship, social gatherings, and prayer meetings? Where will equipment be stored? What equipment and facilities are needed? Where will people park? What about a nursery?

Your meeting place should be attractive and have a minimum of visual distractions. Rumblings and low-pitched noises will bother deaf people.

Select materials and equipment for lessons and worship. You can create your own materials, adapt materials prepared for hearing students, or use materials specially prepared for deaf students. Be sure necessary equipment is available. In earlier years, the typical recommendation (besides things ordinarily found in classrooms and worship centers) was for an overhead projector and a chalkboard. Today, a videotape player and TV should be added as "necessary equipment," and a video camera as "nearly necessary equipment."

Have a formal kickoff. Make it a "big deal." Include some of the following: a special speaker (who signs for himself), a movie or video in sign language, a banquet, homemade ice cream, testimonies, a special announcement about planned services, newspaper advertising, a sports event (softball or bowling), introduction of the leader, a welcome from the minister to the hearing people, a tour of your facilities.

A Growing Ministry

Include deaf people in decision making. This critical idea can be easy to overlook—even when you intend otherwise. Postpone decisions, if you can, until the deaf people can become part of the decision-making process. Attendance, potential leadership, offerings, and attitudes are all at stake.

Include them during the course of church meetings. Get them up front. Put them in charge—more quickly than you might feel you should. Let them gain experience. Be sure they know this ministry is not just *for* deaf people, but with, of, and by them.

Meet the needs of their hearing family members. Some hearing children of deaf parents are people without a culture (or they may be bicultural). They have special needs you would do well to identify and meet. Probably one clear-cut need will be for someone to watch the children of deaf people while they meet. A deaf person cannot watch a child and the speaker at the same time, so he may not see a commotion that the child is making.

Administer wisely. The eldership of the church should not just select a leader and turn it all over to him or her. The leader needs wise guidance. Some ministries have been destroyed because of jealousy, doctrinal errors, or other problems that could possibly have been avoided.

Train new workers. Even if you are successful in training deaf people to be leaders, you may always need at least some hearing workers. Be prepared for your current workers to move, retire, die, quit, or get sick. Be ready for expansion.

Shepherd the flock. Until the deaf people have developed their own shepherds, you'll need to do it. Shepherding is no small task, but is a worthy and rewarding one. Provide leadership training for them, opportunities for growth and revival, and new ways to serve. Have patience. Don't expect phenomenal growth–either in number or in spirit–but plan for and be happy with some growth.

Adjust when necessary. Things don't always stay the same. Your constituency will change. So will your building, your methods, and your equipment needs. Be prepared to make adjustments– not so often or to such extremes that your program seems to wildly fluctuate, but certainly when adjustments are needed.

Keep improving. Keep the eldership informed. Do a better job of involving the entire church in the ministry. There will be ups and downs. Some deaf people will expect you to give up. Endure, and finally the harvest will come.

Develop a broader fellowship. Plan fellowships with deaf people in other congregations. Cross rivers, state lines, and even denominational lines. Deaf people need the encouragement that other Christians can give. Attend conventions, seminars, and other meetings, especially those that make a point of welcoming deaf people. Provide means for fellowship with hearing Christians, also–at least at the local level.

Support missions. If it has not happened yet, then lead the deaf people in your congregation to support missions. This can be as helpful for the local congregations as it is for the missionaries. Actually sending a person from your congregation is a thriller– even if it's for just short-term work.

Start new congregations. Multiply yourselves, sharing your knowledge and leadership skills with others.

These steps are not comprehensive. They are meant only to stimulate your thinking and help you plan. Prayer should be part of every step. Likewise, a certain amount of physical strength and stamina is required. Never forget your goal–to lead deaf people to Jesus. Remember that deaf people who are trained and maturing Christians can probably accomplish that goal better than hearing people. Plan to work yourself out of a job!

Seeing With the Heart

Ministry with persons having visual impairments

by Marsha B. Uselton

Janie, trailing the back of her fingertips deftly down the corridor wall, stops for a sip of water from the fountain, locates her Bible-school room door, and enters with a bounce. She returns the cheerful greetings of her classmates with an eager grin, locates a chair, and opens her brailled Bible-school manual to today's lesson. Janie is blind, but she is a fully participating member of her church.

Down the hall Brian has entered his preschool class ahead of his mother, his eyes brightening through thick frames as he recognizes his buddies. They join hands as they scamper toward the table to explore the activity for the day. Brian is visually limited and, like Janie, at home in his Bible-school, where he and his friends are learning about the wonders of life.

This chapter is designed to help you move past the "panic stage" when you learn that a child with a visual impairment will join your Bible-school program. Blindness is a low incidence handicap; in the past most blind children attended state residential schools outside their community. Consequently, many of us know little about how a person with a severe visual impairment moves through daily life and how we can adapt our program to meet his or her needs. Since more visually impaired youngsters now are attending schools in their communities, more churches now have the week-to-week opportunity to share the exciting adventure of learning and growing with a person who has a vision deficit.

Because the incidence of severe visual impairments is low, it is unlikely that you will find an entire church class having this handicap. We will deal with a situation in which a visually impaired person participates in a regular Christian education program.

Visual Impairments

Visual impairments are usually divided into two categories: *blind* and *visually limited.*

A person who relies on senses other than sight to obtain information and requires adapted methods, materials, and equipment for learning is considered educationally blind. This person would use braille and/or listening as the main avenue for learning.

A person who, after correction (glasses), requires adapted methods, materials and/or equipment in order to use remaining sight as a channel for learning is considered visually limited. This person would read with large print or use a magnifier. We will use the term *visually impaired* to refer to both the braille and large print categories.

Other forms of visual problems include lack of color perception and field defects (not seeing on a certain side, seeing only peripherally, or having blind spots). With some eye disorders, vision loss is progressive. Other disorders may require some limitations on physical activity or lighting.

Most blind people have some level of light or object perception. You will want to find out, from the person himself or from his parents, what use he makes of such remaining sight. Does it help him avoid obstacles when he moves around? Does it assist in locating dropped objects or locating "landmarks" in the church building? Be aware that the use he makes of vision may fluctuate with lighting, emotional state, or level of fatigue.

Fortunately, people no longer believe that remaining sight should be conserved so as not to "use it up." Teachers should encourage use of all senses, including vision. The prolonged strain of close eye-work can cause irritability, fatigue, or headache, but do not worry that the use of vision will further impair the person's sight.

People with visual impairments share with other people a full range of emotions from gloomy to cheerful, fearful to confident. Blindness does not automatically bring with it feelings of insecurity or sadness, nor compensating talents of "spiritual" or musical inclinations. The way others treat a visually impaired child's handicap may have as much to do with the development of his personality as his own inborn characteristics or the happenstance of blindness.

Differences

You need to consider certain differences when preparing to include a visually impaired person in your church program, remembering that generalizations can be risky and not always helpful. Educationally, he may be behind others his age. Braille is a complex code and usually takes longer to master than print. For a small child, more time may be needed to teach him tasks others pick up casually by visual imitation. However, do not be surprised to meet a visually impaired youngster who is at or above his age level. His memory may be developed to a greater degree than in sighted peers, and he has learned to rely on this useful skill.

A child may lack certain concepts in cases where touch cannot replace vision. Such ideas as clouds, stars, and flames may require a good bit of creativity to get across. Whenever possible that visually impaired child benefits from concrete tactile experiences to learn about the words he hears and uses.

Facial and body gestures (smiles, shrugs, raised eyebrows) give us much social feedback that a blind person misses. Lack of visual imitation, meanwhile, means that a child will not spontaneously use such social gestures himself unless taught to do so. The combination of both of these factors may put a strain on new social interactions until the ice is broken. Remember, though, that his other senses are at work. The pitch and inflection in our voices, the sounds of our movements, and the feel of our touch convey whether we are angry, calm, frightened, or loving. Our honest intention to accept him as "OK" will shine through.

When the child experiences prolonged periods of insecurity

about his physical and social environment, nervous tension may result in withdrawal. This passivity may bring with it "blind-isms" or repetitive actions such as rocking and eye poking.

The visually impaired child who has not been encouraged to be independent and who must constantly rely on others for assist-ance and information may likewise develop patterns of passivity and dependence. Conversely, frustration may come from trying too hard to accomplish every task independently. Often a person who has learned when to seek assistance has a calmer acceptance of his handicap than a person with some sight who feels pressured to accomplish every task his sighted peers can accomplish.

A person's biggest handicapping factor can be the way he is treated. Because sighted people rely heavily on vision, we have not explored the many ways our other senses can serve us. A blind child can learn to take care of his own daily living needs (tying shoes, turning sleeves right side out, dialing the phone, cutting meat). There are often alternate ways to solve a problem when vision is lacking, leaving the necessary times when aid from a sighted companion is most helpful.

As long as we avoid the extremes of swaddling our visually impaired person in cotton and pushing him to climb every moun-tain independently, we can provide in the church environment a healthy backdrop for his spiritual growth. Calm, firm expecta-tions based on realistic judgment help him grow, contribute, and learn. Our relaxed approach will convey our trust in his abilities.

Suggestions for Interacting

Here are specific ways we can interact with visually impaired people to help us all feel more comfortable and able to benefit from the being around him.

- It is perfectly OK to use words such as "see," "look," and "blind." Do not worry about struggling to find substitutes (blind people "look" with their fingers).
- A visually impaired child's behavior needs guiding just as any child's. Expect reasonable standards of behavior.
- We tend to talk more loudly than usual to communicate with a blind individual. Monitor your voice level.
- Do not talk to others about the person, no matter how

young, as if he were not there. Whispering, gesturing, or "sneaking by with things" in the presence of a person who cannot see is definitely out!

- Physical contact is an important way to share warmth and acceptance, especially with young children. Avoid babying them, however. Encourage independence whenever possible and help classmates learn not to be too helpful.
- Introduce yourself by name until the blind person knows your voice and encourage classmates to do so. Speaking to him by name will let him be sure when he is being addressed. Let him know when you move away, so he is not left talking to air.
- Instead of drawing attention to any repetitive mannerisms a blind child may have, keeping him involved should alleviate the problem. A quiet touch to the head may remind him to hold his head up or still rocking behavior.
- Check your own feelings – be sensitive to their needs, but get any tears out of your eyes and understand that pity is only damaging. Your attitude will be an example to the others in the class.
- Help a child develop a realistic view of himself, with the expectation of success but not perfection. Avoid regarding every accomplishment as amazing, but help him feel that a full, normal life is a realistic expectation.
- Remember that this person is more like other people than different. Treat him naturally. Relax and enjoy the opportunity!

Adaptations

How will the blind person move about the church building and grounds? How do we teach this person when the Bible-school material is so visually oriented? Will the other children reject or tease him?

Having a visually impaired child in your Bible-school class can have significant advantages to both blind and sighted members. With a little preparation and imagination, you can incorporate activities for a special child and enhance the experiences for the whole class. These suggestions and ideas will not cover every aspect of your particular situation, but have faith in your own problem-solving skills. Your creativity can send you soaring!

Mobility

Techniques. A sighted guide should use a procedure that avoids pushing or pulling the blind person and is good for unfamiliar territory. The person takes your arm and walks a half-step behind. If you need to move through a narrow opening, move your arm behind you and the person can move in behind you also. Holding a young child's hand is perfectly acceptable.

With a wall-trailing technique, the backs of the fingertips brush along the wall a few inches ahead of the body.

Blind youngsters, if they have been encouraged from the start, can quickly learn to use their independent mobility skills to get around. "Facial vision," or obstacle sensing (which is actually sound-wave feedback), enables a totally blind individual who has developed the skill to sense when an obstacle is close by. Using a cross-arm protective technique allows a person to move with confidence to avoid a smashed nose when in semi-familiar territory. Orient the child to the classroom by leading him around. For older children and adults, describing parts of the room as if the room were a clock is helpful. "The bookcase is at 12:00, blackboard at 3:00, etc." For small children who are learning to trust their environment, keeping furniture in the same place is helpful and doors either wide open or closed. It is always courteous to let the blind individual know when changes are made in his surroundings.

Physical aids to mobility. A person will not use a cane until he is mature enough to learn this skill, usually in his teens. Trained mobility instructors teach this mode of independent travel, which is useful indoors and out. There are now also electronic mobility devices for sound discrimination of obstacles and step-offs. Guide dogs are an option as the teenager approaches adulthood, depending on the personality of the individual. If your student has a guide dog, have all members of the class respect the rules he or she has about not petting the animal.

Adapted Reading Materials

There are various ways to adapt printed materials for visually impaired children, and several sources of assistance in getting curriculum materials brailled, enlarged, or recorded. The addresses of these are in the Resource Section. If you don't have special materials, you can hand-print an enlarged version of the day's reading or have someone else quietly read the selection. Allow more time for both braille and large print readers to finish any reading material.

Buddy System

A classmate can be helpful as a buddy for a visually impaired child who needs assistance, with the goal of seeing the child begin working as independently as possible. The buddy may quietly narrate a movie, lead the child through a new activity, and provide mobility assistance when needed. Monitor the arrangement to see that it is burdensome to neither party. Arranging opportunities for a visually impaired child to be a helper to a classmate can also be a rewarding experience.

Learning by Doing

Children learn best by doing, and this certainly applies to the visually impaired child. All young children can benefit from first-hand experiences and learn about the wonders of their world.

Sensory Stimulation. Talk about the feel of various natural objects in creation—soft cotton, rough rocks, smooth leaves, bumpy bark, etc. Make a texture collage or a touch box. Smell bottles could hold natural scents (rose petals, cinnamon, coffee beans, mint leaves). Have a taste time, in which all the children close their eyes and identify various food texture and tastes—sweet, sour, salty, etc. Discuss the variety of textures, smells, and tastes around us.

Singing. Although blind people are not naturally more talented in music than others, singing is an excellent avenue for everyone to express and share joy and spiritual feelings. Stepping behind a child to move his arms through the movements will allow him to participate as fully as others (see also Chapter 15).

Art Activities. Fingerpainting, clay modeling, and texture collages are samples of activities that provide avenues for a visually impaired child to express feelings and produce a creation of his own making.

Raised-line shapes (made by gluing string onto the paper or poking pencil dots from the other side) give outlines for a child to color within. Raised lines of intricate figures or pictures are not identifiable to a child who lacks sight, but a simple outline gives him the opportunity to participate in a coloring activity with the others.

Most blind children want to feel included in every activity, whether coloring, pasting, or cutting. Their efforts may not resemble visually the object intended, but provide them valuable experience in expressing their own feelings. It is often helpful to pre-cut the tricky curves, then let the child experience independently his creative art, rather than move his fingers through the art activity. When the child's touch is sufficiently developed, he or she can feel a crayoned line to color within or guide cutting.

Children who can use their sight for activities may benefit from darkening outlines with a black felt pen or felt tip marker. Cream colored paper with non-glossy surface is better than white for background paper, and use of high contrast colors (yellow on black, red on yellow, etc.) gives the child the best chance to discern pictures. Avoiding background clutter in pictures, by whiting out with white tempora or cutting out the main figure to place on a solid background, is helpful for visually limited children.

Listening and Discussion. These activities need no adaptation when a person's listening skills have been stimulated. As the blind person lacks the social feedback of eye contact to help maintain interest, an occasional touch or personally directed comment helps him feel more a part of the group. Some visually impaired people need no such encouragement to participate freely, and may even need to be reminded to let everyone share equally in the discussion.

Prayer or Poem Writing. Braille students may want to bring their braillewriter (a machine that "types" braille) or a slate and stylus, a less cumbersome apparatus for embossing braille. Many braille or large-type students have been taught typewriting from the fourth grade or so, and could use this method to share written communication with others. Visually limited children may prefer to write with a felt pen on cream colored paper with green lines, obtainable from the American Printing House for the Blind (see Resource Section). Other considerations for the use of vision when possible includes a well-lighted room without glare. Face the person so he or she benefits from window light, but does not face it directly. Let him get as close to the paper as needed.

Recreation

A visually impaired child has the same needs for exercise and play as other children. Your creativity will add to the list of these adapted ideas:

- Beep ball. Your nearest telephone company "Pioneers" is a service organization that often furnishes a ball that beeps, allowing a blind child to participate in ball activities. Create your own version by inserting a jingle bell or two into a plastic ball or balloon.
- Ring-run. Thread a large key ring or hoop through a rope stretched horizontally at waist level, so the child can run independently by holding the ring.
- The child might be able to participate in some games by playing a particular position—server in volleyball, center in football, etc.
- Ordinary playground equipment. Swings, slide, seesaw, and merry-go-round need no adaptation, just orientation to their locations and precautions about running into a flying swing or seesaw. (Even so, a few bruises are better than an inactive child).
- Many games can be taught by moving the child gently through the paces until he gets the idea and by adding sound here and there.
- Field trips or youth group outings. Youngsters can enjoy swimming, bowling, horseback riding, skating, etc. A reassuring buddy may or may not be necessary.

Preparing Other Children

You may want to work into your Bible-school lessons a session or two acquainting the class with visual impairments. Often a hesitation to interact with a new blind child is based on ignorance of the disability, and can be easily overcome with some familiarity with blindness. It seems helpful to talk about how everyone is different—hair colors, height, talents, family members, and disabilities. Letting the children try blindfolds and lead each other around gives them the opportunity to use their other senses. The American Foundation for the Blind has helpful pamphlets and a movie, "What Do You Do When You See a Blind Person?" The child may want to demonstrate her braillewriter or other adapted materials. Do make sure the child feels comfortable with such sessions. They should help heighten understanding and benefit all class members.

These resources and suggestions are offered as a springboard to help you create your own solutions, remembering that good sense and thoughtfulness will see you through and turn a challenge into a celebration. Please remember that a visual impairment can be only an inconvenience and not cause for grief and despair. The book *You Are Special* by Tom Sullivan, an inspiring musician, actor, and sportsman, who happens only incidentally to be blind, may be one you would like to read. It gives valuable insights into how a disability need not be a prison and how you yourself may have an opportunity to stretch and grow as you provide opportunities for your children to get in touch with their specialness.

"One sees well only with the heart;
The essential is invisible to the eye."
                    Antoine de Saint-Exupery
                    The Little Prince

Learning Differently

*Ministry with persons having
learning disabilities*

by Sue Abegglen and Linda King

For years, many children and adults with learning disabilities have become frustrated and disillusioned in Bible-school programs. They suffer embarrassment from well-meaning but misunderstanding teachers, youth leaders, and ministers. Children drop out of Bible school in frustration because they do not "fit in" either at school or church. It becomes too much of a struggle to face the daily defeats in school and community and then again on Sundays. Adults avoid situations where everyone takes a turn reading aloud in front of others.

Learning Disabled Students

There is hope for these individuals. Christian education can take place when basic characteristics of learning disabilities are recognized and appropriate teaching is prescribed. Unlike mentally retarded persons, who have limited learning capacity, learning disabled persons are capable of learning but have specific difficulties with perception or with organizing and communicating language.

The term "learning disabilities" is a recent term used in identifying children. There is still some confusion over the accepted definition. The definition stated in the regulations for Public Law 94-142 is as follows:

"Specific learning disability" means a disorder in one or more of the basic psychological processes involved in understanding or using language, spoken or written, which may manifest itself in an imperfect ability to listen, think, speak, read, write, spell, or to do mathematical calculations. The term includes such conditions as perceptual handicaps, brain injury, minimal brain dysfunction, dyslexia, and developmental aphasia. The term does not include children who have learning problems which are primarily the result of visual, hearing, or motor handicaps, or mental retardation, or emotional disturbance, or of environmental, cultural or economic disadvantage.

The individual with a learning disability usually has an IQ in the normal range of intelligence, but his performance of tasks is far below that level.

Learning Characteristics

Several characteristics often accompany a learning disability. The presence of any one of these characteristics may mean nothing, but the presence of several may indicate that a person is experiencing learning problems and needs some special teaching methods. These characteristics are cited most frequently:

- hyperactivity
- perceptual-motor impairments
- emotionality
- general coordination defects
- disorders of attention
- impulsivity
- disorders of memory and thinking
- specific disabilities in academic areas
- disorders in speech and hearing
- soft neurological signs and electroencephalographic irregularities[1]

These characteristics are most likely to be seen in a church setting:

Difficulty in reading and other basic skills may be apparent. Some people may have difficulty pronouncing words; others may have acquired the mechanics of reading but have difficulty comprehending what has been read.

Abstract concepts may be difficult to comprehend. The person may tend to jump to conclusions. He may also have difficulty in distinguishing differences in similar concepts, such as "like" and "love."

Communication may be poorly organized or poorly expressed. Sentences, or words, may not follow in logical sequence. Words may be jumbled or non-synonyms may be substituted.

The student may have difficulty remembering what he hears during the lesson or difficulty remembering from week to week.

Written language may also reveal difficulties. The learning disabled child may be unable to spell or fill in lesson books legibly. Drawings are frequently poor with figures misrepresented or lacking in detail.

Children may have difficulty behaving appropriately in an automatic way. They may interrupt the lesson, talk aloud while working alone, laugh at the wrong time, or engage in annoying habits that irritate the other students.

Visual and auditory perceptual problems may cause difficulties in seeing or hearing words correctly. This could also cause the student to confuse or misunderstand directions. The student may disrupt the class by incorrectly repeating what he thinks he heard. Outside distractions can also make concentration difficult.

Some children will try to avoid being touched; they will pull away from a hug or touch. An unexpected touch from a classmate may cause them to strike out at the unsuspecting toucher.

Motor difficulties and lack of coordination may cause problems in games and other physical activities.

Hyperactivity and restlessness may make a child appear to be in constant motion. If he is not moving the entire body, the activity may be seen in such behavior as drumming fingers on the table, tapping a pencil, wiggling feet, or shifting positions on the chair. He may be tense or irritable.

Peer group relationships are often poor due to the inability to relate to many people at one time. After years of repeated failure, a learning disabled teenager often turns to delinquency to achieve friends and recognition, unless he develops a solid faith in God and sense of personal self-worth.

Due to frequent failures low self-esteem often accompanies the other problems associated with learning disabilities. This insecurity may result in the student assuming a "don't care" attitude or in placing blame for failures on others. Frustration tolerance levels may be low and temper flare-ups may result.

Guidelines

For teachers of all ages. A special self-contained class is not necessary unless you have several students with severe learning disabilities in a general age range. A single student with a moderate learning disability may be best served by placement with his peers. Assign an assistant teacher or aide to that classroom to provide additional help.

Anyone planning an educational program involving learning disabled individuals should focus on some general goals for the program. A major consideration is development of the students' decision-making skills. This should include helping the student accept responsibility for his decisions. A feeling of self-worth as a child of God should be encouraged. Social skills that include competent interactions and friendship building should receive attention. The ability to communicate feelings and ideas should be a program goal. An understanding of God's love and the plan of salvation should be an ultimate goal for every learning disabled person.

- Teach children to use gestures to accompany songs, poems, and stories.
- Provide jumbo-sized pencils and crayons for young students.
- Provide help with cutting and pasting activities.
- Display sets of capital and lower case letters in elementary level classrooms.
- Allow enough space for pictures and answers to be drawn large size.
- Don't distribute worksheets until you are ready for them.
- Don't pass out pencils until the directions have been given. If the students already have pencils, ask them to lay their

pencils on the table in front of them until the signal to pick them up is given.
- Use a chalkboard and visuals with stories and lectures.
- Simplify tasks and the terms of instruction.
- Read aloud the directions given on workbook pages so they can be both seen and heard.
- Besides giving directions orally, write them on the chalkboard so they can be heard, seen, and remembered.
- Keep extraneous classroom noise to a minimum.
- Allow students to verbalize their feelings and perceptions without fear of ridicule from other students or the teacher.
- Encourage the desire to learn by making learning fun and exhibit a good sense of humor yourself.
- Show love and concern as well as discipline.

For teachers of elementary children
- Use a modern Scripture version.
- Encourage students to use a bookmark to help them follow along as you read each line of Scripture or lesson passage.
- Plan several activities; attention span may be short.
- Read memory verses in unison several times.
- Use visual aids throughout the lesson.
- Practice problem-solving in hypothetical situations.
- Help students verbalize the main idea and application of the lesson.
- To teach memory work use visual clues, partially completed sentences, and associated words to facilitate recall.
- When beginning a lesson or giving directions, make sure you have each student's full attention.

For teachers of teens and adults. Avoid "round robin" reading of the Scripture or lesson in which each person automatically takes a turn. Let students volunteer. If a student volunteers, call on him. Help him with the hard words if he hesitates several seconds. Do not immediately correct every mispronounced word. Other students listening will automatically fill in the correct word. Do not allow others in the class to correct him, as this is devastating to self-concept. If the meaning is missed because of mispronunciations, talk about the passage or background a short time. Then say, "Let's look at this passage again," and read enough of it to give the meaning. Do not allow another student to reread it, and do not draw attention to the errors.

Use discussion groups to apply the lesson. Help guide the students' thinking and decision-making.

Give directions both orally and visually when possible.

Refuse to become involved in theological arguments based on faulty logic. Do not become obsessed with changing an individual's perceptions and logic in one class period. Insights and logic must be developed gradually. They are most effective when "discovered" by the individual.

As with every other person, each learning disabled person has unique strengths and weaknesses. They are not any less worthy in the Lord's kingdom. Like every other person, these individuals need recognition and praise for accomplishments. With spiritual nourishment and a positive self-image, people with learning disabilities can enhance any church program.

A Class for Learning Disabled Children

Have you ever had to install a special bolt lock on your Bible-school room door after one of your prize pupils had broken through? Or had a seven-year-old chase one of your teacher's aides around the classroom with a vacuum sweeper? It happened in our class for hyperactive children at First Christian Church in Springfield, Ohio.

Learning disabled children have average or above-average intelligence but each learns differently than the normal learner. The problem might be perceptual—the child sees and hears perfectly, but the brain can't make perfect sense out of the information received. A motor difficulty might be involved—poor fine or gross motor abilities are frequent areas of inadequacy. Hyperactivity, the common "curse" that haunts many children, makes learning nearly impossible not only for the child himself but also for the classroom of pestered students and weary teacher who falls under the influence of his uncontrolled motion. Failures are the rule rather than the exception.

The Springfield program was begun because some children needed the program, their parents wanted the program, and church leaders saw the need for the time and effort that would go into the program. We called our class the Bible Activity Class, and in it we tried to provide means of success for children with learning disabilities in a Christian learning situation.

Class Procedure

We divided into two age groups: five to eight and nine to twelve. The younger group met during the Bible school and worship hours, while the older group met only during the worship hour. We used two converted storage rooms for our classrooms. One was named the Quiet Room and the second the Activity Room.

Bible school began with the Bible story in the Quiet Room. The teacher had to know the lesson well and be able to act it out enthusiastically to hold the short attention spans of these easily distracted youngsters. If a student got too distracted, the teacher quickly incorporated him into the story. One curly-haired boy became a tree in the garden, so we could get on with Adam and Eve.

After a quick lesson review each child got his own personal folder and went to his cubicle-like desk to begin work on his quiet activity sheets. The materials stressed areas of visual and auditory discrimination, left to right progression, object constancy, closure, and language ability. These activities might involve circling the picture that looked most like what the women saw when they came to mourn for Jesus, or filling in spaces marked "A" with red, "B" with blue, and "C" with green until the fish from the story appeared. These were not unusual activities and could be found in most workbooks. We merely provided more activities and adapted them to learning level rather than age.

After a brief refreshment break in which the older children joined the younger ones, the older ones went to the Quiet Room for the Bible story and activities. The younger children remained in the Activity Room for perceptual and motor activities such as walking around Jericho seven different ways on a walking board, completing a picture of a cross on a pegboard, identifying objects by the sound they make when shaken, or following the color-coded footprints around the room in search of the hidden idol.

With about a half hour of class time remaining, the two groups traded rooms so that the older children could do the activities while the younger ones finished their remaining quiet activities. Then both groups joined to review together and hear the lesson aim. Because most of these children had difficulty with abstract reasoning we decided to give some tangible application to remind them through the week of the point of the lesson. For example after the lesson which told of our need to join forces with God to share in His strength, we gave each child a short piece of rope. We reminded each child that while he alone was only as strong as one weak string in that rope, when teamed with God he would be strong enough to handle the many crises he would meet in the classroom or on the playground in the week ahead.

With the end of class, the students went happily on their way and teachers sat down to rest and breathe a sigh of relief.

Results

We felt we accomplished the goals we had set when we began the program. We knew we could not remediate the learning disabilities, but we hoped to provide each student with a positive attitude toward Christ and His church. We wanted to relieve the tension in the regular classrooms brought about by outbursts of bad behavior, yet we wanted to return these children to their regular classrooms as soon as each was ready to handle the situation and learn there as well.

We saw abundant evidence of a positive attitude. One of our younger boys told his brother that if he was real good, maybe someday he could come to the Bible Activity Class. Our most hyperactive little girl showed the first signs of really knowing who Jesus was when she got to hold the doll representing baby Jesus while reenacting the story of the birth of Christ. She would not put the doll down for the rest of the morning. Later, when we sang "Shine all over Springfield," she held "Jesus" up for all to see.

After the class, our regular classrooms were able to function more smoothly. We heard fewer complaints of classes being disrupted by the outbursts of a few.

We were able to slowly work these children back into the regular classrooms. Each still had problems learning, but each had succeeded and felt more secure with the other children. After a few years we had worked our class out of existence.

Special Considerations
Student selection. We had twelve children who had been diagnosed as having learning disabilities. Not all of these children enrolled in the class, because several parents were hesitant. We were careful not to force a parent's decision. A public health nurse brought two more children (and so outreach became another plus to the program).

Teacher training. At first I taught the class with assistance from several of my students. Then I taught an extension course in learning disabilities to seventeen ladies from the Springfield congregation; they began working into leadership of the program.

Facilities and materials. Several men in the congregation remodeled the storage rooms that served as classrooms. They also helped make some of the larger equipment we needed, such as walking boards and balance boards. The students and the ladies from the extension class designed the lesson worksheets as well as making yarn balls, sound cans, bean bags, tactile letters and numbers and other compact materials.

Evaluation
The class was not completely successful. On some mornings it seemed nothing was accomplished but corraling children and keeping them contained in the two rooms. There were poorly planned mornings that led to discipline problems. We made mistakes, but with God's help we were able to do good for His kingdom.

Our experience gave us all an awareness of the individual learning needs of every child. It helped us to understand that the use of activities was an important way of learning. It caused us to be more dependent upon God for His wisdom and guidance in accomplishing His work.

Everyone should have the privilege of learning God's Word so he can come to know Christ. But some are not able to adapt to conventional learning situations. If you know people like this, perhaps you will want to plan for a specially adapted learning class to open up the wonderful truths of God's Word to them.

Jesus spent a lot of time with people with special problems, and they as a result became very special people. May we always be looking for those who have special problems and try our best to help each of them as Jesus did, so that His church might go forward, whole and complete.

---

[1]M.C. Reynolds and J.C. Birth. *Teaching Exceptional Children in All America's Schools.* Council for Exceptional Children, 1977.

Emotional Disturbance

Ministry with persons having behavioral disorders

by Carol Carrington

There is a big difference between having an emotional *problem* and being *emotionally disturbed.* Hardly a day goes by that a person does not have an emotional problem. A person with a serious emotional disturbance, or behavior disorder, has prolonged, frequent, and severe emotional difficulties. This condition can involve an inability to learn, an inability to build relationships, inappropriate behavior, feelings of depression, or the development of fears or physical symptoms.

The emotionally disturbed person wants to cultivate close friendships, but has considerable trouble doing so. He may have a large number of associates or superficial friends, but no close ones. This condition persists over a long period of time and affects most of his relationships. On an educational level, this disturbance will be severe enough to affect his academic achievement.

Behavioral Disorders

Symptoms

Symptoms fall into four main categories. Listed here are some specific ways in which we see such symptoms acted out in persons' lives. The appearance of any one symptom or combination of symptoms does not necessarily indicate a behavioral disorder.

Withdrawal
- Regularly refusing to communicate or participate in familiar surroundings
- The last one in, the first one out, always sitting in the back of a group alone
- Always quitting their job or moving
- Being inactive in a classroom or home setting
- Excessive fantasizing or hallucinating
- Depression
- Autism, the extreme example of withdrawal to the point where even physical contact is avoided

Anxiety includes all the traditional phobias such as, fear of water, fear of heights, fear of closed spaces, and fear of open spaces. Recently, other phobias have gained attention that could reflect behavioral disorder: fear of leaving the house ("housewife syndrome") and fear of being overweight.

The biggest, most overriding anxiety of the emotionally disturbed person is the fear of rejection!

Aggression
- Fighting
- Arguing
- Name calling
- Graffiti
- Self abuse: using drugs, homemade tattoos, scarring the body with sharp objects or writing utensils, deliberate carelessness with personal hygiene
- Getting pregnant to punish a friend or family member
- Lawbreaking of all kinds

Other symptoms. These behavior patterns either overlap the other categories or seem to demand a class by themselves.

- Physical ailments, self-induced by fear, neglect, or anger
- Short attention span
- Easily distracted

- Hyperactivity
- Impulsiveness

Contributing Factors

No one knows what "causes" a behavior disorder, but the following problems can contribute to it. The appearance of any one or a combination of these factors does not mean that emotional disturbance necessarily follows.

Chemical/biological
- Tumors
- Injury due to accident or abuse
- Congenital or hereditary defects
- Poor prenatal or postnatal care

Severe emotional shock
- Frightening experience
- Death of a loved one
- Divorce
- Loss of job or home
- Abuse
- Inconsistent parental behavior (showing affection for the child one moment, screaming at him or abusing him the next; setting up one standard of right and wrong for parents and another for children)

Severe deprivation or hyper-stimulation. Severe deprivation is a complete or near complete lack of attention and affection. Hyperstimulation is a complete or near complete lack of privacy made more difficult by a constant high level of noise and/or activity.

Remember, the above are "contributing factors." It is extremely difficult to name exact causes in any specific case of behavioral disorder.

Background

History. Not until recent years has this specific area of disorder been identified and made the focus of positive treatment.

Through the 1940's, people with behavioral disabilities were lumped into a few general categories and committed to institutions or prisons or ignored.

During the twenty-five years following World War II, and as a result of studies done on "shell shocked" veterans, an explosion occurred in the field of special education. The number of special education courses and schools doubled or tripled during that time. The Kennedy family made public their efforts to work with an emotionally and mentally disordered sister. This effort encouraged people by the thousands to "come out of the closet" with their own, or a family member's, emotional disorder and seek help.

The 1970's saw a big push toward recognizing emotionally disturbed people as a group with special problems and needs of their own. The right to a free, public education has supposedly been available to every citizen of the United States for generations. But it was not until the passage of Public Law 94-142 in 1975 that many school systems were made to comply with that right. Until that time, many school systems could and did refuse to educate children with special needs because, they reasoned, it would be impractical to alter facilities, curriculum, staff and budget for "just one child."

Statistics. Emotional disturbance has strong ties to the educational system. Estimates on the number of emotionally disturbed public school students vary from 10% to 20% (I prefer the figure of 12%). To this point, behavior disorder shows up more in school-age boys from 7 to 12 years and girls from 9 to 14. One early study of 441 children already diagnosed and enrolled in a program for the emotionally disturbed showed that 83.2% were boys and 16.8% were girls.[1]

Except in the more severe cases, emotional disturbance usually appears to decrease once a student has left the school system and passed into adulthood! Of course there are emotionally disturbed adults. But the pressures that may trigger such behavior are usually more frequent and more intense for a student. And, due to the nature of a daily school schedule, there are more opportunities for disturbed behavior to show itself.

Emotional disturbance is an Equal Opportunity Disturber. It can affect any person regardless of race, color, creed, or social or economic background.

Emotional Disturbance and the Scriptures. While it can be stated simply that sin is the root cause of all the world's ills, emotional disturbance included, sin itself is not a simple matter. A person's emotional difficulties may be the consequence of his own sin. "The sins of the fathers" may still be visited upon the children due to years or even generations of poor child rearing and unhealthy family environments.

However, in many cases emotional disturbance cannot be directly attributed to a person's own sin or the sin of people close to him. The contributing factors to his behavior disorder, like a physiological problem or a traumatic emotional experience, can be beyond his control or the control of those around him.

In dealing with the emotionally disturbed victim of the world's sin, the Christian will have to cut through layers of unreasonable guilt, grief, fear, hopelessness, discouragement, anger, bitterness, and ignorance.

Some persons having behavioral disorders will already have become Christians. These are among the "timid" and the "weak" whom Paul admonishes us to encourage and help in 1 Thessalonians 5:14. These are among the people "caught in a sin" whom we "who are spiritual should restore ... gently" (Galatians 6:1). It takes a good amount of digging into the Scripture, heavy duty prayer, and serious counsel to break through the layers of these problems that are more varied, more deeply ingrained, and more insidious than normal.

Within the Church Program

The Christian dealing with emotionally disturbed people within the church structure has his work cut out for him! You cannot exclude them and yet their presence, whether adult or child, creates extra problems and extra work. What's a teacher, preacher, or worker to do?

Facilities and Equipment

The room. Choose a room away from parts of the building where noise outside would be a distraction to the class and where class noise would be a distraction to others (if necessary, go to a nearby building). The room should be large enough to handle a variety of activities in addition to necessary furniture. The smaller the child, the more room necessary.

Do not hold class in open spaces subject to a lot of audio and visual distractions. Acoustical ceiling tiles and carpeting will help contain noise. The carpet could cover a portion of the floor and one or two walls. Keep windows above students' eye level or use heavy curtains to cut down on visual distractions.

Install good, even lighting.

Furniture and Decoration. Keep designs and decorations simple, and locate them at what should be the center of attention. Have one visual focal point; that is, a display area, temporary or permanent, where object lessons and props are located. This will help keep their attention where you want it. Use light, pleasant, subdued pastels for surface colors.

Steer clear of furniture that is too comfortable. It is easy to turn off your mind when you are too comfortable. All furniture must be especially sturdy! Furniture easily broken often encourages an emotionally disturbed child's destructive tendencies. Use a rocking chair for a hyperactive child. He can vent his hyperactivity on the chair and pay attention at the same time.

Teaching Supplies. Use some means of producing soothing background music, which is especially helpful in room settings where there is considerable noise outside. Audiovisual equipment must be sturdily encased. All equipment must be kept in good working order. It is discouraging to have ineffective or inoperable equipment. Such conditions say, "You don't really care."

Use staples instead of push pins or tacks for bulletin boards. Staples are less likely to be used for inflicting injury.

Decorative knickknacks or toys should be of a sturdy nature. Choose wood over plastic.

Use films occasionally. They are an excellent means for conveying a message, and for focusing attention on the lesson.

Teaching Approach

Time. All segments of class time should be shorter than usual. (A lesson series will, therefore, take more weeks to cover.) Break each class period into segments of "quiet times" and "energy burn-ing times." If you do not make allowances for energy burnoff, your students will do it for you in unacceptable ways. Allow for small group activities. Don't make everyone do the same thing all the time.

Plan every minute in detail. If necessary, print an agenda for yourself and display it prominently in the classroom. There must not be a time when your class has "nothing" to do. Even so, be flexible enough in attitude to follow through with expression of genuine interest, even if it prevents the completion of your tight class schedule. Better too much than not enough to do!

Structure the room to fit your schedule. Keep things out of sight until you are ready for the class to concentrate on those things.

Method. Have a single lesson aim for each class time. Your purpose is to communicate one thought well, not to bombard them with large amounts of information.

Emotionally disturbed people cover the whole gamut of intellec-tual ability. The depth of material can be identical to that of any other group. You will need to simply and carefully explain all important terms and ideas. Though they may be of normal or above normal intelligence, they may not use the same speaking vocabulary you do. Their inability to concentrate affects their ability to understand.

Know some of each student's background, so you'll understand which approach to take or avoid with that person. Do not demand discussion if they are reluctant to talk, and do not expect a talka-tive student to stop talking just because it is class time. You must kindly help this person understand why silence is sometimes im-portant, and when. It is a real chore for this student to stop talking.

Discipline. Be full of praise and reward! Discipline is as much reward as it is punishment. Emphasize character development and spiritual attributes rather than athletic prowess or academic achievement. Praise them for nice things they say and do and make these the important items in your class.

Use another person as an aide or a team teacher to help control the crowd while you are directing activities.

Make your expectations clear. Phrase your explanations in such a way that you do not insult your students' intelligence or patronize them.

Be kind but firm in your correcting and rebuking. Do not humiliate them. Do not lose your temper. You are not in a contest with your student. But neither should a soft tone of voice or touch of the hand disguise your seriousness.

Be fair and consistent. Do not administer a punishment that has nothing to do with the infraction or magnify the seriousness of small incidents. Do not demonstrate firmness on one occasion and apathy on another. Do admit it when you are wrong and apologize when the occasion occurs.

Do not fear the student or the student's family. Let the family know what difficulties you are experiencing and work with them (if they are willing).

Maintain a good sense of humor. Be concerned but not shocked by what your students say and do.

Develop skills in "active ignoring." If a certain behavior pattern is not obviously distracting the rest of the class or yourself, ignore it.

Suggestions for Worship

The preacher and worship leader face the perennial problem of trying to meet many needs at the same time with one service. Rather than expecting each aspect of worship to meet everyone's needs, rely on creating an overall atmosphere of love, forgiveness, acceptance, power, and authority. You can do this as much by your tone of voice and a leader's attitude as by specific methods.

The emotionally disturbed person many times has difficulty in concentrating and handling more than one idea at a time. Make sure everything in a worship service takes these items into account.

Use different methods of preaching that will grab peoples' attention. "Children's sermons" or object lessons can be used either as service openers or during the actual message time.

Use songs with simple, one-thought messages, take time to explain the words and ideas in traditional hymns.

Explain the meanings and origins behind furniture in the sanctuary (or other furnishings throughout your building).

Make Communion meditations a time for short, powerful, and novel messages.

Have well-trained, strategically placed staff to help calm down excitable listeners.

Cultivate "active ignoring" skills and skills of impromptu confronting. At times a disruptive person must be dealt with *right then* by the person in charge of the worship service.

Outside the Church Schedule

It is hard to imagine a congregation having an effective ministry for the emotionally disturbed persons within the church schedule if such service is not carried on *outside* those walls.

Get to know how your school-age students are doing academically. Visit with their teachers; see how the two of you can work together. Provide tutoring if possible. Let the school system know if your congregation has made allowances for emotionally disturbed persons within your Bible school and worship.

Provide for or refer to private counseling and support groups that have experience in dealing with these problems. Never just "turn over" an emotionally disturbed person to a professional. Make it a shared responsibility between the two of you to serve this person.

Express an interest in the person's family, not just in him. Invite the person and/or his family to your house for special or just relaxing times. Provide helpful services for the family; babysitting, transportation, supervision of older children, relief of household responsibilities. Allow family members to "get away from it all" for a while and spend time with other family without the tense presence of a problem person. Inform the families that your congregation does have Bible school and worship with the emotionally disturbed person taken into consideration.

Provide special classes, seminars, and literature for adults or parents of emotionally disturbed persons on such subjects as parenting, hygiene, nutrition, health and safety, home finances. Make these churchwide opportunities; do not single out the emotionally disturbed person or parent.

Help the person pick out mini-goals to work on daily or weekly.

Mini-goals are small parts of the overall problem. Outline a step-by-step process of achieving each mini-goal. Help him keep track of his accomplishments on the way to achieving that ultimate goal—elimination of the behavioral disorder.

Avoid "non-involvement." If immediate intervention is called for in a health-threatening or life-threatening situation, do not hesitate to call the proper authorities!

Within the church setting, the most important guideline in working with emotionally disturbed people is to *plan, plan, plan!* Do not have any idle moments. Keep them busy. Let their energies work toward a planned goal, something of a constructive teaching nature, no matter how unorthodox! Emotional disturbance can be reversed. It may be that we have not yet found the key to that change, but it is there. Many emotionally disturbed individuals do become effective and well-functioning people.

---

[1]Morse, Cutler, and Fink, 1964

PART THREE

Building a Caring Ministry

This section will give you a greater background about disabilities in general and ways that the church can serve (and serve *with*) persons having disabilities.

- Why we should care
- Overcoming physical barriers and barriers of attitude
- The importance of one-to-one relationships
- Relating with group home staff people
- Camping as a ministry tool
- Music as a ministry tool
- Serving the families of disabled persons
- How to set up a church ministry program

A Model of Compassion

*The role of the church with
persons having disabilities*

by Robert O. Fife and Jim Pierson

A Biblical Perspective

"Whatever you did for the least of these brothers of mine, you did for me." These are the words of the king who will sit upon his throne on the Day of Judgment. They are addressed to the righteous who have asked the surprising question, "Lord, when did we see you ... ?" (Matthew 25:31-46)

These righteous people had indeed ministered to the needy, but not for reward or praise. True, they had been moved by the compassion learned from Jesus. But they did not realize that in serving others, they had actually ministered to Him. How could this be? Because Jesus identifies with even the least and most needy people on earth.

Surely this is sufficient reason for modern followers of Jesus to be concerned when they see the special, real needs of people.

Such compassion had an ancient tradition in Israel. You can read about David's concern for Mephibosheth, the son of Jonathan. The young king cared for him by taking him into his own household (2 Samuel 9:13).

The Hebrew family traditionally provided for those who were disadvantaged. The immediate household *(beth)* was marked by intense mutual devotion. But the widow or the orphan were cared for by the *mishpahah*–the larger family group.

In contrast, the ancient Romans showed little sympathy for the weak. The Roman father had unquestioned authority over his family. He could reject an infant that displeased him because of its sex or because it was not "normal."

But if caring was an ancient tradition in Israel, it was not always honored in Jesus' day. People had even devised a "religious" way to avoid responsibility for his aged, needy parents. This was a process called "Corban," in which a prosperous Jew could dedicate his wealth to God. Then he might say to his impoverished parents, "I'm sorry. I wish I could help you. But my possessions are not my own. They have been devoted to God."

It is not surprising that Jesus condemned such a practice. It used the name of God as a pretext to avoid the law of God expressed in the commandment, "Honor your father and mother" (see Mark 7:6-13). In the judgment, the words of the king will radically repudiate all such efforts to separate Him from the disadvantaged of the earth: "Whatever you did for the least of these brothers of mine, you did for me."

Throughout His ministry, Jesus revealed the ultimate concern of God. How often it was said that Jesus had compassion (Matthew 9:36; 14:14; 15:32). To have compassion is to "feel with" someone. Compassion is one's costly identification with the plight of another.

Jesus gave us a perfect example of compassion. He responded to the need for love we all have (Mark 10:21), but neither was He unmoved by the special needs of many people.

Jesus' miracles were "signs" because He revealed the complete self-giving of the heavenly Father, poured out for the world of human need. Power flowed out of Jesus with every miracle of healing (Mark 5:25f). His ministry was so exhausting that He once fell asleep amidst a terrifying storm (Matthew 8:23). Such is the cost of compassion.

The disciples had to learn Jesus' compassion. This did not come easily, for they often seemed to think that persons and their needs were getting in the way of God's kingdom. They considered the little children an intrusion in the midst of a busy day. But Jesus knew there is nothing more important than a little child. Indeed, it is of such the kingdom consists (Matthew 19:13-15). The disciples thought blind Bartimaeus' urgent cries for help were a nuisance. But Jesus heard, and said, "Call him" (Mark 10:46f). They would have sent the multitude away hungry. Jesus said, "Give them something to eat" (Matthew 14:16).

But perhaps the greatest impediment to learning Jesus' compassion was what has been called in modern times the "I/It" relationship. This is a way of looking at another human being as an object – a "thing" – rather than as a person. Such was the attitude of the twelve disciples when confronted by a blind person. They asked, "Rabbi, who sinned, this man or his parents, that he was born blind?" (John 9:1-3) They saw him as a problem to be discussed – not as a person who needed help. He was what moderns so aptly called a "case study." This was an "I/It" relationship.

Jesus refused to treat the blind man in such a dehumanizing manner. Here was a person, made in the image of God. He deserved better than to be treated as a mere object of discussion.

First, Jesus' rebuke of the disciples, who assumed the man was born blind because of sin, should forever warn Christians against making such judgments. Then, with the most humble means – clay and spittle – Jesus established an "I/Thou" relationship, healing the blind man. In so doing, He judged the attitudes many have toward persons with disabilities. All too often we are uncomfortable in their presence; sometimes we are profoundly embarrassed. Tongue-tied, we look the other way. We fail to see them as persons, living souls to be lifted up.

Even in the name of charity, well-intentioned Christians may treat others as objects to be cared for – not *persons* to be related to. We may devise "programs for the disadvantaged" because they are different. *But they are not different in their humanity.* We are all persons for whom Jesus died. We all have ultimate worth.

Programs for handicapped people – especially those sponsored by the church – should be designed to further the "I/Thou" relationship that always characterized Jesus' relationships.

The acts of the early church show that the disciples did learn the compassion of Jesus. The "community of the resurrection" was immediately noted for its remarkable care. We read, "All the believers were together and had everything in common. Selling their possessions and goods, they gave to anyone as he had need" (Acts 2:44, 45).

The church would continue the sensitive ministry of Jesus in many ways. Peter and John healed the lame man at the Beautiful Gate (Acts 3:1f). Now they really saw the man with compassionate concern. He was not an object of charity to be dismissed with a few alms. He was a person worthy of their personal care. Fastening their eyes upon this man, Peter and John said, "Look on us!" Here was the "I/Thou" relationship of Jesus, living on in the church.

Paul exhibited the same compassion of Christ when he liberated a Philippian slave woman from an evil spirit. Her plight was being used by her masters to their profit, but to her degradation. The apostle was so troubled by the sight, he cast out the demon. (Acts 16:16f). Paul, a former persecutor, had now become a minister of compassion.

The early church had thus become the community of ultimate concern. That concern has never been completely lost. Even so, it is distressing to see how easily the acquisitive, self-centered spirit of the age may distract the body of Christ from His ministry. In some cultures the church has developed vast wealth amidst squalor and want. In other societies—especially in nations whose governments have assumed major social responsibility, such as the United States and Australia—churches have not been so wealthy as indifferent.

Perhaps government's new role may be interpreted at least in part to the influence of the church. But the church can never abandon to the state that compassionate "I/Thou" relationship, which is a dimension of Christian love. Government has resources of wealth, enabling it to do some things the church cannot do. But the church also has resources—spiritual resources—not available to the state.

For this reason, the contemporary church dare not be indifferent. Followers of Jesus ought to be in the forefront of efforts to remove the barriers people face, or at least make their burdens easier to carry.

Caring in the Pew

For the past twenty years, I have observed and participated in the exciting changes that have brought improved services to persons with handicaps. Working in an agency that serves young-sters with developmental disabilities, I have watched physical, occupational, and speech therapists (as well as social workers) improve the lives of children and their families. Teaching in col-leges, I have observed student teachers, Christian educators, and ministers become excited about their involvement in the lives of persons with handicaps.

The government has mandated a free and appropriate educa-tion for all disabled children through Public Law 94-142. Na-tional television shows discuss the problems of individuals with various disabilities and the resultant problems of their families. Public buildings have become more accessible. Many fields (archi-tecture, law enforcement, business) have become more responsive to the needs of persons with mental retardation, cerebral palsy, autism, blindness, and deafness.

The religious education community has responded to the spiri-tual needs of persons with handicaps. A small stack of materials to help Christian educators with the task of teaching the person with handicaps in Bible school and Vacation Bible School has grown into a large one. Christian education journals have added columns and/or devoted entire issues to Christian special educa-tion. Multimedia materials have been developed. Many churches have opened Bible schools, worship services, recreational pro-grams, and day-care programs for persons with handicaps.

Involvement

In all of this positive development there is still a problem. The person in the pew does not sense the need or feel the personal involvement with individuals with handicaps. A minister of edu-cation in a large midwestern church recently reported to me that many members were unaware that the congregation sponsored a special Bible-school program. An official in another religious group known for its outstanding services to persons with disabili-ties reports that while the members give money to the support of the institutions, they do not show personal involvement. How does involvement happen for the person in the pew?

First, the person with a handicap must be seen as a person. Responding to the handicap and not the person creates a barrier for interpersonal relationships. While the use of labels is determined by the attitude of the user, saying what one means does make a difference in that attitude. There is a real difference in saying "the cerebral palsied" and "persons with cerebral palsy." "Mentally retarded," "Down syndrome," and "von Recklinghausen's disease" are good for research and funding purposes, but they should never hide the person who is so diagnosed. Handicapped persons are more like normal persons than they are different. They want to be noticed for who they are—not for their handicapping symptoms. They want to be loved, to be accepted, to succeed.

A second factor that can change the person-in-the-pew's attitude is to feel the importance of sharing the gospel with persons who have disabilities. While everyone needs to be taught about the wonderful love of Jesus Christ, persons with mental retardation present a challenge. Because of poor cognitive skills, their learning abilities are limited. But a depressed IQ does not lessen the need for the soul to develop. The person with mental retardation has a soul that needs to be exposed to the teachings of Jesus and nurtured in His love. The Lord told His followers that His gospel was for everyone. No one should be denied the right to know the good news.

Frequently, in a discussion of whether or not the church is responsible for working with this population group, the question will arise, "Won't the Lord understand?" Central to providing Christian education for mentally retarded persons is the question of whether or not they can become Christians. Harold Stubblefield, in *The Church's Ministry in Mental Retardation* (Broadman, 1965), summarizes the four most common positions.

- Mentally retarded people are not aware or responsible.
- They are aware of their religious needs but not responsible.
- They are aware and responsible.
- Their awareness of religion and their responsibility to it are dependent on mental development.

I agree with the last position.

The person with mental retardation is classified as educable, trainable, or dependent. Of the total population, eighty-four percent can be educated. A person in this group can peak mentally

Special Class Day

My small congregation (200 members) fully supported our ministry to mentally retarded persons in a financial and official sense. But we were isolated from the rest of the congregation. We held Bible class, VBS, and any special activities separately. Only once a month do we attend worship service with the whole congregation.

To help bring people together, we held a special service honoring our mentally retarded members. It was held during our regular Sunday morning worship hour. We wrote to the families of all the group home residents attending our church and invited them to come, and we also invited the group home staff (about half the people invited came).

We began with our group singing three hymns they had chosen and practiced the week before. Then, one at a time, each class member stood and faced the congregation. I introduced each one and told the people something about him or her—their talents, likes and dislikes, and the ways they contribute to our class. We concluded with a three-minute slide presentation.

After the service, our class members and their families were the guests of honor at a congregational dinner, followed by games and fellowship outside.

The occasion helped class members and congregation alike by bringing them together. The class members dressed up for the occasion, wore name tags, and enjoyed the spotlight for a day. The congregation appreciated the chance to connect names with faces and learned a lot of valuable personal information. They sat and ate with the class members, called them by name, and later played games with them outdoors. After that day, several people have visited us during our regular class sessions.

It's helpful to have another church committee planning the day's activities so you can concentrate on the worship service and on meeting the family members. In our case, this work was done by an active Missions ministry.

The day was a great way to gain publicity and good will for our class and to break down barriers between people. We now plan a day like this every year.

(R.E.K.)

around nine to thirteen years of age, the age at which most normal children become Christians. The church definitely has a responsibility to provide Christian education for persons with handicaps. The success of this endeavor will depend on the support of every member of the congregation.

Another factor that can make a difference is letting persons with handicaps give. It is easy to do for them. They have too long been the objects of our charitable concern. Robert Perske wrote a marvelous, worth-reading book, *New Life in the Neighborhood* (Abingdon), which relates the delightful account of thirty-two teenagers in a state institution who wanted to exercise the basic human right of giving to others. During the Christmas season of 1962, Perske reports, the institution was packed with several community agency groups singing carols for the residents. The teenagers were bothered. Seventeen-year-old Harold observed that they could sing as well as the visiting troubadors. Surely there were groups out there they should sing for. Ten homes serving persons who were elderly became the recipients of the successful giving of self from these teenagers. Allowing the person with a disability to give to any relationship builds that relationship.

Understanding

The person in the pew often feels uncomfortable in the presence of a person with an obvious handicap. I have asked students and seminar participants on two continents to summarize their feelings if a person with cerebral palsy walked up to them on the street and asked the time. The responses vary, but the most common ones are "fear" and "I'm afraid." Those responses imply that the person might do them harm.

From the days of the Salem witchcraft trials, many have believed that persons who are not normal are bad. Perhaps the modern version of this attitude began early in this century, when noted psychologists and sociologists believed that people with "good blood" were noble and virtuous while those with "bad blood" were ignoble and morally loose.

A 1912 bestseller by Henry Goddard, *The Kallikak Family* (Macmillan), made the theory popular. Goddard told the story of Martin Kallikak Sr., a Revolutionary War soldier full of good English blood who cohabited with a "feeble minded" girl at a tavern. The result of this union was a son named by his mother, Martin Kallikak, Jr. From this son, Goddard claims to have identified 480 descendants. Their numbers included the mentally retarded, the sexually immoral, epileptics, paupers, perverts, horse thieves, and alcoholics. Mr. Goddard continued his study by reporting that upon leaving the army, Martin Sr., improved his ways and married a girl of good blood. From this marriage came 496 descendants—you guessed it! They were all normal, not one problem. They started universities, married into the best families, entered the best professions, and were signers of important documents.

Even though scientists now believe that the Goddard study was spurious, I wonder how much current public attitude is flavored by the "study." Jesus' response should lessen our fears of handicapped persons and motivate us to assist them in displaying God's works in their lives.

A Perfect Model

Finally, if the pulpit spoke clearly of Jesus' response to persons who are handicapped, the listener would have a perfect model to follow. His was a personal involvement. He saw them as individuals with a problem. First, His touch changed lives. The leper who asked for cleansing never dreamed that Jesus would extend His hand and touch him (Matthew 8:3). Second, Jesus' ministry was not limited to cures; He followed through. After healing an invalid of thirty-eight years (John 5) Jesus looked for him in the temple and discussed sin with him. Third, Jesus was sensitive to the feelings and situations that affected the lives of people. When the disciples could not heal the young epileptic, Jesus' first response was to show His concern by asking the father, "How long has he been like this?" (Mark 9:21) His divine example should help us rightly divide the truth to persons who are handicapped.

As I have watched changes in services to handicapped persons over the last two decades, I wonder what the next one will bring, especially in the Christian community. Those projections I won't make, but I am sure that the changes will be in proportion to the level of love, interest, and support shown to persons with handicaps and their families by the person in the pew, and to the strength of the belief that the gospel is for "every creature."

Overcoming Barriers

*Making your congregation accessible
in architecture, attitude, and communication*

by Harold H. Wilke

"I heard the church bells this morning toll the death of an infant, and I was hoping it was your poor little crippled baby."

I was three weeks old when these words were spoken to my mother by a well-meaning acquaintance from church at a chance meeting at the grocery store. I was the "poor little crippled baby," born with no arms, delivered by a country doctor who told my parents, "I've never known anything like this before." My birth caused a stir in our small community, a torrent of tormenting, accusing questions for my parents, and a string of experiences: rejection and acceptance, pain and healing.

My mother had ample occasion to rely upon her strong Christian faith. The encounter with the woman in the grocery store was indicative of a greater struggle she—and eventually I—would have to face. There were bitter hours when she felt utterly alone with what she had brought forth. At first, my father went to pieces. His firm foundation of what *is* in the world came all undone. Nothing had prepared this self-reliant, strong, caring man for what he now had to face—even consoling my mother seemed beyond him.

My grandmother, who made her home with us, cried whenever she thought of me or cared for me during my first year of life. My older brother, able-bodied and only a year older than I, needed nurture and much attention. My mother, constantly confronted by a pool of panic, experienced rejection in many areas. In a few years, the public school was firm in their refusal to accept me as a student.

Rejection is an all-too-common experience for persons with handicaps and their families—and, in some cases, *from* their families. Our society, which so prizes normality, conformity, and physical perfection, has fostered a tragic history of rejection—even the church has sadly acquiesced throughout much of its history.

My own experiences of handicap and rejection—as well as my struggles in faith—have been an intimate education in the meaning of health, healing, and wholeness. So have experiences of care and acceptance.

"Send this child away to an institution where he can be fitted with arms and can go to school. I'll pay the expenses." The well-to-do, well-meaning resident of our town who said these words to my father was acting out of the highest motivation. Surely, he felt, this little armless child could have no chance of a future without new arms and adequate schooling. Wasn't an institution necessary for this?

Had my father accepted the offer, my life would have been radically different. It was surely tempting for my parents after the countless experiences of pain and rejection.

Institutionalization always seems tempting in cases of persons with handicaps. It is easier to take the problem away from the immediate relationship. A good institution will certainly provide a highly professional understanding and a different environment. It may take away the additional financial burden; it may seem to provide an escape from social isolation.

But our society has for too long taken the easy option of institutionalization—often with an enormous cost; in fact, institutions are frequently another form of painful rejection. More and more we need to consider alternatives to the institution as we seek to provide health and wholeness to persons with handicaps.

My own parents resisted institutionalization for me; instead, I was blessed with the greatest of healing factors: a caring community.

Many neighbors and friends within our church and community, once they dealt with the trauma of their own brush with vulnerability, came forward and rallied to our support. Shy at first, like

that curious, limited woman in the grocery store, they soon offered me and my family what they had: the stability of a caring
congregation, a caring fellowship. Through their caring acceptance, I was enabled to get involved in various church activities,
even teaching in our church school.

Perhaps the most significant factor in my growth was my home
life, rooted in the solid faith of my parents. One of their gifts was
inculcating in me a sense of self-reliance and personal responsibility. Such "self-starting" certainly wasn't guaranteed at home—
any parents' tendency to "smother-love," caused by guilt feelings,
may radically inhibit growth. Nor is self-dependence impossible
in an institution. But I was lucky. My parents had a high level of
expectation for me and they worked with me to help me achieve
it.

Once when I was two or three years old, sitting on the floor of
my bedroom, trying to get a shirt on over my head and around my
shoulders, I was having an extraordinarily difficult time. While I
grunted and sweated, my mother stood watching. Her arms must
have been held rigidly at her side; every instinct in her wanted to
reach out and put my shirt on for me.

Finally, a neighbor who was visiting asked in exasperation why
my mother wasn't helping. My mother responded through gritted
teeth, "I *am* helping!"

Her painful withholding of love was helping me. And my pain
and sweat level, while high in that moment, was being reduced in
the long run as I learned the crucial lesson of responsibility and
self-motivation. That was for me an important component in my
own health and wholeness. So were my father's imaginative efforts at helping me to learn to swim. Or the countless other caring
gifts they gave me—and helped me to give to myself.

The Church and
Disabled People

Socially alienated persons are far too often rejected by the local
congregation. They are responded to, if at all, primarily in terms
of a "mission" on the part of the church to these groups—to alcoholics, the mentally retarded, the physically disabled, returnees

from mental hospitals, the violence-prone, former prisoners, and the aging. These are the persons who are wounded or ill on the road to Jericho wherever we travel.

Our comfort is disturbed, our feelings are jolted by the presence of such a person in church (and as much on the way to church). We do not want to be reminded of the presence of such alienated persons in overwhelming numbers in our society, and of Christ's response to them.

Their name is legion. People with physical or developmental disabilities, for example, number over 30 million persons in the United States. But they are seen only when one consciously bothers to notice. They are seen only when we remove our blinders, for they exist outside the comfortable purview of most church members. Alienated persons are in every third home on the block, and they are spread throughout our society; but far too often these persons in wheelchairs and otherwise incapacitated remain "in the attic," where society has placed them through the years. We have a history of keeping people "out of sight, out of mind."

In the U.S. it has been thought the proper thing for the church to institutionalize such persons, and in many cases the church has turned over to secular society the keeping of such institutions. Several of our denominations have been leaders in the establishment of institutions to care for disabled people, work that is motivated by humanitarian concern and that often is necessary. But it is not always true that institutions can best take care of alienated people.

In considering ways in which the church has responded to the needs of persons with disabilities (and alienated persons in general), we must keep in mind the church's contribution to the systems of institutional and community care we now have. While these may be mostly supported by tax dollars, their inherent motivation derives from Christian understanding, and their policies and guidelines reflect a basic Christian concern.

As for the church itself, specialized ministries are carried out for specific target groups, such as the deaf or the blind, often by a single church or by several churches cooperating at a local level. For example, within a local area, churches might point out to those needing such a service that "signing" for the deaf is carried on at one or more specific churches in the city. Deaf members in a church where such signing is not practiced are in effect invited to the church where it is, even though that church may be of another denomination.

Separatist attempts have been made, in which some congregations minister only to disabled persons. Work is also being done by many denominational organizations and councils, relating the church to the various secular institutional responses available.

I am most in agreement with the church's efforts to "mainstream" persons with special needs. In thousands of congregations a minister or leader had raised the question of why a disabled member of the congregation has to go elsewhere. "Of course we must make it possible for him (her) to attend here," they say. Then they begin working to overcome three kinds of barriers: those of architecture, communication, and attitude. For a church to be truly accessible, all three of these barriers must be overcome—the ramp is not enough. The most difficult and pervasive barrier of the three is the barrier of attitude.

The Worst Barrier

Barriers of attitudes stand in the way of understanding and acceptance. They stand between person and person. On either side of the barrier, each person extends outward to many other persons, institutions, and even countries. A ripple effect takes place; these attitudinal barriers may be immensely more difficult to overcome than the architectural ones, difficult as those are in accessibility.

This barrier of attitude begins inside the individual; it is in "me." It is not something "out there." It is not a thing, such as a building with many steps. Since it is within myself, it may not even be based on fact in regard to the other person—but it clearly is real to me!

How can I deal with this barrier of attitude? Do I even want to deal with it? I feel deeply within myself the need to walk away from this barrier: I don't even see the point of attempting to scale it or beat it down. Why must I deal with it at all? How much should it really concern me?

So I simply move away. Even as I turn aside irresolutely, or sharply turn my back and go the other way, I feel nagging questions within me. These questions have to do with how much that barrier of attitude really reflects something within myself, and I have to ask whether I have dealt with this internal problem of my own. I have the haunting feeling that my accepting the reality of this attitudinal barrier actually has to do with my acceptance of myself: it involves questions of my own identity and my own place. Is my acceptance of this barrier on the outside, so to speak, really a reflection of my failure to accept myself?

Lacking a sense of acceptance, feeling that we are not wanted, we may develop all kinds of armor plate and personal protective devices: "I won't accept it"; "I won't deal with it"; "I don't believe it's really true"; and so on.

Yet the nagging question persists. My barriers of attitude toward others may actually be a reflection of the barriers within myself, of my difficulties in accepting my own being.

Recognizing the Fears

At this point, I can turn around once more to face the reality of that barrier–of that attitude of nonhandicapped toward the handicapped. I can see the way it reflects some of my own feelings about myself, and I can also see how my dealing with that barrier may actually help me deal with the more personal barriers within me. I am after all a human being, and as such subject to these tensions and anxieties.

I begin by recognizing the need for acceptance as universal. I have something in common with this handicapped person I see! He needs acceptance just as I do! She wants to be wanted, and so do I!

Having taken this one positive step, I can now begin to look at the total picture of attitudinal barriers and consider the other ways of overcoming my fears and hesitations. To begin with myself, I must recognize in all honesty that these hesitations are present. To say "I will do this" really starts with "I must first see all the underbrush in the way before I can take this step." Make no mistake about it, this underbrush is present. These impediments in my own emotional responses are very real. I must be able to recognize the fact of their existence and learn how to deal with them.

My first fear is that somehow this disability of the other individual is "catching." It might actually infect me. As soon as I say this in words I recognize how foolish the concept is, but the fear (usually unconscious to me) is actually present.

A second fear is related to this first one – that this unknown "thing" out there attached to this person, who seems so different from me and others, is threatening to me in still other ways. I don't understand how the threat exists. I only know that I am afraid. The person with the obvious physical handicap represents the unknown, and we're all scared of the unknown. Whether it is ready to pounce on me or not, I don't know. But somehow I must defend myself. This feeling too is unconscious, but it forces its way into my conscious level and I may well break out in sweat and stammering.

The third fear is even more agonizing because it represents something that is actually in me. It symbolizes my own weakness and my own inability; it makes me cry out in recognition of my own handicaps and my own shortcomings. In this case, the fear is not something created by that "thing" out there, but rather what that thing induces within me, so that I am now torn within myself.

To all of these fears, spirit and body respond. The philosopher William James placed our responses to these fears in two categories: "fight or flight." Either I fight back, defending myself from this thing – this fear – or I flee from it, getting as far away as I can.

In being honest with myself, I look at this fear for what it really is. I do not try to squelch it or ignore it in other ways, but recognize and deal with it. I lift it to my consciousness and attempt to look at it as openly and clearly as possible. As I look at myself, I see the other fears and anxieties intertwined with this one, and I recognize a whole new series of tasks on which I must work.

A fourth fear is one many disabled people have. It comes out of the three mentioned above – the fear of rejection. It is the opposite of the universal need for acceptance. Defenses against rejection may indeed take various forms.

To accept myself, it is good to know that the problem is not mine alone. We are all in this one together; most of us have psychological and emotional difficulties. Many of us feel something of the pain experienced by that tremendously large number of persons around the world confined to various forms of ghetto existence:

poverty creates such; racism creates such; sexism creates such. Each of these is a handicap primarily because of the attitude of others (that there is something inherently wrong with having an ethnic difference that shows, for example). Seeing the problem in this worldwide perspective and therefore with the lengthening of the list of handicapped—that which makes people unacceptable—we begin dimly to see the universality of handicapping conditions. All of us are involved.

Dissipating the sense of rejection is far more painful than an appeal to humor or to a sense of other persons' involvements suggests. A whole process may be involved, one to which I have given the name of "healing process." In terms of a physical disability, for example, the feelings a person has in response to the event which has overwhelmed her or him usually include these: shock, disbelief, bitterness, rebellion, guilt, anxiety, hostility, depression, painful awareness. The actions of the individual, which may more or less correspond with these feelings, include the following: denial, running away, overacceptance, martyrdom, isolation, preoccupation with loss, inability to return to usual activities, gradual awareness of unreality of present attitudes, readjustment to reality. These are the steps in the healing process.

Certainly these steps are not followed easily or routinely or regularly. Some people will never achieve the final step. Some may retain at least some of the feelings all their lives—guilt or anxiety or hostility or depression. Honest, if painful, reappraisal of one's image is required.

Some Marks of an
Accessible Congregation

An accessible congregation is one that has overcome three barriers: physical or architectural barriers that make it difficult for persons with handicaps to enter, communication barriers in sight, sound, and understanding that impede the communication of the message and inhibit participation, and attitudinal barriers that make persons with handicaps feel unwelcome.

Attitudinal Barriers

The attitudinal barriers, intensely psychological in nature, include the ones of embarrassment, inability to respond helpfully, fear of the symbolic meaning a person with a physical disability has for others ("I don't want to be reminded of my own difficulties, even though they do not show.")

An accessible congregation in the personal area of acceptance, then, is one in which the members:

- Clearly see their own psychological discomfort and attempt to deal with it.
- Remember the words of Job and Jesus, that sin has no causal relationship with many of these disabilities, and shame is not to be connected with them.
- Understand that the mission of the religious community to the world includes persons with handicaps as active agents in that mission, rather than as merely recipients of that mission.
- Know from Scripture that persons with handicapping conditions have a privileged place in the kingdom.
- Recognize that although ramps are not enough, an open attitude must move toward an open sanctuary.

Architectural Barriers

An architecturally accessible church is one where the building itself, and the milieu of worship, does not inhibit persons with handicaps or prevent entrance into the building or participation in the service.

Accessibility means that the basic program of the congregation be available to a person with a handicap. It does not mean that every room or unit of the building be accessible. The following worship and education areas must be opened to persons with handicaps:

- the worship center, including area of worship leadership
- the educational wing
- the main hall for banquets and other functions
- the lounge, if many functions are held there
- a toilet

- the study
- the parking lot, and on into the building

Communication Barriers

The message is proclaimed in verbal, visual and intellectual ways. But the words, verbal or written, need to be heard, seen, and understood. Sign language and lip reading, braille and large print, imagery and drama, overcome the communication barriers for many.

Some Criteria on Accessibility

Persons Who Are Physically and Mobility Impaired
- Ramps, in addition to steps. The ramp does not necessarily have to be at the main entrance, but it should not be at an entrance deemed inferior or second rate.
- Toilets.
- A place within the main worship area in which wheelchairs may fit without being conspicuous.
- Opportunity for worship leadership and participation in governance (lay reader, board membership, etc.)

Persons Who Are Blind and Visually Impaired
- A "Welcome to the Congregation" and at least the major parts of the service of worship in braille and in large print.
- A large-print hymnal; brailled hymns if possible.
- Large-print Scriptures in the pew racks.
- Adequate lighting during reading and singing.
- Opportunity for leadership in worship and governance.

Persons Who Are Deaf and Hearing Impaired
- A person proficient in signing available to interpret the sermon, lecture, or program to deaf members of the congregation.
- Inexpensive versions of the Scriptures in the pew racks.
- A "sign-sing-speak" chorus and sign language training increase involvement.
- Pew rack hearing aids should be not only "up front." New technologies in hearing systems are available.
- Adequate lighting.
- Opportunity for leadership in worship and governance.

A Congregational Reading

The church, the source of Christian education and worship experiences, should remove the physical and attitudinal barriers and welcome all persons into its community. The welcome should be more than just a casual invitation. It must be an energetic effort to seek out this segment of the community. The scope of ministry is more than what we can do for them: it must include what they can do for us.

The following responsive reading speaks directly to this concept. It would be useful in a church service designed to encourage inclusion of handicapped people.

The congregation in unison: *Lord, we do not understand all there is to know about Your interest and how You look after it. We do not understand why some people are disabled, even though we know some of the causes like accidents and diseases.*

Teach us, Lord, to remove any barriers between people. We stare at those who do not look like us; we turn away from those who are different, and give up listening to people we do not understand well.

Help us, Lord, to be sensitive to the feelings and needs of others, and also to understand our own handicaps.

Persons Who Are Developmentally Disabled
- The worship service must go beyond being primarily verbal, vocal and intellectual in form. Drama, procession and recession, clothing, and other visual imagery and nonverbal activities involving sights, sounds, and emotions are helpful.
- Opportunity for leadership in worship.

The Congregation's Response

After we go beyond our individual selves, we can begin to work with our congregation's response to persons with disabilities. The

Leader: We know that the family of the church includes both "disabled" and "able" persons and that we must be open to meet with all people.

People: *We hear Your Word, O Lord.*

Leader: "Disability" as a world problem is increasing because of accidents, illnesses, and other causes. Many are emotionally and physically handicapped because of the pressures of life through social change, genetic disorders, famine, and war.

People: *Let Your wisdom lead us, O Lord.*

Leader: Handicapped persons have much to teach about strength and Christian acceptance. They have the same duty to do the Lord's work according to their God-given talents and abilities.

People: *Help us to see Your truth, O Lord.*

Leader: We affirm the continuing need for adequate institutions in which the most severely disabled persons may experience love and care.

People: *Lead us in loving concern, O Lord.*

Leader: We affirm the need for the acceptance, within all congregations, of those who are handicapped, and encourage their full participation in church and society, so that they will reach their full potential as persons of dignity and worth.

People: *Let Your strength move us, O Lord.*

(J.P.)

---

congregation's response begins with a quantum leap. Our ministry is no longer primarily one of a mission *to* or *for* disabled persons, but *with* them in a common mission to the church and to the world.

The difficulty in changing this attitude is complex, because some forms of ministry *to* disabled persons are still necessary. Some institutions must be maintained, for a large proportion of disabled people still need some kind of institutional care and protection. But the attitude change we call for now is to go beyond this sense of mission *to* these persons to one of mission *with*!

Words

*One-to-one relationships with persons
having mental retardation*

by Shirley L. Leutton

Words come easily to many of us. Sometimes we use them in
ministry with disabled people to cover up our lack of ability to
help and our embarrassment, to "put off" dealing with a situation,
or to "put down" the person with less ability than ourselves. Our
own words can be shockingly patronizing when we truly analyze
what we have said. Often in working one-to-one with disabled
persons, words are inadequate. We need to allow God to teach us
deep within our being, words that are acceptable to Him.

My personal experience has been mainly through the avenue of
recreation. Crossroads (Queensland, Australia) Christian Fellowship with Handicapped Persons has a vacation program that
gives us opportunities to bring the gospel to persons with disabilities through "living" experiences.

Many persons have a bad self-image and have lost their sense of
self-worth. Many are not even heard because of their inability to
verbalize. Often they are forgotten people who exist within families or institutions. Crossroads aims at reaching them where they
are, bringing them into a different environment, providing them
the opportunity for interaction with both able-bodied persons and
persons with other types of disabilities. As Christian educators,
we have specific areas of ministry of which the above vacation
program is only one.

Some Friends

Stephen

For our regular biweekly meeting of Crossroads the week before Easter, I chose five Easter teaching pictures for display—the garden of Gethsemane, the trial, Jesus carrying His cross, the crucifixion, and the empty tomb. I placed them in a row at eye level on the window panes about a yard apart. Our mentally retarded friends, all adults, were able to walk along at any time during our two-hour program and follow the sequence of events. Stephen (19, with moderate mental retardation) walked up and stood immediately in front of the crucifixion picture. He just stood. After a few minutes he walked away. A little later he came back and stood again, longer this time. He went away again.

Suppertime came and Stephen was missing. I found him again standing in front of the same picture. I moved over and placed my arm around his shoulders.

"Stephen, you are missing supper."

Stephen dropped his shoulders and turned and looked at me. Quiet tears were running down his face.

"Shirley, look at the blood."

I looked.

"Shirley, look what they did to Jesus."

He had taken his own time to see and understand the picture. He is one of a Christian family and attends church regularly. Lots of things must have fallen into place for him at that moment and few words from me were needed.

He said, "I love Jesus."

How many of us have taken the time, and felt the pain enough, to cry over the crucifixion?

James

James, a 7-year-old slow achiever at special school, is a member of my weekly public school religious education class. The first morning after his arrival from the "normal" school, he was withdrawn and sobbing inside—no visible tears, but slight muscle movement in the chest was evidence of the sob he couldn't quite control. When I greeted the children and responded to their hugs,

James drew back from physical contact. His eyes told me he was frightened and suspicious. I could not move too close too soon; it was to be a slow process over many weeks.

The class, including me, sat on small chairs in a circle. Eye contact on the same level helps to overcome inhibitions and give the children confidence to interact. We sang familiar and bright choruses and James observed the other children's involvement. He still held back.

Each week I would give a different child the privilege of pushing the "play" button on my tape recorder. When I asked James if he would like to push the button, he went to do it and then drew back. I quickly pushed it myself. After that day, each week I watched his eyes and body movements for signs of acceptance.

One morning upon arrival I found James sitting on the chair next to the one he knew was mine. I casually took my place without giving him any special attention, but I knew he had changed. He had grown to trust me–no tears, a shy smile, and expected anticipation to push the button.

On departure he allowed me to touch him.

Steven

Steven, 22 years old, came away with us for a 10-day tour of the Northern Territory of Australia. With the group of 35 persons, 20 had some disability that prevented them from traveling without assistance. Steven is mentally retarded and has a badly turned eye. He is a quiet young man, well-groomed and unobtrusive– someone you could easily forget to notice in the group. From his appearance one might make a hasty judgment that there is not much going on behind those eyes.

For several days he was "just there." Then on Sunday morning, we decided to have our worship service right there in the moving bus in the middle of nowhere. This simple service proved to be a deeply spiritual experience. Spontaneous contributions were made by both disabled and able-bodied persons.

By far the greatest highlight in that worship service came when we invited people to come up and sing. Steven went to the front of the bus, picked up the microphone, and sang all the verses of *Amazing Grace* from memory.

Once more we stood amazed at God's dealings with people. We

would have thought this impossible from our little knowledge of Steven.

David

David, 38, has lived with his father all his life. He is unable to communicate. His mother died when he was three. He had not had exposure to the gospel before his father brought him along on a Crossroads tour. Both father and son have responded to the caring of our Christian Enablers. We don't know how much David understands, but if we can interpret his responses, he feels joy and sadness, satisfaction, and frustration. When he laughs it brings happiness to those around him. Dare we withhold the gospel from one such as this?

Living experiences with those who interpret words into actions consistently have already brought a change to David's life.

Christians cannot make the presumption that "God will take care of them." The Great Commission doesn't say that at all. We are to "go into all the world and preach the good news to all creation" (Mark 16:15).

Paul said in 1 Corinthians 9:22, "To the weak I became weak, to win the weak. I have become all things to all men so that by all possible means I might save some."

We have a responsibility to interpret Christ to those with mental retardation by whatever means we can use.

Margaret

Margaret, 60, was from one of the state government institutions. She came away with us for a few days. She appeared to be "turned off," simply doing as requested like a robot. She was assigned to my group, which meant I was responsible for her well-being.

After the first 36 hours it seemed hopeless as I looked into her blank eyes. Our director suggested that I take her for a drive along the beach. As we drove I was talking, when Margaret suddenly spoke.

"That's Palm Beach," she said.

I got excited. "Margaret, that *is* Palm Beach. How did you know?"

She replied, "My husband and I used to come here on vacation with our children."

From then on it was like a flood was released. She told me her story up to the time that she became ill and was placed in the center for the mentally ill.

When we returned to where we were staying, she was brighter and more responsive. As we were going to bed that night, I was tying the bow at the neck of her nightie when she suddenly looked up into my face.

"Shirley, why do you love me?"

Stunned, I answered after a moment, "Margaret, Jesus loves me, and Jesus loves you too. That's why I love you."

She hugged me and said, "I know, I know."

Qualities You Need

I learned the value of one-to-one ministry in my own life. God knew that I myself needed to have my life straightened out on a one-to-one basis, and that I would need continuing one-to-one counseling to enable me to share this type of ministry with others.

My second child, Vicki, suffered brain damage at birth. At eight months she began having epileptic seizures. I couldn't believe it. I just wanted it all to go away. After five years, I had become bitter and antagonistic and had cut myself off from family and friends. But at that time Jesus Christ came into my life through people who were willing to take the time to care about me and counsel with me on a one-to-one basis.

No, my daughter was not miraculously cured. Neither did all our problems melt away. But my Christian life grew more wonderful every day, and I also had many opportunities to do the same kind of one-to-one witnessing and counseling that I had benefited from so much in my life. Years later, our family went through hard times because Vicki was found to be unemployable (she had lost five jobs in eight years for reasons beyond our control). At this time I again sought one-to-one counsel, this time from a friend who was a Christian psychiatrist. He encouraged me and supported me, and he finally challenged me to help others as I had been helped.

I became involved as a volunteer and later as a full-time worker with Crossroads Christian Fellowship with Handicapped Persons. I believe God has called me to a ministry of reconciliation and encouragement to all those who are led to me in the desperation that I recognize was once part of my own experience.

Faith

"Without faith it is impossible to please God" (Hebrews 11:6). Faith to believe God is in control.

My earliest visitor from a neighborhood church, a Bible-school teacher, had the faith to believe that God's Word would not return to Him void. She had no specialized counseling skills, but she trusted God's guidance and saw her simple ministry of visitation as God's will for her. Oh that more Christians would be involved in such a ministry! My heart aches for those families who are still waiting in every community. Jesus himself went to where the people were, bringing hope, life, encouragement, and peace. Much of His ministry was on a "one-to-one" basis, as the Gospels reveal.

As we sing, "I will follow Jesus," let's learn His methods.

Truth

Sincerity and honesty is discernable even to those with severe disabilities.

Jesus said, "I am the way, the truth and the life" (John 14:6). Perhaps mentally retarded persons have difficulty understanding "the way" or "the life," but they certainly understand "the truth." The one-to-one worker needs to recognize that it is impossible to hide the truth. If you can't help, say so. If you are too busy at the moment, say so. If you can't understand what is being said because of communication difficulties, say so. Complete honesty will give the disabled persons a sense of self worth because you care enough to be sincere with him or her. You will be blessed by their openness, but you have a responsibility to guard their vulnerability.

Love

"Love your neighbor as yourself" (Matthew 22:39).
Sometimes the person in front of you is unlovely, even repul-

sive, as you see through human vision. This is natural and normal and shouldn't make us feel guilty. But Christ's love in our lives overcomes all barriers. Jesus touched a leper on the street (Luke 5:13). Overcome your repulsion by physical contact. When you feel in your stomach that you can, move forward and wipe away the dribble or touch the face that has repulsed you. Let the love of Jesus in you flow through you. Physical contact is important in acceptance. Until the fear, repulsion, or pity is dealt with by the Holy Spirit, we cannot be channels of God's love.

Wisdom

Learn what to do and when to stop. Knowing when to speak and when to be silent is not easy. To know when to hug and when not to hug is even harder (for me anyway).

Desley has been committed to many institutions over the past 20 years but has always run away. I met her through Crossroads and felt drawn to her because of her loneliness. Her handicap includes hyperactivity. She is a loner and keeps moving, unable to sit without rolling a piece of paper or tape in her fingers. She smokes heavily and drinks coffee to the point of obsession. Her family has done what they can, but how much can any family stand?

Her first 10-day tour away with Crossroads was a traumatic experience for her—and a test of my faith. Could she stay within the group life? Would the cord of love I had begun to weave hold? Would she run away? Would she accept the discipline necessary to keep our scheduled itinerary? Several times she pleaded with me to let her go. She just wanted to "do her own thing" and yet she wanted the security, the fun and the family atmosphere of our group life.

Her mother is a Christian and Desley has already obtained a lot of head knowledge about Christ. She knows the Scriptures. My role as I saw it was to bring her to a place of appropriating what she knew into a living reality. She knew I loved her. I *told* her so. I told her often. She accepted my discipline, which was exercised where necessary, privately but firmly—"you cannot go. You chose to come with us, now you must fulfill your responsibility." The next to last day arrived. Desley had deep black rings around her eyes, evidence of the inner struggle. She walked on the other side of the street, but she "hung in" with us. When we arrived home she was exhausted.

Shortly afterwards she ran away and was missing for several weeks. This was not unusual for her. After her return she came back to Crossroads. Since then she has been involved in many activities including a Pacific cruise and a tour of New Zealand. I built a relationship on love and trust until it bore real fruit.

Friday night I arrived home from work at 5:45 p.m. While I was watching the news the front doorbell rang. My daughter answered. It was Desley, almost incoherent with panic.

"Desley, what's the matter?"

"It's an emergency," she said. "I had to come. Let me come in!"

I didn't move. Desley came to the big lounge where I sat and lay like a frightened animal with her head in my lap. I said nothing. She twitched and trembled. I held her and stroked her hair—pointless to say anything—just "Shhh! ... Shhh!" and keep stroking. She eventually quieted down. My family is fairly used to this kind of happening and was at ease. We then went about the normal dinner routine, setting an extra place for her.

After dinner, when she was calm, I said, "OK, Desley, what happened?"

She told me of a domestic argument, which would be part of the experience of most families, but she couldn't cope with it and she ran. She had been walking for several hours and deciding whether to run away again, but she didn't. She came to me. I called her mother, who was sitting in fear by the telephone (again) and heard the relief in her voice—a breakthrough for us all. I kept Desley for 24 hours, then took her back home. No doubt this will happen again, but she knows that I will not be "used." We have been totally honest with each other. Her mental health is improving day by day as Christ's healing power brings love and acceptance into her life.

Humility

"If anyone thinks he is something when he is nothing, he deceives himself" (Galatians 6:3). You need to see the other person as equal with yourself.

If the thought, "he can't understand" or "he's like a child" even comes into your mind, this is evidence that you have prejudged the person's capacity to understand. This will be revealed in your words, body movements, and attitude. We are not ready to reach the mentally retarded person for Christ until our own minds have been convinced, through the study of the Word of God, that all persons are equal in God's sight. Beware of the "us/them" attitude. Remember we are "them" and they are "us." We are all one in Christ Jesus.

Building Relationships

Sharing

Learn to really listen. Many things we feel are trivial and insignificant are important to persons with mental retardation, who may live a limited lifestyle. If we are too busy or preoccupied to really listen, we might hurt someone whose simpler understanding sees this as personal rejection.

Sometimes our friends need time—that precious commodity we don't seem to have much of—time to understand themselves. If they are happy, we need to laugh with them. If they are hurting, we need to share the hurt and absorb some of their frustrations. Our sensitivity should make us aware of these needs as they arise.

A precious gift we need to share continually is our joy. Laughter is contagious. It is free. We don't have to study it. A keen sense of humor will compensate for many of our inadequacies. It is the basic skill required by all who work with persons who have handicaps.

Each counseling situation develops into something quite unique. While methodology has its place, the method will never be the same as the last time. Meet each new situation as that—a new situation.

Never go beyond the immediate need or your own limitations. Don't hesitate to ask for help from others more experienced. If a situation is more than you can handle, first consult your disabled friend and then bring in somebody else to help—a trusted friend or a professional person.

Be available. A mentally retarded person cannot "make an

appointment" to share with you the way he feels now. If we have sorted out our values and priorities it will make it easier to handle unexpected "emergencies."

Don't withhold your natural emotions. "Feel" with the one you are counseling. As this happens naturally more freedom will be experienced between you both.

Family Life

Growing up in a family with other children, the time arrives when comparisons are inevitable. The mentally retarded child notices he is not able to do "running writing" and in little things he is different from his siblings. Somehow the family tries to survive those childhood years, but it is difficult when brothers and sisters go off to clubs and recreation and there appears to be nowhere to take the handicapped child that would be a satisfactory substitute. So often he just stays at home.

In his late teenage years his big brother, who is younger than he is, gets his driver's license and then a little later gets engaged and married.

As Christian teachers and counselors, we need to be ready to support the family as early as possible. We must help them find ways for their disabled family member to keep his self-esteem and continue striving to reach his full potential.

These ways are now being made available in education and employment. Within a Christian environment, Bible school, worship, recreation, and social activities, we need to be alert for opportunities to build up the handicapped person. These opportunities may present themselves when least expected—a question, "Why can't I go to the youth club?" a body movement, a certain look, a smile of expectation, or an act of frustration or anger.

Touching Lives

Prayer comes easily and naturally into a one-to-one ministry with persons having mental retardation. It is important to be included at every opportunity. The person becomes "God conscious" as this happens, and often brings Jesus into your discussions spontaneously. Our responsibility to handle God's Word carefully comes into the spiritual experience—never a God of judgment without a God of love. Although it is necessary to teach right from wrong on a Scriptural basis, we must never use God as a weapon. Our disabled friends need to be left always feeling the warmth and encouragement of God's love to them. Jesus needs to be presented through you by both word and action, and your behavior will make Jesus easier to interpret.

Never underestimate the power of "touch." Jesus touched people and made them whole. Be ready to squeeze a hand, touch a face, put out your hands in invitation, hug somebody who needs to be hugged. Be sensitive and gentle with a quiet spirit.

Say "I love you" and mean it. Say it often. Working one-to-one with handicapped persons will bring you closer to Jesus as you see Him at work in their lives.

Priceless Friends

*Ways to bring your ministry
to the local group home*

by Laura Knoop Burton

*We have only begun to sense the tragic wounds some mentally
retarded people may feel when it dawns on them that the only
people relating to them—outside of relatives—are paid to do so.*
                                                    —Robert Perske

The church can help change this awful situation. Except for a
few staff people and a handful of devoted family members, the
residents in group homes do not have the support and closeness
most of us could not live without.

I once heard the mother of an autistic person say, "We used to
have friends, people we would pay to spend time with our son." I
thought, wait a minute—you don't *pay* friends to come see you.
Can you imagine having no one to share your excitement in good
times or your sorrow in sad times? Mentally retarded individuals
need these experiences just as much, if not more, than we non-
retarded people do.

Serving people living in a group home can be a great benefit to
them and to you. This chapter is for those of you about to take
that first step in contacting a local group home. You'll be far more
likely to make that step a successful one if you keep in mind the
needs of the residents, the staff, and the agency (private, church,
or government) operating the group home.

Needs of Group Home Residents

Personal

We all need physical contact with others. But life in a group home can be devoid of hugs, intimate chats, and real emotional support. Busy schedules often leave only enough time for the staff to assist with basic daily tasks, and little time to spare for relationship building. You, their friends from church, can make the difference between a group home that just gives basic care and a quality program that addresses all of the residents' needs.

Residents look forward to crafts and physical games in which they can feel successful. Fun and laughter can wipe away much of a day's frustration and can help create an atmosphere in which learning can take place by leaps and bounds—one in which we can laugh at ourselves and learn from our mistakes. Fun and laughter can be had just as much at the group home itself as during a "special class" at church.

For the most part, group home staff are young and female. Male friends can be a much-needed influence for many male residents. Their guidance and interest in sports are very welcome in a group home. The maturity of friends over 30 years old can also be helpful to the residents. Many young group home staff have never had to deal with death and grief or with issues related to aging. A sympathetic ear from a friend can ease fears ranging from reduced physical capacity to the death of a family member.

Sometimes a shoulder to cry on or just a hug can be the difference between a minor incident and a major emotional outburst. Emotions must be acknowledged and dealt with quickly. Simple fears can be major upsets to a mentally retarded person. You can help provide immediate attention to these needs.

Medical

Medical needs can be taxing to even the best staffed group homes. Seizures, corrective surgeries, diabetes, diet and exercise control, and emotional problems can require months of preparation and counseling. Church members can visit the residents when they are in the hospital and provide encouragement. Most of the time they just need simple, direct answers and lots of reassurance.

The hospital staff will be more comfortable in caring for a mentally retarded person if they can see how easily the members of their church and the group home staff deal with the minor daily care issues that come up.

Moral/Spiritual

Mentally retarded people need to be reminded daily with concrete examples of moral issues. Spiritual thoughts are not dealt with nearly as often. Once or twice a month a resident will come to us with questions about God, especially when family events happen, like births or deaths. Sometimes they have questions about what happened at church that day, or if someone steals from another or hurts another.

I try to answer the best I can according to whatever religion they have or their family has. In that respect I'm like a chaplain, a support to them. In the same way, the staff in many group homes have been instructed to remain neutral regarding spiritual issues. The residents are looking for answers from people they trust, and you can help them in this way. Communication with group home staff is essential in this area. A resident often has serious reasons for asking a certain question about God or about the teachings in the Bible, and the staff may be able to give background for why he or she is asking it.

Even if your congregation has no formal program, you can help just by transporting the residents to and from the worship services and sitting with them during the services. Some will be able to understand the sermon, and you can help them by discussing the content of the sermon in concrete terms. For those residents who are severely retarded or for those who find communication difficult, a smile and a handshake may be all it takes to help that person feel accepted and welcome. As time passes, he or she will be proud to be a part of your congregation.

Because retarded people are used to frequent staff changes, they find it difficult to depend on people and to trust others to be there for them. Their group leaders are their friends, but when a staff person leaves for another job, he or she seldom comes back to visit. Another person leaves their lives; the trust is broken.

Do not be discouraged if trust and deep feelings take time to develop or if the group home residents are hesitant to express their true feelings. It's important to be consistent and dependable in your relationship with your mentally retarded friends. They'll remember you forever!

Staff Needs

When you first approach a group home director with the idea of having the residents come to your church, you need to understand some of the issues he or she faces. A church-operated group home may already be affiliated with a local congregation. A state- or county-operated home must remain "neutral" with regard to area congregations and responsive to the needs of each resident.

Such a program immediately means more work for an already busy staff. Not only is it additional work, but some of the staff people may be unwilling to attend church services with a resident because of some personal issue.

Group home residents have the right to attend the church of their choice, and the staff have to make that option available to them. Those in charge of the group home know it's the residents' right. It is possible that you could go to them and make the staff people comply—if you could show that attending your church is something the residents want. But this approach is not going to win you the good will of the staff people, who may already want nothing to do with church.

A much better approach is to help them see the benefits of an association with your church—like having volunteer help available for their people if they really need it. They will also respond better to you if they can see you are serious about your proposal to help and that you will follow through with it. (Staff people tend to view community volunteers the same way. They think, "You're not really invested in these people. You're going to start and then give it up.")

Offering to hold services at the group home may not be a workable option, either, even though a congregation might think they are providing a convenience. A worship service held in a group home would have to be a "generic" religion that does not favor one form of religious doctrine over another. More importantly for the residents themselves, we prefer that they have the opportunity to participate in all the normal experiences most people have – and that includes worshiping in a local church that they choose. A small Bible study, for which it was made clear that participation was voluntary, might be possible. A private church-sponsored group home might be a more receptive place for holding worship services.

When you approach a group home, be persistent. Be concerned about the needs of the residents and staff and any requirements of the agency running the home. It would probably be helpful if you could offer to provide transportation. Be willing to show some friendship and commitment to the residents there. As the staff get to know you they will become more receptive to your plan to bring the residents to church.

You will need to notify the group home about any special activities you plan. They will need to plan accordingly for more or less staff during the time period. The activity may not be possible unless you have enough members of your congregation participating. Another concern is the time at which one staff member ends his or her workday and another begins. The group home staff needs to plan ahead for shift changes.

Church members can help the often overworked group home staff. They come to look forward to times when regular, supportive friends lend help and give attention to the residents on evenings when no special outings are planned. One way of helping the staff is to lead activities or crafts in the group home so they will have the time to deal with the major issues of a few.

Church friends who become involved with mentally retarded group home residents often find that they begin to reap many of the rewards of friendships, including love, laughter, gentleness, and fun. They can also affect every aspect of a retarded person's life. They can help these individuals become a part of the communities in which they live. A church "special class" can be a stepping stone from isolation to companionship and love for handicapped people as well as church members. The relationships you build can be priceless. As one resident says about her church friend, "She's precious! I love her berry much. Yes, I do!"

Just for Them

*Camping for persons
with disabilities*

by Don Crooker

Laura joyfully waved good-bye to her parents as the bus pulled away. Many of her friends were also on the bus. They all were excited because they were going to a camp planned just for them! Laura and her friends are mentally retarded.

Many children look forward to attending camp as a normal part of childhood and youth. A Christian summer camp for disabled people is special. At camp they can be with friends and loving counselors for a whole week! They can hike through tall pine trees, see a scampering squirrel or a cautious deer, play special games, take a boat ride on the lake, or go to a weiner roast. They can enjoy lots of singing, listen to Bible stories, participate in Special Olympics events, or attend a special dress-up banquet the last night together. These activities mean fun, achievement, and new friends. Successful experiences mean greater self-confidence.

While Laura was at camp, Mom and Dad left for a vacation. It was their only break that year from the supervision of their daughter. Their routine for the week was different, and they experienced a "release." They were able to focus on each other and their other children, and just relax together. As the week concluded they looked forward to resuming their responsibilities with Laura.

Brother and sister appreciated the break, too, because they got some special parental attention. Since Laura is a family "project," they too experienced a release.

At camp Laura sensed love and acceptance. She didn't always receive that at school, in shopping centers, or around the neighborhood. In those places she sometimes is teased, shunned, or avoided. Laura knows the difference.

Her camping experiences included stories from the Bible about Jesus at a level she could understand. She loved that. She could sing from the joy in her heart, even if she was off-key.

Craft projects are always beautiful. She made them with her own hands.

Laura and the other campers took part in special recreational activities. They were fun, and miscues were not noted. She was comfortable doing her best. Self-worth and esteem could grow easily here. Some of the games were new this year. She looked forward to each recreation session.

Jeff was a smiling nine-year-old boy suffering from a terminal disease. His parents wanted him to go to a Christian camp because Christian values are important to them.

Jeff had never been to camp before. This frail youngster loved the outdoors. He was home-schooled and made frequent visits to the hospital. As camp approached, it appeared he would be strong enough to spend the week.

His brown eyes, which frequently reflected pain, showed only excitement. One experience awaiting him filled him with delightful anticipation. He'd never done it before, but he'd seen others who had. Jeff was going to ride a pony.

He grasped the saddle horn and was helped up onto the saddle. A smile spread across his face as he bounced up and down. His counselor walked beside him to hold him upright. That special moment was captured on film and printed in the camp newsletter.

Jeff went home to meet his Lord before Christmas.

Life's expectancy for many disabled children is just a few years. They have to do a lot of living in a short period of time.

Summer camp for mentally retarded, blind, deaf, physically disabled and learning disabled people is an effective method of evangelism. Eighty percent of the families with a disabled member do not attend church. Some of the reasons for the situation is lack of accessibility, steps, narrow doors, or no curb cuts.

Congregational acceptance is another barrier. One church architect who has designed over four hundred church facilities has each client fill out an extensive survey to help him to design a church to meet their objectives and goals. One question he asks is, "Would your church consider a ministry to the handicapped?" The answer in ninety-eight percent of these churches is "No."

Families with disabled persons often do not feel welcome when visiting a church. Considering the effort it takes to ready that family member for church (bathing and dressing may be a lengthy procedure) and the extra motivation required, families often just avoid the hassle and stay home.

Summer camp is viewed differently by parents. It's a place with activities planned for the campers' level and provides happy experiences. It can be a day-long experience or as long as a whole week! It represents a real break for the parents. They like that so much that they will gladly pay to send the child or adult to camp.

Summer camp is a time to have new experiences. There are many to choose from.

At a Christian camp for disabled people, or where such campers can be mainstreamed, they come into an atmosphere of love and acceptance. There they will hear about Jesus Christ for an entire week. Often they will receive Him as their Savior.

A Christian camp for disabled people alters the lives of the counselors. Often assigned on a one-to-one ratio, their hearts are captured. They may discover a greater understanding of God's love from mentally retarded people. Their love is unconditional, their forgiveness instant; their hugs are genuine and can come at any time.

Persons with physical disabilities can teach a counselor about absolute dependence. They may need to assist with bathing and dressing. Spoon-feeding may also be a necessity. Some campers require complete assistance with bathroom needs, and that includes the wipe after a bowel movement.

Total care and dependence is a hard lesson of life to submit to. They know and lead the way for their counselors; because of them, the camp counselors re-examine their walk with God: "Am I really dependent on my Savior?"

Campers with disabilities can also teach their able-bodied counselors how to acquire a servant's heart. Their attention is forced from themselves to the needs of another. With humility and patience they experience the Savior's attitude of being a servant.

Another benefit of a Christian camp for disabled people is the valuable training aquired by the high school and college students who serve there. Because of their summer camp experience, many of them sense God's call to prepare to serve this special population.

Sam was a college student who felt it might be a neat experience to spend a summer at camp working with disabled people. Well, by the last session, Sam was hooked. When he returned to college he had no doubt God was calling him to prepare to serve the multitude of disabled people.

God's love, encouragement, and lots of hugs brought tears to Laura's eyes as she prepared to board the bus home. That's it until next year.

The counselor's eyes were not dry, either. Laura's love, innocence, sense of discovery, appreciation, and her untimely lengthy hugs have changed her counselor's life. Tammy, her counselor, didn't expect all of that!

Belonging

*Music as a ministry tool
for persons with disabilities*

by Deborah Shell

The Sunday morning worship service is a time when God's people come together as one. We praise Him for His greatness, meditate upon His goodness, thank Him for the gift of His Son, learn about Him, and submit our lives to Him. Music serves as an excellent facilitator for each of these acts in worship.

Music can also play an integral part in Christian education. It encourages participation in a social activity and can teach and strengthen Christian concepts and attitudes.

These three basic principles of music therapy are useful to consider in any group music experience.

- *Establishing interpersonal relationships.* Membership in a group music experience gives a person a sense of belonging, of contributing his part toward the common goal, and of closeness toward the others in the group.
- *Bringing about self-esteem through self-actualization.* An individual can participate in a music experience on his own ability level and in his own area of interest, and he can achieve a feeling of success and accomplishment.
- *Using rhythm to energize and bring order.* Rhythm is the common bond that allows two or more people to share together in a music activity. Rhythm is also the element in

music that provides energy. It can stimulate activity or it can soothe and encourage relaxation.[1]

Music and the Special Learner

Music is adaptable to the needs and capabilities of any individual, however severe his disability. The teacher should be prepared to use any and all means through which music can be experienced—singing, playing, listening, moving, or creating. For the special learner, all of these experiences can be avenues to growth in the knowledge and understanding of Jesus. A child should be encouraged to learn and to express himself. If he cannot participate in one way, perhaps he can in another.

Singing is an excellent means for teaching from the Bible. Songs can also teach appropriate responses of reverence. A prayer song can be sung softly and slowly to prepare hearts for quiet thoughts, and a song of praise can be sung boisterously and at a faster tempo to help exude feelings of joy and happiness.

Children love to play instruments. Learning to play an instrument can give a child a feeling of accomplishment. Instruments can be used to enhance the feeling and understanding of a song. Playing an instrument will also give a child something to do with his hands; this process may help to hold his attention.

Even though it is difficult for them, children should be taught to listen quietly for short periods of time. The attention span of the special learner, particularly the young, is often short. Brief music listening activities can help to lengthen attention span.

It is natural for people, especially children, to want to move to music—clapping to the beat, swaying to the time of a lilting melody, or in the case of young children, using simple fingerplays in acting out a story. Movement helps children to internalize music and meaning. Appropriate and structured movement to music will help fulfill a hyperactive child's need to move and also help hold his attention.

Children should be encouraged to create, to share something that is uniquely theirs. The teacher should provide structured opportunity for children to suggest new movements for songs and new ideas in using instruments, and even to perform for one another and the church.

People With Mental Retardation

Those who have seen the smiles of children clapping and singing enthusiastically during a music activity will realize the great value in the use of music with these children. They often respond more readily to a music activity than to any other activity.

Music an help meet five needs characteristic of persons with mental retardation.[2]

Communication. Music, in a non-threatening way, encourages the use of words, however poor the speech skills or limited the language. Music can also function as nonverbal communication in expressing feelings just as it does for a normal individual. If unable to participate verbally in a song of joy and praise, he can express himself through the bright sounds of ringing bells, the exciting rhythms of a drum, or simple physical gestures or movements such as clapping his hands or snapping his fingers.

Group participation. The child often has few social contacts outside his own family. He needs to develop appropriate social behavior by participating in group activities. In group music activities of the church, he can learn good ways of interaction with others and feel that he is a necessary part of the body of Christ.

Security. For many reasons the child often feels insecure. The structure and order found in music establishes predictability and helps relieve insecurity. Familiar songs and activities can be repeated both to facilitate learning and establish security. Security can also be strengthened through the use of music that arouses positive feelings of love and happiness. Through the use of music, the child can feel the love and security found in our Lord.

Gratification and consequent self-esteem. Often the child is aware of his inabilities. This awareness affects his feelings of self-worth. Music offers him an opportunity for enjoyment and success because it encourages participation on whatever level he can contribute. His feelings of inadequacy are soon gone. What better means can there be for teaching the love and acceptance of Jesus?

Aesthetic sensory experiences. People need beauty and aesthetic expression. Music used in worship experiences can enhance any child's appreciation for the beauty found in all of God's creation.

In planning music activities, the teacher must consider both the child's age and his developmental level. It can be difficult to choose music activities that are socially interesting, appealing, and appropriate for a child's level of understanding. When a child partakes in music appropriate for his age and social level, he will fit in more happily with his peers. If he chooses music that seems too young for him, try to expose him to music suitable for his age. Often an adolescent will choose a song appropriate for young primary children. This is probably because of a lack of exposure to anything else. The use of current gospel songs along with the teaching of hymns regularly used in the church worship services will help him to feel a part of the whole church fellowship.

In choosing songs that will provide success, the teacher should look for songs with a simple melody, easy to sing and not confusing. The words should be simple and concrete, because abstractions are difficult for mentally retarded people to grasp. The words must be relevant to him and to his life experiences; the singer must be able to understand what he is saying and what it means. For example, a young child cannot grasp the whole meaning of "sinking deep in sin." He more easily understands the simplicity of "good" and "bad."

A song with repetitive words and melodic phrases can be learned easily and quickly. Repetition within a song and the repeating of familiar songs and activities will also help to instill feelings of security. Most children love to repeat activities at which they have succeeded.

In teaching a song or a music activity, the teacher should present it in simple steps small enough to ensure success, making sure that the child understands. Each step should be practiced again and again; when the child is successful, he should be praised. When learning something new, response from a child will often be minimal, but after much practice he will succeed. The aesthetic experience will be beautiful both for the child and the teacher.

People With Physical Impairments

The physically impaired person has the same needs as his peer who has no impairment. Goals in his Christian education are the same; only their implementations will differ. No matter what his physical impairment, music can provide an individual with a sense of accomplishment and of belonging to the group.

The person having mobility impairments. Music has been used extensively in helping individuals achieve goals in physical development. Appropriate choices in music can encourage relaxation, improve muscle strength, joint mobility, and coordination, and help increase breathing capacity.

In Christian education, music can help him develop his potential and feel part of the fellowship of Christ. Often he has little opportunity to participate in group activities; he is more familiar with one-to-one learning situations. A child will often feel isolated even when in a group. Music is at its best in a group and allows success through all levels of participation. This success helps compensate for other deficiencies and gives the child something to contribute to the Lord and to the fellowship.

Children should be encouraged to sing, play instruments, listen, move to the music, and create. If they cannot play or move, they often will enjoy being helped. They might like to have their fingers brushed across the strings of an autoharp or guitar, or to have their arms or legs moved by the teacher to the music. However helpless a child may seem or however simple his contribution, music can help in diminishing his feelings of isolation caused by feelings of uselessness and incompetence.

The person with speech impairments. Music has been used to improve articulation, increase language and sentence length, and aid in remediation of speech disorders. In Christian education, the major goal is social. Because they lack normal communication skills, persons with speech impairments are often unable to feel a part of their normal peer group. Music can provide a means of communication as well as an emotional outlet and an avenue for success. To facilitate this success in the music experience, the following suggestions are useful.

• Tempos should be slower than normal, but fast enough to afford challenge.
• The teacher should present good sound patterns by enunciating the words clearly.

• Songs should have few words and a regular rhythm.
• Visual reminders of words are helpful.

The teacher and child should frequently use sign language or modified physical gestures while simultaneously saying the words. This method sometimes will help to promote the use of language in children.

The person with visual impairments. The person with a visual impairment will learn about his environment through the use of hearing, touch, and movement. Music can provide him with experiences using all of the above, encouraging the involvement of the whole person. Listening activities in music can help develop better listening skills. Movement activities can help develop a sense of balance and direction.

When participating in movement activities, a child should be placed near the teacher so that he can easily be helped if necessary. He should be given plenty of space to move without bumping into anyone or anything. Directions should be clearly explained and understood. When showing a movement to the class, it should always be explained verbally. Initially, it is helpful to guide the visually impaired child's hands, arms, legs, or shoulders through the expected movements while the music plays. The child can also touch the teacher to learn the movements. When being taught to play an instrument the child's hands should be guided into the correct positions for playing.

The visually impaired child should also be encouraged to use what vision he has. In music activities, this can be done through the use of pictures associated with the music. The child should be placed close to the visual aids in a well-lighted area.

Because music is an area in which visually impaired persons can succeed on a level equal to that of sighted persons, it can help to rid them of a sense of aloneness. It is an excellent means of helping them feel part of the church fellowship.

The person with hearing impairments. Because of the nature of this person's impairment, it might be assumed that music is of no value to him. Not so. This person learns about his environment through sight and touch. He should be provided with surroundings that will help him experience the world of the hearing.

Familiarity with the sound should be developed to encourage a desire to communicate.

Music activities should be selected for his level of comprehension. All movements, instruments, sounds, and pictures should be explained at the beginning of the activity. If an instrument is used, the hearing impaired person should be placed near it and allowed to touch it. He can place his hand or his ear on a piano or an autoharp to feel the sound as the teacher plays.

A child can learn new words by placing his hand on a drum and watching as the teacher speaks the words and taps the rhythm simultaneously. The child should be encouraged to tap or clap the rhythm while saying the words.

Word meanings can be taught by the use of pictures and actions. After learning a song sequence, a child can do the actions while watching the teacher sing, and then eventually sing along with words he has learned.

Music can provide the hearing impaired person with a sense of accomplishment—communication with the world of the hearing.

Tips for the Music Leader

A series of songs should flow together as one, rather than jumping around directly from a song such as "Jesus Loves Me" to "Give Me Oil in My Lamp" to "Into My Heart." The meditative mood would be lost in the middle.

All songs should be sung with reverence. They may be fast and boisterous or slow and prayerful, but they must always be sung in a worshipful attitude.

The words and melody of a new song should always be taught first before adding movements or instruments. It may take several class sessions for the children to feel comfortable with the words. When reasonable success has been gained with one step, the teacher can add another.

If the teacher accompanies the group on an instrument, he should be prepared both to play and to direct the children in their parts. Eye contact and encouragement are necessary in eliciting response. A guitar or autoharp helps in allowing this interaction between teacher and students. Sometimes a recording is the best choice, especially if there is only one teacher.

Instruments that might be purchased for class include an autoharp, a set of resonator bells (individual bells that can be given to several children, and when played give a full chord sound), and a set of classroom rhythm instruments (tambourines, jingle bells, finger cymbals, triangles, blocks, sand blocks, maracas, drums).

It is amazing what children with disabilities can do when given the opportunity. We in the church should cultivate their abilities and forget their inabilities; we should be thankful for and receptive to what they *can* do.

---

[1]E. Thayer Gaston, *Music in Therapy.* New York: Macmillan, 1968.
[2]*Ibid.,* p. 50-52.

Meet the Outsiders

Ministry with families having persons with disabilities

by Bonnie G. Wheeler

Let me introduce you to two families: the Insiders and the Outsiders. From the day Mrs. Insider discovers that she is pregnant, her days are overflowing with joyful anticipation. The last weeks of her pregnancy are filled with showers, preparation, and presents as friends, family and church share her coming joy.

When little Susie Insider is born the smiling faces of the doctors and nurses reflect the joy of the proud new parents. Words such as "beautiful" and "blessed" float around the delivery room.

At three weeks old, Susie attends church for the first time with her beaming parents. People jostle each other to get a closer look at that "darling baby." Susie and her proud parents are on their way to becoming an established part of the church family.

As the years swiftly pass Susie never misses a Sunday. She wins more attendance awards than any other student and after Sunday school she skips straight over to junior church.

Church camp and the Christmas program are the two highlights of Susie's year. Potluck dinners are a family favorite. Mr. Insider insists, "there's no finer way to get to know the church family than the fellowship of a good potluck dinner."

As the Insiders become secure inhabitants of the Christian "ghetto" they brag that, "our kids play only with other Christian kids, attend the best Christian schools and we only socialize with other Christians."

Across town Mrs. Outsider knows early in her pregnancy that something is wrong. After tests are run her doctor urges her to have an abortion. She switches doctors. The new doctor reconfirms the dire predictions, and again abortion is offered as the only option.

While Mrs. Outsider fights for the life of her unborn baby, her days are filled with fear and dread. The last weeks of her pregnancy are lonely, frightening days as she and her husband cling to each other. When little Janie Outsider is born, the doctors and nurses exchange grim glances. One nurse covers her face with her hands and runs crying from the delivery room. Words like "retarded," "crippled," and "euthanasia" hang heavily over the room.

Little Janie is sick so much of the time that it is almost six months before the three Outsiders are able to attend church together. A few people speak brief words to Mr. and Mrs. Outsider (words of condolence, not congratulations) but avoid looking at the baby.

As the years pass Janie is seldom able to attend Sunday school on a regular basis. Her surgeries and illnesses give her long lonely times confined to bed. When she is able to attend, there is no class that's appropriate for her. One week Janie stays a few minutes after class to enviously admire the shiny new attendance pin on Susie Insider's dress. The teacher leaves and Susie skips off to junior church. After services, Mrs. Outsider finds her hysterical daughter still in the classroom ... unable to open the door and get her wheelchair over the door jamb.

One Christmas Janie gets to practice for the program. On the day of the big event, Mrs. Outsider gets a call from Janie's teacher. "There's just no way we can get that chair up on the platform ... and anyway, there weren't any wheelchairs in Bethlehem."

When Janie is old enough to consider going to camp, her parents are told to send her to a camp better equipped to handle "kids like her."

Potlucks are out of the question. The fellowship hall is in the basement and inaccessible to Janie's wheelchair. So are the bathrooms and the baptistry.

Week after week, church becomes more of a haven for peace, fellowship, and restoration for the Insider family. Week after week the Outsiders are pushed more and more into the outside world as they seek services, programs, and provisions for their child.

A Child Is Born

A child is born. When this miraculous event happens, it is truly life-changing. As new parents we spend sleepless nights, visit a bewildering assortment of doctors, rearrange our social lives, rethink career goals, rearrange our homes. We are surprised at the strains and stresses a new baby—a new, healthy, normal baby—can put on our marriage.

When that new baby has a mental and/or physical disability, we have all the just-mentioned experiences, only they are intensified and multiplied. We have more sleepless nights, more doctor appointments. We are often confined to our homes for long periods of time as our children are prone to more illnesses and surgeries. Instances of sibling rivalry are intensified as brothers and sisters cope with jealousy, embarrassment, and fear. Career plans come to a halt, social lives to a standstill. Four out of five of our marriages are failing.

We spend our week literally and figuratively fighting ... for a proper diagnosis, proper medical treatment, appropriate education for the acceptance of society. We long for the blessed peace of Sundays—the love, affirmation, and comfort that we envision as part of church.

Unfortunately, most churches are geared for the average family. They have little room or provision for those who don't fit the established mold. One out of every five families has a disabled member, yet nowhere in the church is this number represented.

C.S. Lewis said that "suffering is harder for Christians to deal with because we expect so much from God." We finally manage to get to church and the frequent response—both spoken and unspoken—is about as comforting as Job's friends:

There is *scolding:* "How dare you question the sovereignty of God."

There is *judging:* "This must be God's punishment for some unlearned lesson or unconfessed sin."

There is *chiding:* "If you only had more faith, your child would be healed."

There is *faint praise:* "Ah, exceptional parents for an exceptional child. I could never deal with this."

Or they ignore us. I once had a pastor candidly confess that he avoided our children because they made him uncomfortable. "I just can't explain them to myself theologically," he said.

Modeling Christ

"But what can I do to help?"

What difference can one person make? All the formal church programs that I have known started because of one concerned person. You can be that one person.

If you feel a call to start a formalized program, tell your church leadership of your heart's concern. Be prepared with suggestions and resources that can help your church become known as a caring church (see p. 294 of the Resource Section).

We usually think of "ministry" as a Sunday-kind-of-thing, but the times that our family has experienced ministry in its truest sense have been those times between Sundays when people have dared to walk beside us in our everyday lives. Following are a few simple examples of this specialized, personalized type of ministry.

Doctor Appointments

During our numerous appointments we have been blessed by a variety of ministering friends. Our foster daughter used to have massive temper tantrums in the car; taking her for appointments was both nerve-wracking and dangerous. But friends would go with us and either drive, so I could watch Melissa, or entertain her so I could drive.

One summer Becky was scheduled for orthopedic surgery and the doctor wanted to store a supply of her blood for transfusions. That required six trips (120 miles each time), a scary experience for Becky, and then the long hours at the blood bank. Another friend helped drive us into the strange city and we took turns entertaining Becky and diverting her attention.

One mother told me of a companion who went with her on appointments and took shorthand notes of all the specialists said.

Visits

We can't get out as often or conveniently as others. At times when Becky was recovering from surgery, I have been confined to the house for weeks at a time. Our family has been blessed by friends who realize that, and for much of our friendship these couples have to come to us.

"We're bringing dinner to you. We just realized how much you're missing out on fellowship, so we're bringing some to you." With these warm words new friends brought us dinner on several festive occasions—paper plates, napkins, drinks, and even their teenage daughter to keep Becky company. Another lady would occasionally bring a big pot of soup and a pan of rolls, "for whenever you need it." An older couple played grandparents to our kids and often brought dinner over and treated us like guests.

Housework and Baby-sitting

Glynnis was thrilled when friends realized how important having a clean house was to her. They set up a schedule to take care of her daughter while Glynnis caught up on neglected housework.

A friend had numerous physical problems and was limited in how she could help. "Please let me do your laundry during this time," she pleaded. It was hard for me to let her play servant to me, but I eventually realized how necessary it is for us to allow people to minister to us in any way they can.

"I'll watch any of your children—except Melissa—anytime you need help." Far from being offended, I was grateful for my friend's honesty. I took her up on her offer on those numerous times when I had to take Melissa to see a specialist. A teacher friend used to come and take Melissa out for a few hours to either give me time alone or time to concentrate on the other children.

Being a Friend

Often we take the everyday, "normal" events of life for granted. Birthday parties, sleep-overs, outings. However, our children so often miss out on the "normal."

It takes just a little pre-planning on the part of the hostess, but being included is possible. We have had birthday parties that included physically disabled children in walkers, wheelchairs, and body casts; we have had parties that included classmates from Melissa's deaf-blind program. When I mailed off invitations to Melissa's party, one mother responded in tears. "It's my nine-year-old's first ever invitation and it's so normal!" she cried.

When people include disabled children in public outings, trips to lunch, shopping, etc., it does wonders for them to be out, gives them a break from their parents, and sends out strong messages of "I'm proud to be your friend."

We have a few treasured friends who have been faithful over the years. They have continued to come to our house when we were confined. They have proudly gone out in public with our kids, bravely baby-sat so we could go out. They have brought us meals, played chauffeur, washed our clothes, and cleaned our house. They have shown us Jesus' love as Jesus did—not in the confines of church walls, not on a Sunday schedule. Through them the love of Jesus has permeated our everyday lives.

A Ministry Program

Starting a formal ministry program for persons with disabilities in your local congregation

by Marie B. Latta

In America today over 10% of the population has some type of disability. Every church is within touching distance of disabled people. My local church is a large one in a metropolitan area. Yours may be a small rural one or a size somewhere in between. The need—and the possibilities—are the same. We are responsible for meeting them.

No matter what your location, church size, denomination, or specialized need, you can follow some basic organizational guidelines to begin a ministry with disabled people. This chapter focuses on the development of a teaching ministry for children with mental retardation, C-HANDS (Children with Handicaps Developing Spiritually), at Mt. Carmel Christian Church in Stone Mountain, Georgia. It is a step-by-step process that can be applied to beginning any type of ministry to people having specialized needs. It can work for you.

Before You Start

Ingredients

Seven ingredients must exist to have a successful ministry with handicapped people. These ingredients can be found or developed in any church. A spiritually healthy church will be able to blend the ingredients into a rich mix and produce a ministry centered on the local needs.

Two or three lay persons. In our Bible-school class for four- and five-year-olds, two teachers were wondering how we could minister to the needs of disabled people. One of them has a teenage granddaughter with Down syndrome and knows firsthand what can be learned and what tremendous unconditional love can be given by a child with Down syndrome.

When I began to inquire about what other churches were doing, I was directed to a lovely lady in a Southern Baptist church who had started a class for persons with mental retardation. She had begun with no previous experience.

Ministerial support. There must be a commitment from your ministers. Our two teachers approached our children's minister, who shared the same concern. He did not have the expertise either, but he spoke about this concern to the church leadership at a regular board meeting.

When I heard that our church leadership felt we should be ministering to disabled people but weren't sure how, I went directly to our children's minister and asked if I could direct a program.

A vision and a goal. An incurable crusader will do fine! Someone has to have the burning desire that starts with nothing and envisions a program fully functioning.

That vision must be translated into a reasonable goal. The stated goal will give a focus and the framework for accomplishing it by setting appropriate activities. The goal must be workable and attainable.

Initial brainstorming and planning sessions led us to establish goals for a ministry to children up to twelve.

Commitment. Those involved must be persistent and willing to see that the program is maintained over time. Disabled people and their families face too many disappointments for the church to let them down too.

The program needs are bound to change. You will occasionally find that your needs will change or something you planned didn't work. Stay committed when you have to adjust.

A focus and flexibility. Decide on the type of ministry you will begin. Narrow the focus so it is manageable, then do it well. A personal battle I continually fight is the temptation to start too many projects. Too many projects at once can lead to burnout, frustration, and failure, no matter how workable the ideas are.

Even when you are on the right track, you will make mistakes or things will change. Be flexible enough to admit mistakes and alter plans when the need arises. After all our planning, we made changes after our first Bible-school class.

A positive we-can-do-it-together outlook. This is a must. The entire church must be sold on the idea. While support from church leadership allows you to make decisions and implement the program, the support of the church members is a prerequisite for assuring a climate of acceptance and love for people with handicaps.

Acceptance cannot be legislated or dictated. It must be modeled, taught, demonstrated—and seen in your actions, your face, your life. Acceptance will always precede integration of handicapped people into the church life.

Timing. If the above ingredients are in place, you have set the stage. God will provide the timing necessary to orchestrate the ministry.

When the Christian Church Foundation for the Handicapped was formed, the idea captured the heart and imagination of our church. We were involved through prayer, financial support, and physical labor from the beginning. This involvement throughout our congregation set the stage for the development of our own ministry programs.

Around this time other opportunities came to us. During this time the directors of Friends of Disabled Adults, Inc. (FODA), came to our senior minister to ask if adults in wheelchairs would be welcome at Mt. Carmel. Seven other area churches had been unable to accommodate them. Several of the FODA folks have since joined our congregation. They are involved in Bible-school classes and even have Sunday lunch with the ministers.

For years Mt. Carmel has had interpreters and a comprehensive ministry with persons having hearing impairments. They are integrated into the church life as participants and leaders.

Experience as Christian lay and professional leaders tells us that when we surrender to God and begin on faith, God will open up avenues for service.

Accessibility

You do not have to wait until you make your church totally accessible. Mt. Carmel was full of physical barriers when the programs began. Our new barrier-free building has changed that, but we started in a building full of physical barriers. You will find ways to improvise. As you prepare, check the physical barriers:

- *Parking Spaces*. Do you have several parking spaces marked close to the entrance? Stencils can be purchased or reusable ones made out of plywood to save money.
- *Ramps*. Someone in your church can build a wooden ramp to place on the steps where needed. At the curb, it can be constructed of wood or poured from concrete.
- *Bathrooms*. We removed doors from two stalls in one of the rest rooms to give needed wheelchair width.
- *Seating Spaces*. We took out one of the back pews to allow room for the wheelchairs.

Use what you have. Adapt. There is no excuse good enough not to start.

Decision and Planning

What happens *before* your doors open to a formal ministry is critical to the successful implementation and maintenance of the ministry. Do not rush this stage by trying to do it in two or three weeks.

In January 1986, the idea for our ministry was conceived. The program was implemented on promotion day, September 7, 1986. During those eight months, we took the following eight steps.

Decide to Act

Any person, lay or ministerial, who wants to begin ministry with persons with disabilities should start *saying* so. It is not necessary to wait until you know for sure what you want to do or if someone else will care. Start saying, "We need to act." Someone with authority will need to say, "Let's run with it."

Ideally a layperson (you don't have to be experienced) should begin the program rather than saddling the minister with one more organizational task. But the minister should be involved as an advisor (in whatever way suits your church needs and leadership style).

A minister, a layperson who is willing to direct the program, and an assistant make a great start.

Set Long- and Short-Range Goals

Now it is time to go into your brainstorming mode and look at your church calendar for the next year.

Your scheduled brainstorming sessions should include discussing and recording all ideas and possibilities about what your program could be. Include even the ideas that sound farfetched. There are no right or wrong answers at this point.

After doing your homework and brainstorming, begin to narrow your focus and make initial decisions about what specifically you will do. You cannot be all things to all people at all times. Consider the following:

- *Facilities.* What space can be made available? (No classes in back corner, out of the way rooms!) Consider proximity to entrances and bathrooms. Where can ramps be placed? (Small children can be carried up and down stairs.)
- *Existing needs.* Do you have members with mental retardation, cerebral palsy, or mobility impairments?
- *People in the community.* Contact local agencies to research the need: school systems, human service agencies, training centers (see the Resource Section for more suggestions).
- *Resources.* Don't try to reinvent the wheel. Use what is available. Contact the local agencies you've found and ask, "What resources (materials, speakers, training, information) and services are available in the community?"

Start with a manageable goal. Do a good job, then expand if you need to. Keep your eye on your goal, but always be fluid and flexible. In 1986 at Mt. Carmel, our first long range plan was to begin serving handicapped children through age twelve during Sunday morning services. Once you establish your goals, make sure your activities are designed to accomplish these goals.

Win the Heart of Your Church

People are afraid of the unknown. Your first big job is to provide information, exposure, and support – in short, to win the heart of the church, the people. Doing this means having church members accept responsibility for a ministry instead of having two people teach a back-corner class that no one else knows much about.

You can implement your ministry by going around stomping your foot and saying, "These people *do* have rights!" Or you can educate your church members. Involve them by asking for their help and thanking them for what is happening.

Educating the church is your key to success. It can be done by:

- Placing articles and announcements in the church bulletin.
- Getting the minister to support your plans from the pulpit.
- Doing special programs in the children's classes.
- Speaking to adult classes and ladies' groups.
- Publicizing your plans in community media.
- Give your program a name. A name is an important way to promote your ministry. When we did select a name, a church member who is a commercial artist developed a beautiful "C-HANDS" logo as a donation.

Using the above suggestions and just talking the work up in your everyday contacts will break down the barrier of fear of the unknown. Wave your flag! Blow your horn! Elevate the plan to a high plane by your enthusiasm. It will take on an air of importance.

Develop a Service Model

Once you have decided what population you will serve, decide how you will do it. Apply the old adage, "Plan the work and work the plan." Your decision about age groups and types of disabilities should be based on the goals you have already established.

Your next major decision will be whether to have a separate class or to integrate your disabled students into regular classes with the help of your workers.

A separate class is called *self-contained.* Integrating into regular classes is a resource model known as *mainstreaming* (these are standard terms for serving handicapped children in school).

In deciding between the mainstreaming and self-contained models, you will need to consider age, severity of handicap (a person with physical disabilities who has normal intellectual functioning probably should be in a regular class), available teaching staff, accessibility of space, and resources.

At first we included children with severe behavioral disorders in the same self-contained class with children with other disabilities. This did not work for us. Many trained special education teachers are not comfortable with this combination. Don't expect volunteers to be able to handle it.

Enlist Workers

If you have won the heart of your church, you will be pleasantly surprised. People will want to help. Announce that you need workers. Talk it up. No experience necessary, just a desire and a love for the Lord.

If you have experienced professional people in your church, enlist their help. But inexperienced people can learn. They have much to offer and they can be reliable and creative.

Insist that your workers be members of your local congregation. The ministry is an integrated part of your church family staffed by members. Your goal is to present Christ, the Redeemer.

Because you have won the heart of the church, you have before you volunteers (maybe two, maybe eight or twelve) looking directly to you for leadership. Most or all of them will not have had any experience with persons having disabilities.

- Act like a leader so they will have someone to follow and over come their fear of the unknown.
- Give them information to break down fear and help build confidence.

• Reinforce their interest.
• Be enthusiastic (a fearless leader, not a fearful one, conquers new terrain).

Search for Prospects

Start looking as soon as you have decided what population to serve and have a target date to begin the ministry. Announce the beginning of your ministry to the congregation and ask them for the names of people you might be able to serve. Follow up on any prospects that come to your attention. You can also make announcements in media resources at your disposal like your church bulletin, community newspaper, or the newsletters of local social service agencies.

Every county or community in America has available human service agencies through the State Department of Human Resources or Human Services. There are training centers for persons with mental retardation, rehabilitation services, and many other agencies. By letting your community and county social service agencies know what you are doing, you will get referrals.

Contact the families of the referrals you receive. Get information. Find out about their past disappointments and present needs. We usually receive a positive response to such contacts. Families appreciate groups who are trying to meet their needs in a genuinely caring way. Some families will also read or hear about you and initiate a contact.

Promote Your Ministry

Promotion goes beyond the things already discussed. Do everything with an air of excitement and expectancy. Create in your church members a sense of being a part of something wonderful.

We found that speaking to classes in the church greatly enhanced the work. For the adults we took a report of what we were doing and asked for their prayer support. They have readily given us their prayer and financial support. Most classes will be willing to give you five minutes during their announcement time. Be upbeat and concise, and stay within the prearranged time limit.

In children's classes we have taught special lessons to increase their awareness and acceptance. Group activities, stories, and coloring books can be used to make acceptance of differences a reality. Many times children have more exposure and are more comfortable than their parents because of interaction with handicapped children at school.

A strong emphasis on educating young children will pay off. They give unconditional friendship. Teaching acceptance early and continuing it as they grow through the children's program will cultivate a climate in which all people will be comfortable and have true Christian fellowship. The early training will buffer children against the middle and preadolescent years when they are self-conscious and want to be exactly like their peers. At a time when conformity is paramount in the child's mind, it is difficult to expect them to readily accept differences.

One good strategy is to identify some strong peer leaders among your elementary age children. A few moments of observation will tell you which children the others follow. Win those young leaders over. Teach them that it is personally rewarding not only to accept but be involved in the lives of handicapped people. Remember, you are building for the long haul!

There is no room for an attitude of pity for the downtrodden or a do-gooders' syndrome. You are involved in the process of making friends with and serving the spiritual needs of handicapped people and their families ... of sharing Jesus.

Spending time on winning the church members and helping them have more knowledge about persons with disabilities will probably do more than anything else to successfully launch a long-lasting, well-supported ministry.

Train Your Volunteers

When people volunteer, they do it on faith and expect your leadership. Map out a clear-cut training strategy and carry it out *before* implementing the program. Training does several things for those fantastic people who called you and said, "I don't have any experience, but I'll do whatever you need me for."

At Mt. Carmel we had our initial training on four consecutive Wednesday nights in August 1986. Since our goal was a children's ministry, our topics were:

- Characteristics and behaviors associated with various disabilities.

- Affective skills (skills having to do with feelings). Positive ways to work with and talk to children and parents.
- Teaching techniques, alternative strategies, equipment demonstration.
- Behavioral strategies—behavior modification, modeling, prevention, intervention.

Training materials are listed on pages 278 and 279.

If you are new at these, don't be intimidated by the necessity of planning training, but *do* have it. Plenty of professionals and parents of handicapped children will assist in your training, probably at no charge. They will be grateful you are planning for handicapped people.

Even though your workers should be members of your church, your skilled resources who do the training need not be members. Use the best people you can find.

The county or community Mental Health/Mental Retardation Board, special education teachers, members of advocacy groups, Down syndrome association, and the Association of Retarded Citizens are organizations that can provide both materials and speakers/trainers.

Looking back over my involvement with special education training centers and human services agencies, I believe that training (both formal and informal) in behavioral management techniques is the single most important need. It cuts across all types of disabilities and through the whole range of functioning, from dependent to mild.

The oft-repeated question is, "Do we make them mind like other kids (people)?" Yes, yes, a thousand times yes!

During our initial training, we presented information, role-played, shared experiences, did activities, and had tremendous fun. Taping the sessions has provided a reusable training tool.

Something special and lasting happened at those training sessions. A strong bonding process began developing among the workers. That bond still exists today.

Working with handicapped people is intense. The burnout rate can be high if workers do not receive training and leadership support. Time spent sowing the seeds and cultivating the fruit of good leadership will be one of your keys to success and longevity of the program.

Implementation

Service Model

You have decided on your service model. This will, to a great degree, dictate how you will implement the ministry.

Almost immediately after our start-up, we shifted from a self-contained to a combination self-contained/mainstreaming model. There is nothing like doing it to show you how things really work (or don't work). This is what we learned by doing:

- Some children need a self-contained classroom all the time.
- Some can function with self-contained class for Bible school and mainstreaming into children's chapel (with an assigned teacher) for worship service.
- Some can be mainstreamed into a regular class for Bible school and chapel.
- Children with physical handicaps (cerebral palsy, spina bifida) who have at least average intellectual functioning will have their needs met best in a regular class with a special help teacher. Small children can be carried to class if necessary.
- If you have only one mentally retarded student, a self-contained class is too isolating and fails to provide for him the structural framework of a classroom setting.

We didn't initially develop a strong program for preadolescents and adolescents. We are working on it. Children do grow up. People who are mentally retarded go through the same developmental stages and have the same needs as others. If your church does not have enough of this age group for a self-contained class, it is often hard to meet their needs in the regular setting. Young people without handicaps do not automatically accept their disabled peers at a time in their lives when looking and acting like a clone of their brightest, prettiest, most popular peers is critical. They have to be educated and taught acceptance.

Curriculum

Consider adapting your own existing curriculum materials for a while. Often that will work well. As you proceed, you will change your perception of what you need. For more on adapting Bible lesson material, see Chapter 3. Other alternatives include adapting the lesson plans in this book or buying ready-made curriculum (see the Resource Section). In any adapting work, consider the following:

- Use of all the senses.
- Visual aides.
- Hands-on activities.
- Participation.
- Focus on one thing at a time.
- Short attention span.
- Instructions given *one* step at a time.

During your planning stage, look at bibliographies and materials available. Buy materials when you know what you need.

Since the dawn of special education, teachers have done something with nothing. Create handmade materials, get classes and individuals to take you on as a project to buy needed materials and equipment. Ask merchants to give promotional items or overstock.

Your Expectations

We considered the overall church activity timetable and decided to begin the ministry at promotion time to heighten the probability of success. Treat the beginning of your ministry as an event, a happening. Schedule it and promote it.

What happens if you have made all those plans and no one shows up? The workers and the congregation must understand that this type of ministry will start slowly.

Even though I had cautioned my co-workers not to expect too much, we all had the opening-day jitters. But the contacts had paid off. On the first Sunday five children showed up. All the workers wanted to be there. Workers were tripping over each other. Excited church members came by to see if children had come.

One of the first things we had to do after that first Sunday was to alter the schedule and classroom arrangement. Some Sundays we had a big group and other Sundays no children came. That's

OK. Expect that and prepare your workers for it. Some Sundays new children came, about whom we had not previously known. Be ready, be flexible. Always get information about each new child for the records.

During the early implementation stage, encourage each other as workers, contact the prospects and parents, and pray without ceasing. The one in charge needs to be visible, a decision maker, and most of all, an encourager. Avoid trying to do it all on your own as a leader.

Maintaining the Ministry

A ministry to handicapped persons is like a marriage. Saying "I do" is the easiest part. Maintaining it and making it work are the real tests of commitment. Three keys will help you maintain your program over time.

Keep Your Focus

Whatever your plan, think of it as a long-term commitment, not a short-term project. Whatever you choose to do, do it consistently! You are providing people the opportunity to know Jesus.

Over time, we have seen several children coming, no children coming, and one or two children coming. That makes a long-term goal critical to making the program work. Otherwise we would give up during the down times and miss blessings.

The long-term goal is the target. A short-term objective or activity is a step toward the target, a gauge. The special education director in your school system can give you more helpful information about long-term goals and short-term objectives for people with handicaps.

At times while you are getting started, you can feel like you are in charge of a runaway horse as you see things you want to accomplish. Some things just don't get done immediately. That's OK. Forgive yourself. Keep pacing yourself. Focus on goals and objectives.

Your list of mistakes may be different than ours, but accept the fact that you are going to have a list. Then when the mistakes jump out at you, you won't be ready to give up.

Stay in continual prayer so you can tell the difference between what God wants you to get done and what you want to get done. I have to continually relearn that difference. Remember that you are human.

When you are feeling like "throwing in the towel," talk to your minister or co-workers, or call someone at one of the community agencies. Tell them you need a listening ear, a sounding board. You can be assured that the problem, even if new to you, is not new. Building yourself a support system is mandatory for longevity.

Be Flexible and Ready

Notice, over time, what is working and what isn't. Keep what works and toss out what doesn't. We have maintained the combination self-contained and resource (mainstreaming) model because it works for us.

We started the children's ministry as a Sunday morning program for children twelve and under. We since have written an individualized program to integrate a thirteen-year-old with dependent mental retardation into the total church program. On the other hand we have another young teen who functions in the educable range of mental retardation. We are struggling to know how to most appropriately meet his needs.

You will be more successful if you start small, do the job well, then expand. The need is so great that there is temptation to bite off too much.

We have had to revise our goals and objectives. Regular attendance does not come easily, but we believe that what we're doing is just as important for one as it is for thirty.

As the leader, regroup periodically with your minister for debriefing and planning. Update and make necessary changes. Ask these questions:

- Are the people you serve learning about Jesus, integrating into the church life, making friends, getting moral support?
- Are the other church members aware of needs, becoming more involved?
- Are your workers staying with the ministry?
- Are the families involved and pleased?

Fit Into the Church Life

Your goal should be to integrate people with handicaps into the mainstream of your church.

Get to know the population you serve and their families. In the same way you would get to know the members of any Bible school class, you will get involved in the lives of those in your ministry. This is not losing the focus. It is, rather, providing the ministry. You should become a resource for help and information and a much needed sounding board for families. People with handicaps may have a high number of illnesses, surgeries, and other needs. They need the support of the church family. Utilize your church members to minister to these varied needs. Grandparents are wonderful at giving emotional support.

Keeping your church involved and informed about successes, needs, and new ideas will keep the program going through both exciting and discouraging times.

Some of the fun and meaningful things we've done:

- A kickoff luncheon to initiate the program. (Can you imagine how it feels to be honored instead of derided as a handicapped child or his parent?)
- A Christmas party for children and a simultaneous tea for parents.
- Visit children in their public school environment.
- Provide additional ongoing training.
- Act as an information network.
- Prayer and financial support during difficult times.

The Challenge

The purpose of this chapter has been to give you a framework for starting the ministry that your church needs.

One individual can be the catalyst that starts the ministry in your local church. Act on the desire. Learn as you go. God is your leader. But you must *start.* There are no other choices. You are where God put you. Don't wait for a windfall before you start. To deny the opportunity and responsibility is to deny people an open door to Christ.

You can do it. You are an important, capable person ... God's person for the chosen time. Believe Him and believe in yourself.

Developing your local congregation's ministry to handicapped persons will change your life.

PART FOUR

Resources

This is a section of resources for your ministry program.

- 52 lessons for a class of mentally retarded students
- A strategy for finding resources available to you in your community
- A list of Christian and secular resources
- A test for determining the knowledge of your beginning mentally retarded students

A Year of Lessons

by Gloria Fife Lacy

The following lessons are to be used as a foundation on which to build your daily plans. After you discover the individual strengths and weaknesses of your students, you will know which lessons will be appropriate for the members of your class. The lessons of the final quarter, concerning the church, are the most complex and abstract. Your decision should not only consider the chronological age but also the student's mental abilities and emotional needs.

The emphasis verse is not for memorization, but rather to be used as focal point for the lesson.

The songs are suggestions only. If the students do not have a strong background in church music, you may want to choose one or two songs and use them throughout the quarter.

The most important point to stress in teaching these lessons is the JOY one finds in learning about God, His Son and His family. I hope you will find much joy in your teaching.

PART 1

God

1. God Created Everything
2. God Cares About Me
3. God Is My Heavenly Father
4. God Protects Me
5. God Leads Me
6. God Listens to Me
7. God Is Love
8. God Is Powerful
9. God Is Everywhere
10. God Knows Everything
11. God Lives in Me
12. God Has Feelings
13. God Helps Me Know What Is Right

Theme song: "Blessed Be the Name
of the Lord"

LESSON 1

God Created Everything

Purpose: To realize God created us all.

Scripture: Genesis 1:26, 27; 2:7 (also Genesis 1:1-31; 2:1-25; Isaiah 40:12, 22, 26)

Songs: "God Thought of Everything" (group)
"All Things Bright and Beautiful" (group)
"This Is My Father's World" (group)
"Praise God From Whom All Blessings Flow" (group)
"God Made Me a Specialty" (special)

Lesson: *Tell the story of creation.* God created the light and darkness (day and night); the sky; the dry land and the seas; the plants and trees; the sun, moon, and stars; seasons, days, and years; sea creatures and birds; land animals; and *people!* As you tell about His creation, show pictures of the different wonders of His world. Emphasize the special place people have in God's creation.

Application: God made each one of us. He loves us. He gave each of us a soul so that we could love Him back. He has made each one of us special.

Activity: Have the students draw a picture or color a drawing of a happy face. Then write underneath the picture in large capital letters, GOD MADE ME–I'M SPECIAL!

Emphasis Verse: "Know that the Lord is God. He made us, and we belong to him. We are His people, the sheep he tends" (Psalm 100:3).

LESSON 2

God Cares About Me

Purpose: To discover God's caring love.

Scripture: Genesis 21:14-19 (also Isaiah 40:27-31; 41:10)

Songs: "He's Got the Whole World in His Hands" (group)
"God Will Take Care of You" (group)
"O God Our Help in Ages Past" (group)
"His Eye Is on the Sparrow" (special)

Lesson: *Tell the story of Hagar and Ishmael in the desert wilderness.* Hagar was running away with her boy, Ishmael. They were in the hot, dry desert, all alone. They ran out of food and water. Hagar gave up hope. She did not want to see her son die. She cried. But God heard. He showed her where to get water. He cared.

Application: God knows our needs. Even when we give up hope, God wants to help us. Discuss with the students the implication of this story in their lives.

Activity: Talk about how hot and thirsty one gets in the desert. Show them pictures of the desert. Bring some sand and let them feel how dry it is. Then let them put their hands in some cool, clear water. Talk about how hot, tired, and thirsty Hagar and Ishmael were. God answered their needs.

Emphasis Verse: "The Lord gives strength to those who are tired. He gives more power to those who are weak" (Isaiah 40:29).

LESSON 3

God Is My Heavenly Father

Purpose: To learn that we are children of God.

Scripture: Romans 8:15

Songs: "God Is My Father" (group)
"Our Father, Who Art in Heaven" (special)
"Great Is Thy Faithfulness" (group)
"A Child of the King" (group)
"I Am Adopted" (special)

Lesson: *Talk about God adopting us as His own children.* God becomes our Father who lives in Heaven. When we decide to believe in God and do what He says, we become a part of His family. He even wants us to call Him "Father." Then all the other people who believe in God become our brothers and sisters!

Application: Discuss the concept of "family." Talk about how we take care of one another and care about each other's problems. We are special. We are children of God!

Activity: Using pipe cleaners, help the students form the words FATHER and GOD in capital letters. Then connect the two words with several more pipe cleaners.

Emphasis Verse: "The Spirit that we received is not a spirit that makes us slaves again to fear. The Spirit that we have makes us children of God. And with that Spirit we say, 'Father, dear Father'" (Romans 8:15).

LESSON 4

God Protects Me

Purpose: To discover God's protecting love.

Scripture: Daniel 6:3-23 (also Psalm 121:1-8)

Songs: "Dare To Be a Daniel" (group)
"A Mighty Fortress Is Our God" (group)
"Under His Wings" (group)
"When the Storms of Life Are Raging"
(special)

Lesson: *Tell the story of Daniel in the lions' den.* Daniel
believed in God. He worshiped only God.
When the king tried to make Daniel bow
down and worship him, Daniel would not do
it. So the king's men threw Daniel into a place
where lions lived. They even put a big rock
over the opening of the lions' den to be sure
Daniel couldn't get out. But God protected
Daniel. He didn't let the lions hurt Daniel.
The next day the king came to the lion's den
to see if God had protected Daniel during the
night. When he saw Daniel was safe and
sound, he wanted to tell everyone what a
great God Daniel's God was!

Application: God wants to protect His children. Everyone
who believes in God is His child, no matter
how old that person is. We can tell other people about God just like the king did in the
story. For our God "will guard you from all
dangers."

Activity: Bring pictures of lions you have found in
books or magazines. Show how big and fierce
they can look. Then let the students paste the

pictures on cardboard. Collect all the cardboard pieces and make a circle with them by
connecting them together. Then cut out the
figure of Daniel from paper (or mold it from
clay). Lower the figure into the "lions' den"
and seal it shut with another piece of cardboard. Talk about Daniel being in the den all
night long. Afterwards, open the den and find
that Daniel is safe. God closed the mouths of
the lions!

Emphasis Verse: "The Lord will guard you from all dangers. He
will guard your life" (Psalm 121:7).

LESSON 5

God Leads Me

Purpose: To learn that God can lead us through hard
times.

Scripture: Exodus 13:17-22 (also Psalms 25:9, 10; Isaiah
40:11)

Songs: "He Leadeth Me" (group)
"Follow, I Will Follow Thee" (group)
"Walking in the King's Highway" (group)
"I Know Where I'm Going" (special)

Lesson: *Tell the story of God leading Moses and the
Israelites through the Red Sea wilderness.* The
Bible tells us about a man named Moses, who
was taking some people out of slavery. These
people were called Israelites. They had to
travel across a desert. Moses was not afraid
that they would get lost because he knew that

God would lead them. God chose to lead the people by a pillar of fire at night and a pillar of cloud during the daytime. The cloud and the fire were never out of sight. Moses and the Israelites knew that God was with them.

Application: The Bible says God will lead us, too. When we trust God, like Moses trusted Him, He helps us know what to do. When we read the Bible, we find answers to our questions. God doesn't want us to be afraid. He wants to lead us. He is always near.

Activity: Blindfold each student, one at a time. Then you the teacher, lead them around the room. Take them around obstacles: tables, chairs, people, things on the floor. Talk about the trust and faith they must have in the person who leads them. Apply this to trust in God.

Emphasis Verse: "All the Lord's ways are loving and true for those who follow the demands of his agreement" (Psalms 25:10).

LESSON 6

God Listens to Me

Purpose: To learn that God listens to us when we talk to Him.

Scripture: Acts 16:22-26 (Psalm 91:15)

Songs: "Whisper a Prayer" (group)
"Hear Our Prayer, O Lord" (group)
"God Is So Good" (group)
"God Is Always Listening" (special)

Lesson: *Tell the story of Paul in prison.* The Bible tells us about a man named Paul who was thrown in jail because he believed in God's Son, Jesus. The people were angry with Paul and his friend Silas. They hit Paul and Silas with sticks. The man in charge of the jail tied up their feet and threw them into a dark place. But this did not make Paul and Silas sad or afraid! Instead of giving up and crying, they prayed to God and sang songs to Him! They sang so loudly that the other prisoners heard them.

Suddenly, the earth began to shake. The ground moved under their feet. The bars of the prison began to rattle. All of the sudden the doors of the jail opened! God had heard the prayers of Paul and Silas. He set them free from prison!

Application: Even when we feel that no one is listening to us, even if we feel all alone, God listens and He cares. Paul and Silas were down in a deep dark jail and were locked up and tied up. They weren't free to move where they wanted to go or do what they wanted to do. But they didn't get discouraged. They prayed to God. They even sang! And God listened. The Bible tells us He listens to us, too.

Activity: Have everyone join in building a jail with popsicle sticks and glue. Make some men from clay or cut some out of cardboard. Then act out the story of Paul and Silas being put in jail, of praying, of singing, of the earthquake, of the jail falling apart, and of Paul and Silas being free.

Emphasis Verse: "They will call to me, and I will answer them. I will be with them in trouble. I will rescue them and honor them" (Psalm 91:15).

LESSON 7

God Is Love

Purpose: To learn about the depth of God's love and how He wants us to love one another.

Scripture: John 3:16, 17 (also 1 John 4:7, 8, 20, 21; Romans 8:38, 39)

Songs: "For God So Loved the World" (group)
"Praise Him, Praise Him" (group)
"God Loved the People of the World So Much" (special)
"O Love That Will Not Let Me Go" (group)
"Love One Another" (special)

Lesson: *Tell how God sent Jesus to us because He loves us.* God shows His love for us in many ways. But the most beautiful way was in sending His son, Jesus, to us. God expects us to love each other. He says in the Bible that it is impossible to say we love God and then turn around and say we hate someone else. "Whoever does not love does not know God, because God is love."

Application: God wants us not only to *say* we love others, but also *show* we love others. Discuss with the students ways that they can show their love to those around them.

Activity: Using parts of old greeting cards and pictures from magazines, help the students make cards to give to a member of their family, a friend, or a fellow worker. (Make get well cards, friendship cards, thinking of you cards, Christmas cards.) On each card print the words GOD IS LOVE.

Emphasis Verse: "Whoever does not love does not know God, because God is love" (1 John 4:8).

LESSON 8

God Is Powerful

Purpose: To learn about God's mighty strength.

Scripture: Exodus 14:1-29

Songs: "How Did Moses Cross the Red Sea?" (group)
"He's Got the Whole World in His Hands" (group)
"O Worship the King" (group)
"God of Our Fathers" (special)

Lesson: *Tell the story of Moses crossing the Red Sea.* When Moses was leading the people of Israel out of Egypt, he believed God would help him. All the people were excited to be free. They were happy. But then they came to a sea of water. They became afraid. They thought it would be impossible to get across. But Moses believed God would help them. He knew that there wasn't *anything* God couldn't do. He held out his walking stick over the sea. Then God opened a path through the water. The water was pushed back and the people of Israel walked across the sea on dry land! There isn't anything God can't do.

Application: God is powerful. When He saw that His people needed help, He used His great power to help them. But what came before God's help? Moses' *faith* came first. Moses didn't give up when he saw the sea in front of him. He believed God would help him. He believed God had the *power* to help him. God wants to help us with our problems, too.

Activity: This is a fun story to dramatize. Using two large sheets (preferably blue), make the sea. Several students could stand on each side and give the sheets a toss now and then to create "waves." Moses and the people could travel on to the promised land!

Emphasis Verse: "Oh, Lord God, you made the skies and the earth. You made them with your very great power. There is nothing too wonderful for you to do" (Jeremiah 32:17).

LESSON 9

God Is Everywhere

Purpose: To learn that God is always near.

Scripture: Psalms 139:6-12 (also Proverbs 15:3)

Songs: "All Night, All Day" (group)
"God Is Watching Over You" (group)
"You Can't Run Away From God" (group)
"His Eye Is on the Sparrow" (special)

Lesson: *Tell how God is everywhere.* The Bible tells us that God is everywhere. A man named David was so happy that God went with him everywhere. He said, "Your knowledge is amazing to me. It is more than I can understand. Where can I go to get away from your Spirit?

Where can I run from you? If I go up to the skies, you are there. If I lie down where the dead are, you are there. If I rise with the sun in the east, and settle in the west beyond the sea, even there you would guide me. With your right hand you would hold me" (Psalm 139:6-10). God always watches over us.

Application: Discuss with the students the different places they think God may be—not just in the church, not just near us when we pray, not with us just when we are happy and the sun is shining. God goes with us when we go to school and to work. God is near when we are tempted to do the wrong thing. God is close to us when we feel sad and lonely. He is everywhere. He loves us and wants us to know He is there beside us.

Activity: Give each student a piece of black and a piece of yellow construction paper. Then have them cut out a sun or a lamp from the yellow paper. Have them paste the yellow on the black. Print the words GOD IS NEAR on the bottom of the page. Talk about what this means to us.

Emphasis Verse: "'I am a God who is near,' says the Lord, 'and also a God who is far away'" (Jeremiah 23:23).

LESSON 10

God Knows Everything

Purpose: To learn that God knows our thoughts as well as our actions.

Scripture: Psalms 139:1-6

Songs: "Be Careful Little Hands" (group)
"He's Everything To Me" (group)
"God Understands" (group)
"Cleanse Me" (special)
"How Great Thou Art" (special)

Lesson: We have learned that God is everywhere. We have learned that He sees what we are doing. But He also knows what is in our hearts. He knows what we are thinking. This is a wonderful thing! We can talk to God just by thinking the words. We can say "I love you, God" anytime we want to and He will hear us. He even knows what we are going to say before we say it! We need to think good thoughts and do good deeds. This makes God happy.

Application: Discuss with the students the thoughts that might make God sad—angry thoughts, mean thoughts, jealous thoughts; be sure to give examples. Then talk about good thoughts— happy thoughts, thankful thoughts, and peaceful thoughts.

Activity: Ask the class what good thoughts they could send to God. You make some suggestions. If they wish to thank Him for specific things, a list could be made or pictures drawn of their ideas. After everyone has had a chance to decide, have a quiet time. During this time, let them think their special thoughts. Assure them that God knows exactly what they are thinking.

Emphasis Verse: "Lord, even before I say a word, you know what I am going to say" (Psalm 139:4)

LESSON 11

God Lives in Me

Purpose: To discover that God dwells within us.

Scripture: 2 Corinthians 6:16 (also Romans 12:1, 2)

Songs: "Take My Life and Let It Be" (group)
"Higher Ground" (group)
"Open My Eyes" (group)
"The Best You Can Be" (special)

Lesson: The Bible tells us about a man named Paul who wrote letters. He wrote to people who believed in God and in God's Son, Jesus. In one letter Paul writes that people who believe in God should take good care of their bodies because God *lives* there! Paul said we are the home of the living God. It is wonderful to think that God loves us so much that He wants to live in us. He is near us always.

Application: Our bodies and minds are God's home. We need to take very good care of ourselves because we belong to God. We should put only good thoughts into our minds. We should put only healthy things into our bodies.

Activity: Give a short lesson on nutrition. Talk about healthy food and compare it to "junk" food. Talk about good thoughts and actions. We should be filling our minds and bodies with "health food" so that we can present them to God as acceptable places to live.

Emphasis Verse: "The temple of God cannot have any agreement with idols. And we are the temple of the living God. As God said: 'I will live with them and walk with them. And I will be their God. And they will be my people'" (2 Corinthians 6:16).

LESSON 12

God Has Feelings

Purpose: To learn that what we do can make God happy, angry, sad, or jealous.

Scripture: John 3:16; Genesis 6:6; Proverbs 6:16; Exodus 34:14; Deuteronomy 29:23; 1 Peter 5:7

Songs: "Give Me Thy Heart" (group)
"Great Is Thy Faithfulness" (group)
"My God, How Wonderful Thou Art" (group)
"Lord, I Adore Thee" (special)

Lesson: God has feelings. He loves us and cares about what we do. When we do what He wants, He is happy. But when we do wrong things, it makes Him sad. If we care more about other things than we care about Him, it makes Him angry. It is because He loves us that He cares so much. *(Using the Scripture verses listed above, tell about the different emotions of God.)*

Application: The students need to realize that what they do affects God. Discuss the things that we can do to make God happy. Have them think about the things that make God sad and angry. Remind them that God is showing how much He cares about us.

Activity: Have the students act out emotions. Ask them to look angry, sad, happy, jealous. Follow this activity with a discussion about what makes *them* happy, angry, sad, and so forth.

Emphasis Verse: "Give all your worries to him, because he cares for you" (1 Peter 5:7).

LESSON 13

God Helps Me Know What Is Right

Purpose: To discover God's will in our lives.

Scripture: Exodus 20:1-17; John 13:34, 35 (also Matthew 22:34-40)

Songs: "Love One Another" (group)
"Guide Me, O Thou Great Jehovah" (group)
"Make Me a Blessing" (group)
"Angry Words" (special)

Lesson: *Tell the story of the Ten Commandments; then talk about the greatest Commandment.* God does not just tell us to be good. He gave us rules to live by. He doesn't want us to worship anyone or anything except Him. He wants us to use His name only when we are talking to *Him*. He tells us to remember His special day. He wants us to respect our mother and father, no matter how young or old we are. We must not kill. We must be true to those we love. We must not steal. We must not lie. God wants us to be happy with what we have and not want what other people have. These are all important laws. But Jesus gave us the greatest law. He said to love God and love each other. If we do this we will not do anything to hurt them.

Application: Discuss with the class how God has let us know what is right and wrong. Talk about how we act toward those we love. When we care about other people's feelings as much as we care about our own, we will make God happy. We feel good when we are doing what is right. It makes *us* happy, too!

Activity: Cut two "tablets" out of cardboard for each student. Have a list of the Ten Commandments typed on sheets of paper. Give a list to each student. Let them cut them into individual commands. Then have them paste the commandments on the "tablets." On the back of each tablet print the words LOVE ONE ANOTHER. Draw a big heart and let them color it.

Emphasis Verse: "I give you a new command: Love each other. You must love each other as I have loved you" (John 13:34).

PART 2

Jesus

Theme song: "Oh, How I Love Jesus"

LESSON 1

A Baby Named Jesus

Purpose: To introduce the fact that Jesus was a baby in need of love and care.

Scripture: Luke 2:3-24 (also Matthew 1:18-25)

Songs: "Away in a Manger" (group)
"Silent Night" (group)
"No Room in the Inn" (special)
"The Star Carol" (special)
"Sweet Little Jesus Boy" (special)

Lesson: *Tell the story of the birth of Jesus.* There was a man named Joseph. He had a wife named Mary. They had to take a long trip back to their families' home, Bethlehem. It was very crowded in the city. There was no house for them to sleep in. Finally they found a barn where there was some room. That night their baby was born. He had to sleep in a place where cows get their food – in a manger. Angels were excited about Jesus being born!

Application: Emphasize the complete dependency of the baby. Endeavor to help the students understand the need for love Jesus must have felt as an infant.

Activity: After discussing the needs of a baby, bring out a couple of dolls. Let everyone care for them – wrap them up in a warm blankets, etc. Perhaps some students would enjoy putting together a "manger" of boxes. Talk about what they would do if the baby cried. Then have everyone sing the baby to sleep ("Away in a Manger" or "Silent Night").

Emphasis Verse: "She gave birth to her first son. There were no rooms left in the inn. So she wrapped the baby in cloths and laid him in a box where animals are fed" (Luke 2:7).

LESSON 2

Gifts for Baby Jesus

Purpose: To help the students discover the joy of *giving* their love.

Scripture: Matthew 2:1-12

Songs: "We Three Kings" (group)
"O Come, Little Children" (group)
"O Come All Ye Faithful" (group)
"What Can I Give Him?" (group)
"Drummer Boy" (special)
"I Love Thee, Lord" (special)

Lesson: *Tell the story of the wise men.* Some wise men, who learned things from the stars, came to Jerusalem to find Jesus. They asked people where He was. They wanted to worship Him. King Herod heard this. He was very jealous. He wanted everyone to worship *him!* So he decided to trick the wise men. He told them that Jesus was in Bethlehem. He said that when they found Jesus, he wanted to go and worship Him, too! So the wise men went to Bethlehem and found Jesus. They gave Him beautiful gifts of gold, perfume, and spices. They worshiped Him. That night God told them in a dream to go home another way. King Herod wanted to kill baby Jesus. They obeyed God and didn't go back to the king.

Application: Emphasize the point that the wise men brought gifts of love to Jesus. They brought what they treasured or valued. Also explain the obedience of the wise men. Apply this to the students' lives.

Activity: Talk about what each person would want to give to Jesus—something that means a lot to them. Then have everyone paint a picture or draw the object that they treasure. Let them discuss why it means so much to them and why they would want Jesus to have it.

Emphasis Verse: "They went to the house where the child was and saw him with his mother Mary. They bowed down and worshiped the child. They opened the gifts they brought for him. They gave him treasures of gold, frankincense, and myrrh" (Matthew 2:11).

LESSON 3

Where Is Jesus?

Purpose: To realize the importance of obedience to God.

Scripture: Luke 2:41-52

Songs: "One Door and Only One" (group-action)
"Trust and Obey" (group)
"Savior, Teach Me Day by Day" (special)

Lesson: *Tell the story of Jesus in the temple.* When Jesus was twelve years old, He and His family went to Jerusalem for a religious holiday. After it was over, Mary and Joseph started back home. After one whole day, they noticed that Jesus wasn't with them. They looked for Him for *three* days. Finally they found Him in the house of God. He was talking to the teachers. Everyone was surprised that He understood so much. His parents scolded Him for not telling them where He was. They had been very *worried!* He said, "Why were you looking for me? Didn't you know that I must be in my Father's house?" He then went home and obeyed them.

Application: Emphasize the fact that Jesus obeyed His parents. He loved them and wanted to make them happy. We can show our love for Jesus and our parents by obeying them. Also point out that Jesus was in the house of God. We love Jesus because He also obeyed His heavenly Father.

Activity: This is a good story to dramatize. The principal characters would be Joseph, Mary, and Jesus. Joseph and Mary would be with a group, then become worried, look and look for Jesus, find Him with another group, carry on a short dialogue, telling Him that they were worried, etc., then join the first group.

Emphasis Verse: "Jesus went with them to Nazareth and obeyed them. His mother was still thinking about all that had happened" (Luke 2:51).

LESSON 4

Jesus Is Baptized

Purpose: To show that Jesus obeyed God even after He was grown.

Scripture: Matthew 3:13-17 (also Mark 1:9-11; Luke 3:21-22; John 1:29-34)

Songs: "Where He Leads Me" (group)
"Seek Ye First the Kingdom of God" (group)
"Open My Eyes" (special
"I Will Serve Thee" (special)

Lesson: *Tell the story of Jesus coming to be baptized.* John the Baptist was Jesus' cousin. He was at the Jordan River. Jesus went to him and asked to be baptized. John tried to stop Him because he didn't feel that he was good enough to baptize Jesus. But Jesus said, "Let it be done now. *We should do what is right."* So John agreed to baptize Jesus. When Jesus came up out of the water, the heavens opened up. The Holy Spirit came down and rested on Jesus like a dove. Then a voice from Heaven said, "This is my Son and I love him. I am very pleased with Him."

Application: Emphasize the fact that even after Jesus was grown, He still obeyed His Father. He wanted to please God. He made God so happy that God told everyone how pleased He was with Jesus. We want to please God, too. We can make God happy by making our parents and all those around us happy. We can show our love for Jesus by obeying.

Activity: Paint a picture of the sky, the land, and the water. Cut a slit in the sky and in the water. Cut out a figure of a dove and of Jesus. Have Jesus walk into the water. Then have the dove come from the sky and light upon Jesus. Discuss the voice from Heaven and what it said.

Emphasis Verse: "And a voice spoke from heaven. The voice said, 'This is my Son and I love him. I am very pleased with him'" (Matthew 3:17).

LESSON 5

The Devil Tempts Jesus

Purpose: To discover that Jesus was tempted to do wrong things just like we are.

Scripture: Matthew 4:1-11 (also Mark 1:12-13; Luke 4:1-13)

Songs: "I Shall Not Be Moved" (group)
"Be Careful Little Hands" (group)
"Standing on the Promises" (group)
"Yield Not to Temptation" (special)

Lesson: *Tell about the three temptations the devil put before Jesus.* Jesus was in the desert. He went without food for forty days and forty nights. He was *very* hungry. The devil told him to make a rock into bread. But Jesus said it takes more than bread to keep a man alive. Then the devil told Jesus to jump off a high building and let the angels save Him. But Jesus told the devil it was wrong to test God. Then the devil said if Jesus would worship him, he would give Jesus all the nations of the world. But Jesus answered that He would worship only God. The devil finally gave up. He went away. Then angels came and took care of Jesus.

Application: Jesus was tempted just as we are every day. But He never gave in to the temptations. We can love Jesus that much more because we know He understands how we feel.

Activity: Using fingerpaints, have all the students express how they think the devil looks and how they feel about him. As they create, discuss how the devil tries to get us to do things we shouldn't do.

Emphasis Verse: "Jesus said to the devil, 'Go away from me, Satan! It is written in the Scriptures, "You must worship the Lord your God. Serve only him!"'" (Matthew 4:10)

LESSON 6

Jesus Teaches Me That I'm Important

Purpose: Discovering the unique and important place that each person has in God's world.

Scripture: Matthew 5:13-16

Songs: "This Little Light of Mine" (group-action)
"I'll Be a Sunbeam" (group)

"Let the Lower Lights Be Burning" (group)
"It Is Better To Light Just One Little Candle"
(special)

Lesson: *Tell how Jesus taught that we are the light of the world.* Jesus went up on a mountain one day. Many people followed Him there. He began to teach them. He said that we are like candles. A person doesn't light a candle and then put it under a basket. He puts it on a table so it can help people see. Jesus told us to let our light shine in front of others. Then they will see the good things that we do and praise our Father who is in Heaven.

Application: Discuss the important role we each play in our family, group of friends, or work associates. Talk about the different kinds of 'lights.' Some examples are a smile, a good deed, a kind word.

Activity: Have the students dramatize different situations in which they could let their light shine, such as:

1. Mother is running late with dinner. The table isn't set.

2. A friend is really sad. He needs someone to talk to.

3. The newspaper boy didn't throw the newspaper on the porch and it is starting to rain.

4. An older person can't see whether the traffic light is green or red.

Emphasis Verse: "In the same way, you should be a light for other people. Live so that they will see the good things you do. Live so that they will praise your Father in heaven" (Matthew 5:16).

LESSON 7

Jesus Listens to Me

Purpose: Discovering that we always have someone to talk to who listens and who cares.

Scripture: Luke 11:5-13 (also Matthew 7:7-11)

Songs: "Ask and It Shall Be Given Unto You" (special)
"Whisper a Prayer" (group)
"Why Worry When You Can Pray?" (group)
"What a Friend We Have in Jesus" (group)

Lesson: *Tell the picture story that Jesus told about prayer.* Jesus said to His followers, "Suppose one of you went to your friend's house at midnight and said to him, 'A friend of mine has come into town to visit me. But I have nothing for him to eat. Please loan me three loaves of bread.' Your friend inside the house answers, 'Don't bother me! The door is already locked. My children and I are in bed. I cannot get up and give you the bread now.'... But he will surely get up to give you what you need if you continue to ask" (Luke 11:5-8).

Jesus tells us that if you ask for something, you will find it. If you knock, the door will be opened to you. Jesus listens when we talk.

Application: Emphasize Jesus' wonderful love. Even though we do wrong things, Jesus listens to us and through Him we talk to God. He wants to know our needs.

Activity: Take everyone quietly outside the classroom. Explain that they can't enter the room until each one *knocks.* After they re-enter the room, tell them you have hidden some money or food around the room. But they must *seek* to find it.

Emphasis Verse: "Yes, everyone who continues asking will receive. He who continues searching will find. And he who continues knocking will have the door opened for him" (Matthew 7:8).

LESSON 8

Jesus Loves Me

Purpose: Learning how Jesus feels about us as *persons.*

Scripture: Mark 10:13-16 (also Matthew 19:13-15; Luke 18:15-17)

Songs: "Jesus Loves the Little Children" (group)
"Jesus Loves Me" (group)
"What a Friend We Have in Jesus" (group)
"He Tenderly Looked at Me" (special)

Lesson: *Tell the story of Jesus giving thanks for the children.* Parents brought their children to Jesus. They wanted Him to touch them. But the disciples, Jesus' followers, scolded them and said that Jesus was too busy for children. But when Jesus heard this, He was angry with the disciples. He said, "Let the little children come to me. Don't stop them. The kingdom of God belongs to people who are like these little children. I tell you the truth. You must accept the kingdom of God as a little child accepts things, or you will never enter it." Jesus took the children into His arms. He put His hands on them. He blessed them. He wanted good things to come to them.

Application: Emphasize the tenderness of Jesus' love for the children. Jesus accepts us even though we are not perfect. Talk about some ways we can show our love for Jesus.

Activity: This is another good story to dramatize. Pick one person to play the character of Jesus–or the teacher may prefer to play this part. Then divide the others into three groups: disciples, parents, and children. Encourage them to show tenderness (Jesus), anger (disciples), anxiety (parents), and joy (children).

Emphasis Verse: "Let the little children come to me. Don't stop them. The kingdom of God belongs people who are like these little children" (Mark 10:14).

LESSON 9

Jesus Teaches Me I Can Change

Purpose: To discover that, even though we have done bad things, we can always turn to Jesus, love Him, and make changes within ourselves.

Scripture: Luke 19:1-10

Songs: "Jesus, I Want To Be Like You" (group)
"Have Thine Own Way, Lord" (group)
"Oh to Be Like Thee" (group)
"He Plants Me Like a Seed" (special)

Lesson: *Tell the story of Zaccheus.* Jesus was passing through the city of Jericho. In that city there was a rich man. His name was Zaccheus. Zaccheus was rich because he took money from people. When he heard that Jesus was coming through Jericho, he wanted to see Him. But Zaccheus was a short man. He could not see over the heads of the people. So he climbed up a sycamore tree. When Jesus walked by, He saw Zaccheus and said, "Zaccheus, come down. I'm going to your house today." So Zaccheus took Jesus home. There he told Jesus that he was going to give one-half of his money to the poor; and if he had cheated anyone, he would give them much, much more! Jesus was happy! He said that this was the reason that He came to earth from Heaven!

Application: Jesus wants us to follow Him and turn away from our bad ways. It is never too late. We can love Jesus so much for being so kind and understanding.

Activity: Sing the song "Zaccheus Was a Wee Little Man" several times. Then have the students act out the story. The characters are Jesus, Zaccheus, and the crowd. Let each person participate as a central character by rotation. Emphasize the changes that Zaccheus decided to make in his life.

Emphasis Verse: "The Son of Man came to find lost people and save them" (Luke 19:10).

LESSON 10

Jesus Died for Me

Purpose: Learning that Jesus died to take away our
sins.

Scripture: John 19:17-20, 28-30, 38-42 (also Matthew 27;
Mark 15; Luke 23)

Songs: "For God So Loved the World" (group)
"When I Survey the Wondrous Cross" (group)
"Christ Died for Me" (special)
"O How He Loves You and Me" (special)

Lesson: *Tell the story of Jesus' death.* Jesus was told
He would have to die. He carried His cross to
a hill. The soldiers nailed Him to the cross.
They put a sign above His head that said,
"Jesus of Nazareth, the King of the Jews."
Jesus knew He was dying. He said He was
thirsty. They gave Him sour juice to drink. He
took it and said "It is finished." He put His
head down and died. A friend came and took
Jesus' body. The friend had a new grave. It
was a cave in the side of a hill. They wrapped
Jesus' body in cloth. Then they put Jesus'
body in the grave. But after three days, Jesus
came alive again! He rose from the dead!

Application: Emphasize the fact that Jesus died for all of
us. God loved us so much that He gave us
Jesus. Jesus willingly died to save us from our
sins.

Activity: Give each student some modeling clay. Have
part of the class make a large cross. The other
part of the class can make a mountain with a
cave in the side. Then make a round stone to

roll over the entrance of the cave. Discuss how Jesus' friends brought Him from the cross to the grave. Then roll the stone over the opening and seal it shut.

Emphasis Verse: "They nailed Jesus to the cross. They also put two other men on crosses, one on each side of Jesus with Jesus in the middle" (John 19:18).

LESSON 11

Jesus Comes Back to Life

Purpose: Discovering the miracle of the resurrection. He lives!

Scripture: Mark 16:1-8 (also Matthew 18:1-8; Luke 24:1-12; John 20:1-18)

Songs: "I Will Sing Unto the Lord" (group)
"I Serve a Risen Savior" (group)
"Low in the Grave He Lay" (group)
"Christ the Lord Is Risen Today" (special)

Lesson: *Tell the story of Jesus' resurrection.* Three days after Jesus died on the cross, some women friends were on their way to His grave. They were bringing spices to put on Jesus' body. They came early in the morning. The sun was up. As they walked, they began to worry how they were going to get into the cave. A stone was in front of the door. It was too big for them to move. Then they saw the stone was already rolled away! They went in and saw a young man sitting there. He was wearing a long white robe. They were afraid!

But the man said, "Do not be afraid. You are looking for Jesus, who was nailed to a cross. He is not here. He has risen!" He told them to go tell Jesus' followers that He was going to Galilee. They would see Him there. The women were shaking and afraid. They ran from the grave. Mary Magdalene told Jesus' followers.

Application: Emphasize the truth of the resurrection. Jesus came back to life. He is our Savior! We must be like the women. We must run and tell others about this miracle of love!

Activity: Using hand puppets and the cave that the students made last week, act out the lesson. Encourage as much participation of the students as possible.

Emphasis Verse: "You are looking for Jesus from Nazareth, the one who was killed on a cross. He has risen from death. He is not here. Look, here is the place they laid Him" (Mark 16:6).

LESSON 12

Jesus Goes to Heaven

Purpose: To explain what Jesus is doing now.

Scripture: Luke 24:50-53 (also Mark 16:19-20)

Songs: "For God So Loved the World" (group)
"Heavenly Sunshine" (group)
"Crown Him With Many Crowns"(group)
"Yesterday, Today, Tomorrow" (special)

Lesson: *Tell the story of the ascension.* After Jesus rose from the dead, He stayed with His followers a short time. Then He led them out of the city. He lifted up His hands and prayed. He wanted good to come to them. While He was praying, He was lifted up into Heaven. The followers went back to the city with great happiness! They spent all their time in the temple, the house of God, worshiping Jesus and giving thanks to God.

Application: Emphasize that Jesus is sitting at the right side of God in Heaven. He is speaking for us. He is loving us. And we love Jesus. He has given us very much—even His Life!

Activity: Let the members of the class paint what they think Heaven looks like. Talk about it being Jesus' home. (Nothing they paint will be incorrect. Let them know that they can paint anything they want. Since heaven is a perfect place, it can be any way that makes that certain person happy.)

Emphasis Verse: "While he was blessing them, he was separated from them and carried into heaven" (Luke 24:51).

LESSON 13

What I Can Do for Jesus

Purpose: Discovering the *joy* of living for Jesus.

Scripture: Matthew 28:16-20 (also Mark 16:15-18; Luke 24:44-49; John 20:21-23)

Songs: "I'm in the Lord's Army" (group-action)
"Jesus Wants Me for a Sunbeam" (group)
"I'll Live for Him" (group)
"I Will Serve Thee" (group)
"The Longer I Serve Him" (special)
"Is There Anything I Can Do for You?"
(special)

Lesson: *Tell the story of Jesus sending the disciples out.* After He rose from the dead, and before He went to Heaven, Jesus met with His followers on a mountain. When they saw Him, they worshiped Him. Jesus told them to go over all the world and tell people about Him. He told them to baptize people and teach them. Then Jesus said that He would be with them always. He would be with them until the world came to an end.

Application: Emphasize that Jesus is always with us. We are never alone. Then tell how we can show our love for Jesus by telling others about Him and by letting our light shine for Him.

Activity: Sing the song, "I Will Make You Fishers of Men." Then play the game, "Fishers of Men." Divide the class in half. The first half will put their pictures or names in a basket. The second half will use a pole and "fish" out the picture or name. For the rest of the day they will be Jesus' helper for that person.

Emphasis Verse: "So go and make followers of all people in the world. Baptize them in the name of the Father and the Son and the Holy Spirit. Teach them to obey everything I have told you" (Matthew 28:19, 20).

PART 3

People of Faith

1. Abraham and Sarah
2. Rebekah
3. Joseph
4. Moses
5. Joshua
6. Jonah
7. Hannah
8. Samuel
9. David
10. Job
11. Elijah
12. Hezekiah
13. Esther

Theme song: "Faith Is the Victory"

LESSON 1

Abraham and Sarah

Purpose: To help the students learn about having complete trust and faith in God.

Scripture: Genesis 21:1-8 (also Genesis 11–21; Romans 9:9)

Songs: "Where He Leads Me, I Will Follow" (group)
"Faith of Our Fathers" (group)
"God Moves in Mysterious Ways" (special)

Lesson: *Tell the story of Abraham and Sarah's trust in God.* God told Abraham and his wife Sarah to move away from their home and go to a land far away. Abraham and Sarah were both old people, and they didn't even know where God wanted them to go. But they obeyed God anyway. God promised He would give them a son. They believed God even though they thought they were too old to have children. After many years God gave them a son. Abraham and Sarah were very happy. They called their little boy "Isaac."

Application: Help the students see how much faith it took for Abraham and Sarah to leave their home and follow God. Even though their minds told them that what God said was impossible, their hearts believed His promise. Through their acts of faith, the wonderful plan of salvation for all men could unfold.

Activity: Using puppets or muppets, act this story out, or make a tent, a camel, some sheep, Abraham, Sarah, and a baby out of cardboard. Let the students color the figures. Then act out the story using the cutouts.

Emphasis Verse: "Abram believed the Lord. And the Lord accepted Abram's faith, and that faith made him right with God" (Genesis 15:6).

LESSON 2

Rebekah

Purpose: To show the students an example of working cheerfully and following God's leading.

Scripture: Genesis 24:1-67

Songs: "Lead on, O King Eternal" (group)
"Attitudes and Actions" (group)
"To Do Thy Will" (special)

Lesson: *Tell the story of Isaac and Rebekah.* When Isaac was grown up, Abraham sent a servant back to His homeland to find a woman for Isaac to marry. He wanted to find a woman who believed in God. The servant didn't know who to pick. He was afraid he might choose the wrong woman for Isaac, so he asked God to help him. God heard the servant's prayer and showed him which woman would be a good wife for Isaac. Her name was Rebekah. The servant brought Rebekah home and she married Isaac.

Application: Emphasize how important it was to Abraham to find a wife for Isaac who believed in God. When we choose our friends, we should look for good qualities like love for God. Rebekah also had the quality of working cheerfully. Stress the practical aspects of this concept.

Activity: Make jewelry from aluminum foil and cardboard. Make chains from construction paper or yarn and beads.

Emphasis Verse: Blessed is the Lord, the God of my master Abraham. The Lord has been kind and truthful to him" (Genesis 24:27).

LESSON 3

Joseph

Purpose: To learn the bad effects of jealousy and the beauty of forgiveness.

Scripture: Genesis 37:1-36; 45:3-10

Songs: "The Coat of Many Colors" (group)
"I Would Be True" (special)
"Make Me a Blessing" (group)

Lesson: *Tell the story of Joseph.* Joseph had eleven brothers. All but one was older than him. But Joseph was His father's favorite, and he gave Joseph a beautiful coat with many colors. The other brothers were jealous. They took Joseph's coat and sold him as a slave to some people who were going far away to Egypt. Many years later Joseph saw His brothers again. They had come to Egypt to get food, because there was no food in their land. Joseph could have been angry and hurt his brothers back, but he didn't. He helped them. He was good to them. He forgave them for what they did to him years before.

Application: Joseph showed he loved God by forgiving his brothers. How can *we* show God that we love Him? Discuss with the students the concept of jealousy. Ask if they have ever felt jealous. Talk about forgiveness—not only how God forgives us but how we should forgive others.

Activity: Make clothespin dolls. Dress them in cloaks of colorful material. Use yarn for hair and paint on "happy faces."

Emphasis Verse: Joseph said, "God had made me forget all the troubles I have had and all my father's family" (Genesis 41:51).

LESSON 4

Moses

Purpose: To realize that each one of us has something special to offer God.

Scripture: Exodus 4:1-17

Songs: "Take My Life" (group)
"To the Work" (group)
"Ready" (special)
"True-Hearted, Whole-Hearted" (group)

Lesson: *Tell the story of Moses and the burning bush.*
One day a man named Moses was on a mountain. He saw a bush that was on fire but didn't

burn up. God spoke to him from the bush. God wanted him to lead some people out of slavery. Moses didn't think he could do this. He didn't think he had the ability. But he decided to trust God. He had faith that God would help him. God helped Moses lead the people to the promised land.

Application: Even though Moses didn't think that he had any talent for leadership, God used His willing heart. Emphasize that God can use each one of us, even though we don't think we have any special abilities. Discuss with the students the different ways God can use us.

Activity: Give each student a picture of a bush. Let them color in the flames.

Emphasis Verse: "Now go! I will help you speak. I will tell you what to say" (Exodus 4:12).

LESSON 5

Joshua

Purpose: To see that God can help us tear down the "walls" or problems in our lives.

Scripture: Joshua 6:1-27

Songs: "Joshua Fought the Battle of Jericho" (group)
"Give Them All to Jesus" (special)
"Sound the Battle Cry" (group)
"Victory in Jesus" (group)

Lesson: *Tell the story of Joshua and the battle of Jericho.* Joshua was a general who led the army of God's people. God told him to attack the city of Jericho, but this would be hard, because Jericho had great, high walls built all around it. God told Joshua to march His whole army around the city seven times, and to blow their trumpets and shout after the last time. Then the walls would fall down flat, and Joshua and His army could march right in. They did what God told them, and it worked! The walls fell down, and the army went in and captured the city just like God told them.

Application: When we do what the Lord tells us to do, He will give us victory. No matter how high the "walls" in our lives may be, God can help us deal with them. Discuss the challenges that we face today. Encourage the students to share some of their "walls." Also talk about some of their victories.

Activity: Build a wall with cardboard boxes. Dramatize the story of marching around the walls and blowing trumpets. Then watch the walls come tumbling down!

Emphasis Verse: "Everyone who is a child of God has the power to win against the world" (1 John 5:4).

LESSON 6

Jonah

Purpose: To see that *everyone* needs to know God.

Scripture: The book of Jonah

Songs: "Jonah and the Whale" (group)
"Everybody Ought to Know" (group)
"Bring Them In" (group)
"I Love to Tell the Story" (group)

Lesson: *Tell the story of Jonah.* God told Jonah to go and preach in a city called Nineveh. Jonah didn't want to, so he got on a ship going the other way. But God sent a storm, and Jonah was thrown off the ship into the sea. There he was swallowed by a great fish. He stayed in the fish underwater for three days. He was afraid and he prayed to God. Then the fish spit him out on dry land, and he was safe. After that, Jonah went and preached at Nineveh the way God had told him to.

Application: Jonah didn't care whether the people of Nineveh heard about God or not. Talk to your class about the concept of "insiders" and "outsiders." Discuss the second verse of Jonah 4. Compare it to Ezekiel 33:11. *Everyone* ought to know God and His Son, Jesus.

Activity: Using modeling clay, let the students mold a fish, a man, and a boat. Review the story.

Emphasis Verse: "I knew that you are a God who is kind and shows mercy. You don't become angry quickly. You have great love. I knew you would rather forgive than punish them" (Jonah 4:2).

LESSON 7

Hannah

Purpose: To learn the importance of saying "thank you" to God when He answers our prayers.

Scripture: 1 Samuel 1:11, 20, 26-28

Songs: "To God Be the Glory" (special)
"We Gather Together" (group)
"Count Your Blessings" (group)
"All to Jesus I Surrender" (group)

Lesson: *Tell the story of Hannah's sacrifice of praise.* The Bible tells us about a woman named Hannah who wanted to have a baby. She cried to God to give her a child. She had faith that God could help her. When He gave her a baby she dedicated him (gave him) to serve God. This is the way that she showed her gratitude.

Application: Hannah had faith that God could give her the son for which she prayed. In response to her answered prayer, she dedicated her son to God. Not only should we have faith that God will hear our prayers, but we should also thank Him with joyful hearts.

Activity: Discuss with the students what they could do to show appreciation to God for His blessings; sing a song of praise, dedicate a few minutes to prayer every day, show loving care for a pet, be helpful to those around you.

Emphasis Verse: "Thank the Lord because he is good" (Psalm 107:1).

LESSON 8

Samuel

Purpose: To learn that we should not judge people by the way they look on the outside, because God sees their hearts.

Scripture: 1 Samuel 16:1-13

Songs: "Looking Through His Eyes" (special)
"The Way That He Loves" (group)

Lesson: *Tell the story of Samuel looking for a new king.* Hannah's son was named Samuel, and Samuel became a special servant of God. When Samuel grew up, God told him to choose a man to become king over all God's people. God said, "Go to Jesse's house, and choose the one I tell you to choose." So Samuel did. He saw all seven of Jesse's sons. They were all tall and good-looking. Samuel would have picked one of them, but God said no. They had to wait for Jesse's youngest son to come, a little boy named David. When David came in, God told Samuel, "He's the one I want." So Samuel picked David.

Application: God tells us not to judge a person by the way he looks or how tall he is. God doesn't make decisions the way we do. "Men judge by outward appearances, but I look at the man's thoughts and intentions" God says.

Activity: Make a list of helpful actions. Choose appropriate activities that would benefit your particular students.

Emphasis Verse: "God does not see the same way people see. People look at the outside of a person, but the Lord looks at the heart" (1 Samuel 16:7)

LESSON 9

David

Purpose: To learn about the power of faith.

Scripture: 1 Samuel 17

Songs: "Only a Boy Named David" (group)
"A Mustard Seed of Faith" (group)
"Only Believe" (group)
"O For a Faith That Will Not Shrink" (group)

Lesson: *Tell the story of David and Goliath.* When David was a few years older, God's people were at war with another country. The other country had a giant, Goliath, on their side fighting for them. Everyone in God's army was afraid to fight the giant. But not David. Even though he was only a boy, he went out to fight Goliath all by himself. He did not even wear armor on His body to protect him. "God will take care of me," he said. He had only a slingshot, but he took the slingshot and hit the giant in the head with a rock. The giant fell down dead. God had helped David win the battle when everyone else was afraid to fight.

Application: David's faith in God enabled him to face great odds. It not only made him brave, it also make him sure. He had no doubts about God's power and God's faithfulness.

Activity:	Make a drawstring pouch. Cut circles of tough cloth. Give a circle to each student. Have them punch holes around the circumference. Weave twine in and out of the holes. Pull it tight.

Emphasis Verse:	"Be careful. Continue strong in the faith. Have courage, and be strong" (1 Corinthians 16:13).

LESSON 10

Job

Purpose:	To learn about Job's unchanging faith.
Scripture:	The book of Job
Songs:	"I Shall Not Be Moved" (group) "I Know Whom I Have Believed" (group) "Little Flowers" (special)
Lesson:	*Tell the story of Job.* There was once a rich man named Job. One day the devil told God, "Job just loves you because you have given him so much." But God said, "No, that is not true." God let the devil take away from Job the good things He had given him. Soon Job lost his house and his money and everything he had. All his children died and Job had nothing. Then Job himself became very sick. He was very unhappy. He didn't know why God would let this happen to him. But he never stopped loving God no matter what. God was proud of Job, so he made Job well again and gave him a new home and riches and children.

Application: Emphasize how Job never doubted God—even when it seemed he had lost everything. Even when his wife pushed him to curse God, he still remained faithful. Talk about how Satan works very hard to get us to deny God. Then discuss the blessings that Job received when he didn't deny God.

Activity: Make a wall mural from newsprint. Have the students draw Job's blessings: wife, children, cattle, sheep, house, barns. Add flowers, trees, sun, stream. (If drawing is not an appropriate activity, have pictures cut from magazines from which the students can choose.) Then have everyone sing the song, "Count Your Blessings."

Emphasis Verse: "God does great things by His power. No other teacher is like him" (Job 36:22).

LESSON 11

Elijah

Purpose: To learn how important it is to put our trust in the real God.

Scripture: 1 Kings 18:20-39

Songs: "How Great Thou Art" (group)
"The Heavens Declare Thy Glory" (special)
"O Worship the King" (group)

Lesson: *Tell the story of Elijah on Mount Carmel.* Elijah was a preacher for God. But when Elijah lived, most of the people worshiped another god named Baal. Even the king and queen did. Elijah wanted to show them that they should worship only God. He told everyone that only God could send fire from Heaven, and Baal couldn't. So they had a contest. Everyone went up on a mountain. The people who worshiped Baal asked Baal to send fire. They did everything they could think of to get fire to come down. But nothing happened. Then Elijah asked God to send fire from Heaven, and the fire came down and burned up everything there on the mountaintop. All the people could see that they should worship only God.

Application: Elijah wanted the people to decide in whom they believed, God or the false god Baal. When they didn't answer, he decided to force the people to see which one was the *real* God. Elijah stood up for what he believed. We must also take a stand for what we believe.

Activity: Build a small altar with rocks. Put some sticks on top. If advisable, the teacher could light the wood and talk about how Elijah worshiped the true God. Discuss how Elijah even put water on the wood. What are some of the "false gods" people put their trust in today?

Emphasis Verse: "When all the people saw this, they fell down to the ground. They cried, 'The Lord is God! The Lord is God!'" (1 Kings 18:39)

LESSON 12

Hezekiah

Purpose: To learn to stand up for what we believe.

Scripture: 2 Kings 18:1-7 (also Numbers 21:4-9)

Songs: "Holy, Holy, Holy" (group)
"Once to Every Man and Nation" (group)
"Greater Is He That Is in Me" (group)

Lesson: *Tell the story of Hezekiah and the bronze serpent.* King Hezekiah believed in God. He wanted all the people to worship only God. But they had other things that they worshiped. One of these things was a bronze rod that Moses had carried. The people thought that it was magic. King Hezekiah destroyed the rod. He was not afraid to stand up for what he believed.

Application: Moses had not intended for the bronze rod in the shape of a serpent to be worshiped. But people began to worship it instead of God. King Hezekiah was being faithful to God when he destroyed the idol. We must always worship God—not things. We must never be afraid to stand up for what we believe.

Activity: Talk about some things people care about more than God. Discuss some of the reasons we might be afraid to stand up for what we believe.

Emphasis Verse: "Hezekiah trusted in the Lord, the God of Israel. There was no one like him among all kings of Judah. There was no king like him, before him or after him" (2 Kings 18:5).

LESSON 13

Esther

Purpose: To learn that if we have faith in God, He will lead us.

Scripture: The book of Esther

Songs: "Lead On, O King Eternal" (group)
"Seek Ye First the Kingdom of God" (group)
"Where He Leads Me I Will Follow" (group)
"We've Come This Far by Faith" (special)

Lesson: *Tell the story of Queen Esther.* God's people were living in another country. The king there did not believe in God, but his wife Esther, the queen, did. God's people worshiped only God and not the false gods of that country. So the king passed a law that all of God's people would be killed on a certain day. God's people were afraid. They asked Queen Esther to save them. So she made a big banquet for the king and asked him to grant whatever she asked. Esther was afraid because this was dangerous. If the king said no, Esther would die. But the king said he would do whatever she wanted. She asked him to let God's people live in peace. Esther was very brave and trusted God to lead her.

Application: Esther's people, the Jews, would not bow down to anyone but God, even if it meant their lives being taken. Esther trusted God and was faithful to Him. He showed her a way to solve the problem. God is faithful to those who trust Him. He will show us a way to deal with our problems, too!

Activity: Ask the students why Esther fed the king a banquet before she asked for help. Talk about favorite foods and plan a picnic for the following class time.

Emphasis Verse: "It was a time of happiness, joy, gladness, and honor for the Jews" (Esther 8:16).

PART 4

The Church

1. What Is the Church?
2. What Is Baptism?
3. What Is Communion?
4. Who Is the Holy Spirit?
5. Being a Christian—Help From the Holy Spirit
6. Being a Christian—Praising God
7. Being a Christian—Praying
8. Being a Christian—Serving
9. Being a Christian—Forgiving Others
10. Being a Christian—Telling Others
11. Being a Christian—Looking Forward to Heaven
12. Being a Christian—A Full Life
13. Being a Christian—Always Learning More

Theme song: "The Family of God"

LESSON 1

What Is the Church?

Purpose: To introduce the students to the concept of "the family of God."

Scripture: John 1:12 (also Matthew 18:20; Colossians 3:15-17)

Songs: "Come Ye That Love the Lord" (group)
"I Have an Invitation" (group)
"Bless Be the Tie That Binds" (group)
"God's Family" (group)
"God's Wonderful People" (group)

Lesson: What is the church? The church isn't a building. It isn't just a place where people go on Sundays. The church is the *family of God!* Everyone who believes that Jesus is the Son of God and follows Him belongs to the family of God. The Bible tells that God sent Jesus to us to save us from our sins. If we don't believe that Jesus is God's son, we can't belong to God's family. All the people that *do* believe in Jesus are a family. They are brothers and sisters! They are called Christians. Christians love each other. When they get together, Jesus is always right there with them. Jesus is happy when we want to be a part of His family.

Application: Discuss the concept of "family" with the members of the class. Remind them of how God takes care of us and loves us as a father would. Jesus is our brother. We are brothers and sisters in Christ. Relate some different ways families take care of each other.

Activity: Have a family reunion. Explain to the students that this is a get-together for all God's family. Let each person participate by song, prayer, praise, Bible reading, or sharing a thankful thought. Make it a happy, joyful time!

Emphasis Verse: "Some people did accept him. They believed in him. To them he gave the right to become children of God" (John 1:12).

LESSON 2

What Is Baptism?

Purpose: To tell the students what Jesus said about following Him.

Scripture: Acts 2:38 (also Matthew 3:13-15; 28:19, 20)

Songs: "Jesus Saves!" (group)
"If That Isn't Love" (group)
"O How He Loves You and Me" (group)
"Heaven Came Down and Glory Filled
My Soul" (special)
"Now I Belong to Jesus" (group)
"Gone, My Sins Are Gone" (group)

Lesson: God loved us so much that He gave His only Son to us. Jesus came here to save us from our sins. When we believe in Jesus we become a part of God's family. God has promised to take us to Heaven someday. If we believe in Jesus, we want to do what He tells us. We want to obey Him. When we decide to follow Jesus, we ask Him to forgive us for all the bad things we have done. We tell Him we are sorry for doing those wrong things. In the Bible Jesus tells us to be baptized. Being baptized means having our sins washed away. We go into the water and Jesus washes all the sin out of our lives. Isn't that wonderful! After we are baptized, we live our lives for Jesus. We always try to do the things that Jesus would want us to do.

Application: Talk to the students about Christian living. When we believe in Jesus and want Him in our lives, we want Him to forgive our sins. We should also try not to do wrong things any more. Jesus can give us the strength to turn away from evil.

Activity: Talk about baptism. Answer any questions the students have. At the next opportunity., have them witness a baptism in the church family.

Emphasis Verse: "Peter said to them, 'Change your hearts and lives and be baptized, each one of you, in the name of Jesus Christ for the forgiveness of your sins. And you will receive the gift of the Holy Spirit'" (Acts 2:38).

LESSON 3

What Is Communion?

Purpose: To explain the meaning of the Lord's Supper.

Scripture: Matthew 26:26-29 (also Acts 2:41-47; 1 Corinthians 10:16, 17)

Songs: "I Gave My Life for Thee" (group)
"Break Thou the Bread of Life" (group)
"When I Survey the Wondrous Cross" (group)
"Jesus Paid It All" (special)

Lesson: When Christians gather to praise God and Jesus, we have a special time together. There is a special time to remember what Jesus did for us. It is called Communion or the Lord's Supper. During Communion, we Christians think about Jesus dying for our sins. When we drink the juice and eat the bread, we think about Jesus' body on the cross. We think about how He promised to come back again some day. We think about how much He loves us.

Application: Communion is not a time to be sad. It is a time to be thankful for all Jesus did for us. It is a time for all of us to look into our hearts. What do we see when we look into our hearts? Do we see good, happy things? Jesus helps us change into cheerful, helpful people.

Activity: Cover an area on the wall with newsprint. Give each student a marker. Help them draw a person with a big smile (stick figures are fine). Then have all the figures join hands.

Emphasis Verse: "They spent their time learning the apostles' teaching. And they continued to share, to break bread, and to pray together" (Acts 2:42).

LESSON 4

Who Is the Holy Spirit?

Purpose: To introduce the students to the Holy Spirit.

Scripture: John 14:16, 17, 26 (also John 16:7-14)

Songs: "Holy Spirit, Faithful Guide" (group)
"God Is My Father, Jesus Is My Brother, and the Blessed Holy Spirit Is My Guide" (group)

Lesson: When Jesus went back to Heaven, He asked God to send us someone to help us. Jesus said, "I will ask the Father, and He will give you another Helper, that He may be with you forever." The Holy Spirit is our friend who helps us remember what Jesus has taught us. He will be beside us forever. We can thank God for sending such a wonderful friend.

Application: Talk about what the Holy Spirit brings us: love, joy, peace, patience, kindness, goodness, faithfulness, gentleness, self-control. Discuss what each of these words mean.

Activity: Play the record *Music Machine* (or have the youth group present it to the class). After playing each song, talk about the meaning of the words. (This activity may be used over several weeks' time. Perhaps a different quality could be introduced each week.)

Emphasis Verse: "But the Helper will teach you everything. He will cause you to remember all the things I told you. This Helper is the Holy Spirit whom the Father will send in my name" (John 14:26).

LESSON 5

Being a Christian—
Help From the Holy Spirit

Purpose: To help the students see how the Holy Spirit assists in Christian growth.

Scripture: Galatians 5:22, 23 (also Galatians 5:16-26)

Songs: "I Have the Joy" (group)
"I Have Peace Like a River" (group)
"When Peace Like a River" (group)
"Peace, Joy and Love" (special)
"Spirit of the Living God" (special)

Lesson: When the Holy Spirit comes into our lives, He helps us be better people. He gives us love and joy. He gives us peace and patience. He gives us self-control. All these qualities help us be better Christians.

Application: Write the different qualities on cards. Have each member of the class pick a card and talk about the word. Help them see how the Holy Spirit gives us the strength we need to become better Christians.

Activity: Continue talking about the fruit of the Spirit. Use the *Music Machine* record to give a practical example of the lesson. Compare the fruit of the Spirit with the deeds of the flesh.

Emphasis Verse: "We get our new life from the Spirit. So we should follow the Spirit" (Galatians 5:25).

LESSON 6

Being a Christian—
Praising God

Purpose: Learning that God loves to hear our praise.

Scripture: Psalms 35:28 (also Psalms 99:3; Matthew 11:25; James 5:13)

Songs: "Praise Him, Praise Him" (group)
"We Praise Thee, O God" (group)
"O Worship the King" (group)
"Praise Ye the Lord" (special)

Lesson: A man named David loved to play a harp and sing praise to God. Even when he was afraid or worried or tired, he would praise God. David wrote His praises in a book. The book is called Psalms. Jesus praised God, too. He said, "I praise You, Father, Lord of Heaven and earth." We can praise God, too. We can tell Him how wonderful we think He is.

Application: Sometimes when we feel full of happiness, we sing. Sometimes we dance with joy. Sometimes we grin and laugh. Knowing God fills us with joy. We can let God know how happy we are to know of His love, care, and power. He loves to hear us praise Him.

Activity: Cut a harp shape out of strong cardboard or plywood. Cut several holes in the edge. Let the students "string" the harp with strong rubber bands. They can make their own music, just like David!

Emphasis Verse: "If one of you is having troubles, he should pray. If one of you is happy, he should sing praises" (James 5:13).

LESSON 7

Being a Christian—Praying

Purpose: Learning the importance of prayer.

Scripture: Matthew 7:7-11 (also James 5:16; Matthew 6:5, 6)

Songs: "In This Quiet Moment" (group)
"I Must Tell Jesus" (group)
"Sweet Hour of Prayer" (group)
"For You I Am Praying" (special)

Lesson: Are you ever sad? Do you ever feel lonely? Are there times when your troubles seem to get heavier and heavier? God knew that we would have times when we feel this way. That's why He gave us a special way to find relief, a special way to feel better. The secret is prayer. Prayer is talking to God. Jesus told us that if we ask, it shall be given unto us. We don't have to feel alone or sad. Christians also pray for each other. If you find out that one of your friends needs something, pray for him. We all should take time to talk to God.

Application: When we are feeling low, we can turn our eyes upon Jesus. When we do this, the troubles will seem much lighter. Sing "Turn Your Eyes Upon Jesus" prayerfully and thoughtfully.

Activity: Using finger puppets, act out the parable of the Pharisee and the publican. Discuss the attitude that Jesus wants to see in our hearts when we pray.

Emphasis Verse: "Confess your sins to each other and pray for each other. Do this so that God can heal you. When a good man prays, great things happen" (James 5:16).

LESSON 8

Being a Christian—Serving

Purpose: To find the fulfillment of helping others.

Scripture: Hebrews 12:28 (also Romans 12:11; Proverbs 16:3)

Songs: "Footprints of Jesus" (group)
"I'm in the Lord's Army" (group)
"Take My Life" (group)
"Make Me a Blessing" (special)

Lesson: How can we show our gratitude to God for all He has done for us? One way is to serve Him. The Bible tells us to find peace instead of anger. It tells us to try to make other people feel good. We can help them in so many ways. Jesus said that when we do things for others, it is the same as doing things for Him.

Application: Have you ever looked around you to see if anybody needed your help? Sometimes helping others is the best way to make *ourselves* feel better! Serving the Lord with a happy heart is a wonderful Christian habit.

Activity: Working with each student individually, discover their abilities. Then give them a specific task or responsibility in the classroom; dusting, arranging books, distributing music, helping a classmate find his place. Emphasize the fact that every job they do shows their love for God.

Emphasis Verse: "Serve the Lord with joy. Come before him with singing" (Psalm 100:2).

LESSON 9

Being a Christian — Forgiving Others

Purpose: Learning the importance of forgiveness.

Scripture: Matthew 6:14, 15 (Ephesians 4:3-32)

Songs: "Amazing Grace" (group)
"Grace That Is Greater Than All Our Sin" (group)
"When We Walk With the Lord" (group)
"To Do Thy Will" (special)

Lesson: In the Bible Jesus tells us that if we want God to forgive our sins, we must forgive those who sin against us. That means that if somebody does something wrong to us, we must forgive them. If we hold on to our bad feelings toward them, it gets in the way of our love for God. It makes the Holy Spirit sad when we keep our bitterness and anger. He does not want us to talk about other people in a mean way. The Bible says to be kind to one another, tender-hearted, forgiving each other, just as God has forgiven us.

Application: Sometimes it is hard to forgive. When someone does something that hurts us or makes us mad, we want to hurt them back. But Jesus tells us to forgive those who do wrong to us. He wants us to be kind. He tells us to remember that God has forgiven us. We should do the same for others.

Activity: Have the class dramatize the story of Jacob and Esau. Then let them share some experiences of forgiveness.

Emphasis Verse: "Yes, if you forgive others for the things they do wrong, then your Father in heaven will also forgive you for the things you do wrong" (Matthew 6:14).

LESSON 10

Being a Christian — Telling Others

Purpose: To learn about the Great Commission.

Scripture: Acts 2:38 (also Romans 10:13-17; 2 Corinthians 5:18-20; 1 Peter 3:15)

Songs: "Jesus Is the Lord of All" (group)
"Stand Up for Jesus" (group)
"Lead Me to Some Soul Today" (group)
"I'll Tell the World That I'm a Christian" (special)

Lesson: When you believe in God, you have something special. When you believe in Jesus, you have something special. When the Holy Spirit is your guide, you have something special. That something special is *hope*. We can look forward to tomorrow and the day after that. We can look forward to Heaven. We can live life without being afraid. The Bible tells us to tell others about the hope that they can see in us. But we should not brag about it. We should tell them in gentleness and reverence.

Application: Don't you wish everyone could have the hope of living forever in Heaven? Don't you wish that everyone could know Jesus as you do? How can they find out? *You* can tell them. Every Christian has the power to tell anyone about God. You can tell your family and friends. You can tell your neighbors and the people you work with. God *wants* us to spread the good news. We can sing about it, we can whisper about it, we can *shout* about it! Jesus is Lord!

Activity: Place the chairs in a circle. If possible, give each student a candle. Starting with the teacher, light the candle to the person next to you and whisper, "Jesus is Lord." After all the candles are aglow, point out how much light they all make. If candles can't be used, whisper "Jesus is Lord" around the circle. As each one says it, have them kneel or bow their heads. Then the teacher can lead in a word of prayer. Make name tags saying "Jesus Is Lord" and pin them to the students' clothes.

Emphasis Verse: "Jesus is the Lord of all people!" (Acts 10:36)

LESSON 11

Being a Christian—
Looking Forward to Heaven

Purpose: To learn about Heaven.

Scripture: Matthew 5:12 (also Matthew 6:20; Luke 10:20; Philippians 3:20)

Songs: "Walking on the Heaven Road" (group)
"When We All Get to Heaven" (group)
"Is My Name Written There?" (group)
"That Will Be Glory for Me" (special)

Lesson: "Our homeland is in heaven, and we are waiting for our Savior, the Lord Jesus Christ, to come from heaven. He will change our simple bodies and make them like his own glorious body. Christ can do this by his power. With that power he is able to rule all things" (Philippians 3:20, 21). Isn't that exciting! Heaven is going to be wonderful. Everyone will be happy. There will be no sadness or pain. And Jesus is going to take our bodies and make them like His body! We won't hurt anymore. We won't need wheelchairs or canes anymore. We won't be too fat or too skinny. What joy we will find there!

Application: The Bible says that our name is recorded in Heaven. When we believe in Jesus and live the way He wants us to live, our name is written on the book in Heaven. We'll see all our Christian brothers and sisters there. What a family reunion that will be!

Activity: Ask the students what they are looking for-
             ward to the most in Heaven. Write it down on
             a card for them. Tell them to keep it in their
             Bibles as a promise from God.

Emphasis Verse: "Rejoice and be glad. You have a great reward
             waiting for you in heaven" (Matthew 5:12).

LESSON 12

Being a Christian — A Full Life

Purpose: To learn about the abundant life.

Scripture: Philippians 4:4 (also Philippians 2:14; John
             10:10; 15:1-5)

Songs: "Rejoice in the Lord Always" (group)
             "Stepping in the Light" (group)
             "Trust and Obey" (group)
             "In Heavenly Love Abiding" (special)

Lesson: God wants us to look forward to Heaven. But
             He does not want us to be miserable here on
             earth. He has given us many blessings to en-
             joy. Serving Him gives a person a happy life.
             Living in His beautiful world is a pleasure.
             The Bible tells us to rejoice in the Lord al-
             ways. What He has given to us, no thief can
             take away.

Application: Some people are so busy looking toward the
             future and what might be that they forget to
             enjoy the present. Each day brings us oppor-
             tunity to find pleasure in God's creation. If we

are living in obedience to God, we will truly find an abundant life.

Activity: Sing "Count Your Blessings." Then help each student make a list of their blessings, one by one.

Emphasis Verse: "Be full of joy in the Lord always. I will say again, be full of joy" (Philippians 4:4).

LESSON 13

Being a Christian— Always Learning More

Purpose: To learn the importance of growing in grace and knowledge.

Scripture: 2 Peter 3:18 (also Acts 2:42; Colossians 2:6,7)

Songs: "Tell Me the Story of Jesus" (group)
"Living for Jesus" (group)
"Have You Got What It Takes?" (special)
"I Would Be True" (group)

Lesson: When do you know everything about God? When do you stop studying the Bible? Never! Christians should *always* be learning. The Bible tells us that Christians who lived a long time ago did three things. They got together to learn more about Jesus. They met to take Communion together. And they shared their meals with great joy and thankfulness. God wants us always to be learning more about Him. He wants us to grow in knowledge about Him.

Application: It is such a privilege to know God and His Son, Jesus. It is a blessing to have the Holy Spirit as our guide and comforter. The more we learn about them, the more we can enjoy their presence.

Activity: Buy each student a Bible with his name written on the cover or write their names on the front page. Make laminated bookmarks with the letters GOD'S WORD on one side and the student's name on the other.

Emphasis Verse: "Grow in the grace and knowledge of our Lord and Savior Jesus Christ. Glory be to him now and forever! Amen" (2 Peter 3:18).

Additional Resources

How to find help for your ministry

Even if you don't include local chapters of large national organizations, there are hundreds, perhaps thousands, of organizations and publications for disabled people. The aim of this Resource Section is to equip you to find the information, assistance, or service you need for your ministry within your congregation, or for any other disabled person you know.

The list is organized in roughly the same way the book is. On page 275 is a table of contents. At the end of the section, on pages 303-4, are the names and addresses of the publishers listed throughout the section.

We listed religious resources from many different denominations as well as secular resources. We did not list organizations that had only a local ministry or influence. The ones in this list generally have many regional or local chapters, a hotline, or publications. We did not include private companies, such as makers of wheelchairs or hearing assistance devices. Publishers were the only private companies listed.

For religious materials, curriculum, congregational awareness materials, etc., this Resource Section is the first place to look. It will also give you a start on finding secular organizations that can help you. To find out what is available to you locally, even if you live in a small or rural community, try some of the following:

- A local hospital
- Your town or county government office
- Your local school system
- Your local library. A Chamber of Commerce will sometimes put together a reference book listing local organizations.
- The telephone book. This is organized according to products and services–look under Hearing Aids, Orthopedic Appliances, etc.
- Your local United Way or Community Chest
- For persons with mental retardation, your local ARC (Association of Retarded Citizens) chapter. Their national address and phone number is given on page 276.
- Other national information lines for particular kinds of disabilities or the headquarters of particular denominations (addresses and telephone numbers throughout this section).

Contents

Persons With Mental Retardation • 276

Persons With Other Disabilities • 282

Building a Caring Ministry • 294

Sources of Additional Information • 302

Persons With Mental Retardation

Secular Resources

**Administration on Developmental
Disabilities**
**Department of Health and Human
Services**
Room 531D, Humphrey Bldg.
Washington, DC 20201

The G. Allan Roeher Institute
Kinsmen Bldg., York University
4700 Keele St.
Downsview, Ontario, Canada

(Formerly Canadian Association for Community Living) Information exchange network; reference library; audiovisuals; workshops and symposiums; quarterly magazine, *Entourage,* in English and French

**National Association for
Retarded Citizens**
2501 Avenue J, Box 6109
Arlington, TX 76005
(817) 640-0204

Research, employment, family support, prevention, rights, information
Publications: Bimonthly newspaper, *arc,* $15/year; books: *How to Provide for Their Future; Developmental Checklist*; other books on community awareness, overview of mental retardation; employment, fact sheets

**National Down Syndrome
Congress**
1800 Dempster St.
Park Ridge, IL 60068
(800) 232-NDSC

Information, advocacy, help for parents; national convention
Publications: fact sheets, publications list, list of groups by state; *Down Syndrome News,* 10/year

National Down Syndrome Society
141 Fifth Ave.
New York, NY 10010
Hotline (800) 221-4602;
also (212) 460-9330

Sponsors research, provides educational materials, public awareness, mainstreaming of children. Publishes directory of parent support groups; list of publications available for professionals and parents; videos, magazines

**President's Commission on
Mental Retardation**
Cohen Federal Bldg., Room 4723
330 Independence Ave. SW
Washington, DC 20201

Religious Resources

Bethesda Lutheran Home
700 Hoffman Dr.
Watertown, WI 53094
Toll-free number, Resource and
Outreach Service (800) 458-0349;
(414) 261-3050 x284 in WI

National Christian resource center
on mentally retarded persons;
database and library; information
and referral; training tapes (audio
and video); workshops, seminars,
and speakers

**Christian Church Foundation for
the Handicapped**
P.O. Box 310
Louisville, TN 37777
Jim Pierson, Executive Director

Offers materials for helping establish programs in churches; congregational awareness materials,
Christian Education materials;
staff people are available for seminars and as consultants

Christian Overcomers, Inc.
246A Third Ave.
Westwood, NJ 07675

Quarterly newsletter, *The Over-
comer*; lending library (write for
catalog)

Ephphatha Services
Evangelical Lutheran Church in
America
8765 Higgins Rd.
Chicago, IL 60631-4187

Friendship Foundation
2850 Kalamazoo, SE
Grand Rapids, MI 49560

Support groups of parents and
teachers of mentally retarded persons throughout the U.S. and Canada (see *Friendship* series below
under "Curriculum")

Handi*Vangelism
Division of BCM International
237 Fairfield Ave.
Upper Darby, PA 19082

Training seminars; Handi*Camp;
BASIS (grief support for parents);
Hospital Sunday-school classes;
video training materials

**Mennonite Central Committee
Mennonite Developmental
Disability Services**
21 South 12th St.
Akron, PA 17501

Training Materials

**National Apostolate with
  Mentally Retarded Persons**
P.O. Box 4711
Columbia, SC 29240

Publications: book, *Sharing the
Journey,* NAMRP quarterly publication; newsletter, catechism video
course

National Council of Churches
Division of Education and
  Ministry
Task Force on Developmental
  Disabilities
475 Riverside Dr.—Room 706
New York, NY 10115

Shepherds Home and School
Box 400
Union Grove, WI 53182

Residential school for children,
residential training for adults, respite care for adults, workshops
  Bimonthly newsletter, *Shepherds Folder*

Bethesda Lutheran Home
700 Hoffman Dr.
Watertown, WI 53094

Quarterly newsletter *Breakthrough*; book, *Task Analysis* (for
setting objectives); two series of
twelve half-hour videotapes, one
on mental retardation in general,
one on mental retardation and the
church

**Board of Publication
Christian Reformed Church**
2850 Kalamazoo SE
Grand Rapids, MI 49506

Four films/videos on ministry to
mentally retarded people; available from TRAVARCA (800) 828-
8013; (800) 331-2546 in MI

**Christian Church Foundation for
  the Handicapped**
P.O. Box 310
Louisville, TN 37777

Handi*Vangelism
237 Fairfield Ave.
Upper Darby, PA 19082

Reaching the Disabled for Christ, a videotape training course, includes: preparing, accessibility, salvation for mentally retarded people, physical techniques, discipline, friendship

Johnson Bible College
Correspondence Dept.
Knoxville, TN 37998

Offers a correspondence course based on this book, *Reaching Out to Special People*, that can be taken for college credit

**National Apostolate with
Mentally Retarded Persons**
P.O. Box 4711
Columbia, SC 29240

Video catechism course

**Office of Religious Education
Archdiocese of Cincinnati**
100 E. Eighth St.,
Cincinnati, OH 45202

"Catechetical Process in Special Education," a series of 13 videotape programs to train special education teachers

Magazines

KEY to Christian Education
magazine
8121 Hamilton Ave.
Cincinnati, OH 45231

Quarterly Special Education column edited by Jim Pierson

Special Education Leadership
127 Ninth Ave., North
Nashville, TN 37234

Quarterly magazine; $7.50/year; first issue was Fall 1988.
Articles in first issue: "Developing a Ministry," "Autism: A Family Matter," "Self-Esteem in the Physically Disabled Person," "Can You Recognize a Learning Disability," "Do We Need a Special Education Department?"
Also a listing of resources, seminars, camps, and retreats

Curriculum

Books

Harris, Sandy. *Teaching Children and Youth with Mental Handicaps in Sunday School.* Southern Baptist Convention.

Hawley, Gloria H. *How to Teach the Mentally Retarded.* Scripture Press, 1981

Nabi, Gene. *Teaching Adults with Mental Handicaps in Sunday School.* Southern Baptist Convention.

Nabi, Gene. *Ministering to Persons with Mental Retardation and Their Families.* Southern Baptist Convention.

Wood, Andrew H. *Unto the Least of These/Special Education in the Church.* Regular Baptist Press. 1984.

A large array of pictograph, teaching pictures, object talk books, stickers, children's materials, etc. for teaching is available from Standard Publishing. Write for the latest catalog or call (800) 543-1353

If not here, addresses of publishers can be found on pp. 303-4

American Bible Society
National Distribution Dept.
1865 Broadway
New York, NY 10023

"Special Education" pamphlets (two series of eight pamphlets with easy Scripture translation and art); "Good News for Young Readers" similar to above, but for kids

Order from ABS
P.O. Box 5656
Grand Central Station
New York, NY 10063

Bethesda Lutheran Home
700 Hoffman Dr.
Watertown, WI 53094

Quarterly newsletter, *Breakthrough,* provides Bible lessons for the quarter for older children and adults.

Board of Publication
Christian Reformed Church

Friendship series, a three-year curriculum, one for older children and one for adults. Includes Teacher's Manual, Group Leader's Kit, visual aids, and Student Resources

Cokesbury Service Center

Living In Faith, a book of 52 lesson plans and helps for older children and adults

Concordia Publishers

Bible Stories series;
Christian Faith series

Ephphatha Services
Evangelical Lutheran Church in
   America
8765 Higgins Rd.
Chicago, IL 60631-4187

AFFIRM series

National Council of Churches
Division of Education and
   Ministry
Task Force on Developmental
   Disabilities
475 Riverside Dr., Room 706
New York, NY 10015

Expanding Worlds, for adults

Scripture Press Publications

Happy Time course, for children. Includes teacher's book, pictures, and a copy of *How to Teach the Mentally Retarded* by Gloria Hawley

Shepherds Home and School
Box 400
Union Grove, WI 53182

Southern Baptist Convention
Special Ministries Department

Special Ministries Resource Kit, quarterly lessons for youth and adults

Winston Press, Inc.

Two series: *Gift,* for children and youth; *Growing Together in Jesus,* for adults

Persons With Other Disabilities

Physical Disability
Secular Resources

(for Religious Resources, see specific disability or list beginning on page 294).

American Paralysis Association
P.O. Box 187
Short Hills, NJ 07078
APA SCI Hotline: (800) 526-3456;
  (800) 638-1733 in MD

Information and referral, also a network of volunteer peers to help with support and solutions to problems

Candlelighters
1901 Pennsylvania Ave NW
Suite 1001
Washington, DC 20006

An international network of groups of parents and children with cancer; crisis line, residences for parents
  Publications: Quarterly newsletters for adults and for youth; publications list; camp list; *Starting Support Groups*

Children's Defense Fund
122 C St. NW
Washington, DC 20001-2193

Monthly newsletter, *CDF Reports*

Clearinghouse on the Handicapped
Department of Education
Room 3132–Switzer Bldg.
Washington, DC 20202-2319

Disabled American Veterans
807 Maine Ave., SW
Washington, DC 20024
(202) 554-3501

Help with government benefits, transportation, job training, scholarships for children, emergency financial help; outreach to native American, homeless, and incarcerated veterans
  Monthly magazine, *DAV Magazine*

Epilepsy Foundation of America
4351 Garden City Dr., Suite 406
Landover, MD 20785
Hotline: 1-800-EFA-1000 between 9-5 EST; call (301) 459-3700 for nearest affiliate

Monthly newspaper, *National Spokesman;* research, information and education, advocacy, employment programs, resource center

March of Dimes
1275 Mamaroneck Ave.
White Plains, NY 10605

Prevention of birth defects, public health education, prenatal health care, help with high-risk pregnancies; catalog of Public Health Education materials includes *Your Special Child;* also *Families With Special Needs Children* kit (teacher book, ten student, two tapes, filmstrip)

Muscular Dystrophy Association of America
810 Seventh Ave.
New York, NY 10019

Research, patient services, professional and public education, clinics and summer camps; MDA may help with payments for treatment and other services

National Association of the Physically Handicapped
76 Elm St.
London, OH 43140

Advocacy, eliminate barriers, promote leadership among handicapped people, transportation and architecture, provide activities, help with employment; quarterly newsletter, $12/year

National Cystic Fibrosis Foundation
6931 Arlington Rd.
Bethesda, MD 20814
(800) FIGHT-CF

National Easter Seal Society
2023 West Ogden Ave.
Chicago, IL 60612
Phone (312) 243-8880 (TDD)

Therapy, vocational training, recreation, counseling, prevention of disabling conditions; catalog listing publications on attitudes about disabilities, caregiving, recreation, speech impairments

National Hemophilia Foundation
110 Greene St., Room 406
New York, NY 10012

Quarterly magazine, *Hemophilia Newsnotes;* educational materials list; also brochures for sale on general and specific topics dealing with hemophilia; directory of hemophilia treatment centers

**National Multiple Sclerosis
Society**
205 East 42nd St.
New York, NY 10017-5706
Information Resource Center,
phone (800) 624-8236

Research, information, community
service
Publications: Quarterly magazine *Inside MS*, booklets: *Living
with Multiple Sclerosis/A Practical
Guide* and *What Everyone Should
Know About MS*; list of others

National Self-Help Clearinghouse
184 Fifth Ave.
New York, NY 10010

**National Spinal Cord Injury
Foundation**
600 W. Cummings Park
Suite 2000
Woburn, MA 01801
(800) 962-9629

Publications: Fact sheets, quarterly newsletter, yearly directory,
National Resource Directory ($20)
Develop regional systems for care,
rehabilitation, community living;
educate public and professionals
Through chapters, counseling,
motivation, advocacy on accessibility issues

Office of Civil Rights
Department of Health and Human
Services
330 Independence Ave. SW
Washington, DC 20201

Places to call for questions about
rights, accessibility, employment,
education, health care, etc.
Publication: *Your Rights as a
Disabled Person*

**Osteogenesis Imperfecta
Foundation**
P.O. Box 14807
Clearwater, FL 34629-4807

Publications: Quarterly newsletter
Breakthrough, reprints of articles
on osteogenesis imperfecta

**Spina Bifida Association of
America**
1700 Rockville Pike, Suite 540
Rockville, MD 20852-1631
(800) 621-3141

Adult network; research; legisla-
tion; adoption information; public
education
Publications: Bimonthly newsletter, *Insights*; list of print and
audiovisual information

United Cerebral Palsy Association, Inc.
66 East 34th St.
New York, NY 10016
(800) USA-1UCP

Publications on communication devices, wills, baby care, employment, respite care, others

Many lending libraries for visually impaired people offer Bibles, books, and magazines on cassette for people with mobility impairments. See under "Visual Impairment."

Magazines

Accent on Living
P.O. Box 700
Bloomington, IL 61702

Quarterly magazine with articles and ads mainly for physically disabled people; $2 each, $6/yr, $9/for two years
Also books and other publications for physically disabled persons

The Exceptional Parent
605 Commonwealth Ave.
Boston, MA 02215

Eight issues/year; $3.50/issue or $16/year
Feature articles on traveling, instructions for respite care, hospitalization, tube feeding, continuous education programs
Departments: letters, resources, children's page ("If I Ran the Hospital"), family life, news, editorial, book reviews
They also offer books on parenting

Hearing Impairment

Alexander Graham Bell Association for the Deaf
3417 Volta Place Northwest
Washington, DC 20007-2778
(202) 337-5220 TDD/voice

Emphasis on speech teaching
International Parents Organization (IPO) forms support groups
Information, lending library, children's rights, conferences, scholarships
Publications: *Newsounds* newsletter, 10/year; *The Volta Review*, 7/year; *Our Kids* magazine

American Ministries to the Deaf
7564 Brown's Mill Road
Kauffman Station
Chambersburg, PA 17201

Trains and sends out missionaries to deaf people; workshops, leadership training, helping churches, Bible correspondence school; *Hearing Hearts* magazine is free to deaf people

Deaf and Hard of Hearing Institute
7036 Harrison Ave.
Cincinnati, OH 45247
(513) 353-4129

Materials, referrals, "deaf awareness," revival meetings

Deaf Evangelism
Gospel Publishing House
1445 Boonville Ave.
Springfield, MO 65802

Several excellent books on sign language: *The Joy of Signing*, 2nd ed., *Sign Language Made Simple*, and *Talk to the Deaf*
The Joy of Signing is available in video from Joy Enterprises, Inc., P.O. Box 10376, Arlington, VA 22210-1376

Deaf Ministries International
P.O. Box 182
Concord, CA 94522

Book, *No Time to Lose*, about deaf ministry

Deaf Missions
R.R. 2 Box 26
Council Bluffs, IA 51503
Duane King, Director

Materials, referral, "deaf awareness," speakers
Publications: *The Bible, ASL Translation*; *Daily Devotions for the Deaf*, Bible visuals catalog; quarterly report

Deaf Opportunity Out Reach
9920 Long Point
Houston, TX 77055

Sends out teams of deaf people for church planting and assistance, leadership training in deaf churches

Episcopal Conference of the Deaf
P.O. Box 27459
Philadelphia, PA 19150

Annual conference; clergy and lay person training

Helen Keller National Center for Deaf-Blind Youths and Adults
111 Middle Neck Rd.
Sands Point, NY 10050

Brochure, "Without Sight and Sound"
Services: diagnostic, technical assistance, counseling, employment, advocacy

Lutheran Church, Missouri Synod
Ministry to the Deaf
1333 South Kirkwood Rd.
St. Louis, MO 63122-7295

National Association for the Deaf
814 Thayer Ave.
Silver Springs, MD 20910
(301) 587-1788 TDD/voice

Public Information Center; information and referrals
Publications: Monthly newsletter, *The NAD Broadcaster,* quarterly magazine, *The Deaf American;* textbooks on ASL, four books on special signs for religious services; books on signing, novels, research, others. Write for catalog

National Catholic Office for the Deaf
814 Thayer Ave.
Silver Springs, MD 20910

Works within the Catholic church on behalf of deaf people
Publications: Bimonthly magazine, *Listening*; book, *Signs for Catholic Liturgy and Education*

National Council of Churches
Division of Education and Ministry
Task Force on Hearing Impairments
475 Riverside Dr., Room 706
New York, NY 10115

Visual Impairment

National Information Center on Deafness
Gallaudet College
Kendall Green
Washington, DC 20002
(800) 672-6720 x5051 or x5052; voice (202) 651-5051; TDD (202) 651-5052

Information about deafness and related topics; catalog of materials, directory of organizations, directory of church organizations; notebook, *Workshop on Developing Religious Materials for Deaf People*

SHHH (Self Help for Hard of Hearing People, Inc.)
7800 Wisconsin Ave.
Bethesda, MD 20814

American Bible Society
National Distribution Dept.
1865 Broadway
New York, NY 10023
(800) 543-8000

Bible in large print, cassette, and braille (KJV, Good News, and Spanish)

Order from ABS
P.O. Box 5656
Grand Central Station
New York, NY 10063

American Brotherhood for the Blind
18440 Oxnard St.
Tarzana, CA 91356

"Twin-Vision" print and braille books; free semimonthly braille newspaper, *Hotline to the Deaf-Blind;* small braille calendars are available in October; when you write, show on the envelope what department you are interested in

American Foundation for the Blind
15 West 16th St.
New York, NY 10011
(800) AFB-LIND; (212) 620-2127 in Maryland

AFB Directory of Services; Journal (10/year)

American Printing House for the Blind
P.O. Box 6085
Louisville, KY 40206-0085

3500-volume library; publications in braille, large type, talking books, and music; catalogs for each type of publication; includes textbooks and even custom printing

Catalogs for "Instructional Aids; tools; supplies for the visually handicapped." These include braille writing devices, tape players (half speed), and computer hardware and software

Bible Alliance Inc.
P.O. Box 621
Bradenton, FL 34206

Bibles and Bible studies on cassette, free for visually impaired and physically handicapped persons (you must be certified by a doctor); the Bible in 27 languages

Braille Bible Foundation
4096 Northeast 6th Avenue
Oakland Park, FL 33334

Braille Circulating Library
2700 Stuart Ave.
Richmond, VA 23220

Christian Mission for the Sightless
5406 Boy Scout Rd.
Indianapolis, IN 46226

Christian Record Braille Foundation
4444 South 52nd St.
Lincoln, NE 68516

Eleven publications: original magazines, Bible studies; list of camps for visually impaired persons; library, scholarships, also helps for hearing impaired persons

Christian Fellowship for the Blind International, Inc.
P.O. Box 26
South Pasadena, CA 91030

Quarterly Newsletter, *The Bartimaeus Review*

In braille: *Decision, Power for Living,* and 350 titles

On tape: *Decision, Moody Monthly, Focus on the Family, Our Daily Bread, Discovery Digest, Power for Living,* 150 titles

Braille and tape circulating libraries, Christian counseling, information; referral and activity center; training for workers

Episcopal Guild for the Blind
157 Montage St.
Brooklyn, NY 11201

Has braille circulating library, cassette program, including books recorded on request, and tapespondence (personal counseling via cassette by director, blind since birth)

Gospel Association for the Blind
P.O. Box 62
Delray Beach, FL 33447

Monthly magazines: *Gospel Messenger* and *Jottings*; 2500 religious volumes

Helen Keller National Center for Deaf-Blind Youths and Adults
(see above under "Hearing Impairment")

Howe Press
Perkins School for the Blind
Watertown, MA 02172

Has catalog of materials available

Library of Congress
Division of Blind and Physically Handicapped
Washington, DC 20542

Lends in braille, large print, cassette or disc; 49,000 books; 70 magazines; and lends special equipment for playing cassettes or discs.
Music books or scores in braille or large print
Bimonthly publications announce new books and services
You must be a U.S. citizen and blind or physically disabled and certified by a doctor

National Federation of the Blind
218 Randolph Hotel
Des Moines, IA 50309

Has catalog of aids and appliances for visually impaired persons

Learning Disability

Recording for the Blind, Inc.
20 Roszel Rd.
Princeton, NJ 08540
(609) 452-0606

Lends books on tape; 72,000 total, 3000 new each year, to those with visual, perceptual, or physical handicaps; $25 registration fee
Quarterly newsletter, *Recording for the Blind News;* they specialize in college texts

U.S. Association for Blind Athletes
33 North Institute St.
Brown Hall, Suite 015
Colorado Springs, CO 80903

Publications; rulebook for blind athletes, bimonthly newsletter, *SportsScoop*

Association for Children and Adults With Learning Disabilities
4156 Library Rd.
Pittsburgh, PA 15234

Resource center of over 500 publications for sale; film rentals; newsletter, *Newsbrief,* 5/year

Association of Learning Disabled Adults
P.O. Box 9722
Friendship Station
Washington, D.C. 20016

Council for Learning Disabilities
P.O. Box 40303
Overland Park, KS 66204

Mainly professionals who work with learning disabilities
Several newsletters and other periodicals

Foundation for Children with Learning Disabilities
99 Park Ave. – 6th Floor
New York, NY 10016

FCLD state-by-state resource guide

Books

Cherne, Jacqolyn. *The Learning Disabled Child in Your Sunday School* Concordia, 1983.

Evans, J.S. *An Uncommon Gift.* Westminster, 1983.

Behavior Disorder

Association of Mental Health Clergy
12320 River Oaks Pt.
Knoxville, TN 37922

Mennonite Central Committee
Mennonite Mental Health
Services
21 South 12th St.
Akron, PA 17501

National Association of Christian Social Workers
Box 90
St. Davids, PA 19087-0690

National Mental Health Association
1021 Prince St.
Alexandria, VA 22314-2971

Quarterly newsletter, *Focus,* $15/yr; also has catalog of publications
Manual for Law Enforcement: Aiding People in Conflict will be useful for ministers and other leaders as a short "how-to" manual for aiding people in crisis
Educational information and referral
Specializes in the mental health needs of homeless and unemployed people

Seraphim Communications Inc.
1568 Eustus St.
St. Paul, MN 55108

Autism

Mental Illness

Autism Services Center
Douglass Executive Bldg.
Tenth Ave. and Bruce St.
Huntington, WV 25701
Hotline (304) 525-8014; (in WV call collect)

Information, advocacy, training

Autism Society of America
1234 Massachusetts Ave. NW
Suite 1017
Washington, DC 20005
(202) 783-0125

Information and referral; government advocacy
  Newsletter, bookstore

National Alliance for the Mentally Ill
2101 Wilson Blvd., Suite 302
Arlington, VA 22201
(703) 524-7600

National Alliance for the Mentally Ill
Religious Outreach Network
5350 Brooke Ridge Dr.
Dunwoody, GA 30338

Pathways to Promise
c/o Alliance for the Mentally Ill
131 W. Monroe, Suite 8
St. Louis, MO 63122

Funded by Lutheran Church, Missouri Synod, to help congregations work with those having mental illness, train clergy, and build a directory of churches and a resource center
  Publications: six books and brochures; includes *Models of Care* and *An Annotated Bibliography*

Building a Caring Ministry

Disabled People and the Church

Christian League for the Handicapped
P.O. Box 948
Walworth, WI 53184

Mainly for physically disabled people; summer camp, conferences, chapters in nine states
Publications: Quarterly newsletter, *The Bulletin;* pamphlets on accessibility and friendship

Ephphatha Services
Evangelical Lutheran Church in America
8765 W. Higgins Rd.
Chicago, IL 60631-4187

Episcopal Awareness Center on Handicaps
4805 Manion St.
Annandale, VA 22003

Provides information on services required by handicapped people
Religious programs, leader training, referral, information, lending of materials; books, manuals, films

Grace Community Church
13248 Roscoe Blvd.
Sun Valley, CA 91352

Several publications on ministry with disabled people: physical, mental retardation, families, awareness

Handi*Vangelism
Division of BCM International
237 Fairfield Ave.
Upper Darby, PA 19082

Training seminars; Handi*Camp; BASIS (grief support for parents); Hospital Sunday-school classes; *Reaching the Disabled for Christ,* videotape training course

Lutheran Church, Missouri Synod
1333 S. Kirkwood Rd.
St Louis, MO 63122-7295
(314) 965-9000

Write for list of publications. Publishes a series of 18 booklets that can be used in churches or day schools in setting up a program for disabled people

National Catholic Office for Persons with Disabilities
401 Michigan Ave. NE, Room 11
P.O. Box 29113
Washington, DC 20017
(202) 529-2933, voice/TDD

We Are One Flock video, posters; quarterly newsletter, *National NCPD Update; Opening Doors* is a two-volume pastoral manual and resource file designed to help foster participation of people with disabilities in churches

**Special Education Ministries
Church of the Nazarene**
6401 The Paseo—P.O. Box 419527
Kansas City, MO 64141

Network of over 100 volunteer consultants for churches; lists of Christian resources and group homes
Film, *There's No One Exactly Like Me;* brochures and fact sheets on learning disabilities, behavior disorders, other

Stephen Ministries
1325 Boland
St. Louis, MO 63117

Training programs for caregiving in specialized ministries (hospitalization, grief, hospice, suicide, childbirth, divorce, shut-ins). A church sponsors potential "Stephen Ministers" for 10-day seminar at $975 plus lodging
Resource catalog

United Methodist Church Discipleship Resources
P.O. Box 840
Nashville, TN 37202

Catalog of books and resource packets on mental retardation, learning disabilities, deafness, respite care

Magazines

A Positive Approach magazine
1600 Malone St.
Municipal Airport
Millville, NJ 08332

Christian magazine for the physically disabled person; published bimonthly; $12.50/year
Wide range of articles—reviews, news, profiles, practical information, children's section

God's Special People magazine
P.O. Box 729
Ocean Shores, WA 98569

Quarterly magazine, 36 pages,
$10/year

Special Education Leadership
magazine
127 Ninth Ave., North
Nashville, TN 37234

Quarterly magazine; $7.50/year;
first issue was Fall 1988
Articles in first issue: "Developing a Ministry," "Autism: A Family Matter," "Self-Esteem in the Physically Disabled Person," "Can You Recognize a Learning Disability," "Do We Need a Special Education Department?"
Also a listing of resources, seminars, camps, and retreats

Books

Anderson, W., T. Gould, and J.L. Paul. *We Don't Have Any Here.* Discipleship Resources, 1986. Describes specialized ministries and outlines methods of starting them in your church

Bishop, Marilyn. *Ministry with Them/Parish Ministry with Disabled People.* MORES, 1983.

Cook, Ellen, ed. *Sharing the Journey.* William C. Brown Co., 1986. Designed to help families work through issues relating to their mentally retarded child. Published by NAMRP (p. 278)

Haugk, Kenneth. *Christian Caregiving/A Way of Life.* Augsburg, 1984.

Korth, Robert E., ed. *Special Ministries for Caring Churches.* Standard, 1986. Discusses a wide variety of specialized ministries your church can start

Newman, Gene, and Joni Eareckson Tada. *All God's Children/ Ministry to the Disabled.* Zondervan, 1987. An overview on organizing for ministry to persons with disabilities

Perske, Robert. *Circles of Friends.* Abingdon, 1988.

Perske, Robert. *New Life in the Neighborhood;* Abingdon, 1980.

Awareness

Schuster, Clara S., ed. *Jesus Loves Me, Too.* Beacon Hill Press, 1985. Geared toward children's ministry; extensive resources

Tada, Joni Eareckson. *Friendship Unlimited.* Harold Shaw Publishers, 1987. How to overcome personal barriers and be a better friend to disabled people

Wood, Andrew H. *Unto the Least of These.* Regular Baptist Press, 1984. Ministry to mentally retarded persons in the local church, formal and informal

Congregational Awareness
8 Vista Hermosa
Walnut Creek, CA 94596

Provides home-study course, leadership training materials

Christian and Missionary Alliance Special Ministries
Box C
Nyack, NY 10960

The Healing Community
139 Walworth Ave.
White Plains, NY 10606
Harold Wilke, Executive Director

Congregational awareness materials; materials for accessibility

Joni and Friends
P.O. Box 3333
Agoura Hills, CA 91301

Free Handicap Awareness Day materials; resource list; books and videos; tapes from Congress on the Church and the Disabled; films, *Let's Be Friends* and *Meet My Friends,* are available from D.C. Cook Publishers

Power Ministries
1732 Thames Dr.
Clarksville, IN 47130
Jerry Borton, Director

Family

The Service Center
United Methodist Church
7820 Reading Rd.
Cincinnati, OH 45222-1800

Distribution center for United
Methodist Church Board of Global
Ministries. Features accessibility
audit materials

Books

Carder, Stan. *Why Bother?* Grace
Church Publications, 1987.

Jansen, Larry. *My Sister Is Special*
Standard, 1984. A picture book
for children about Down syndrome

Perske, Robert. *Don't Stop the
Music.* Abingdon, 1986. Novel.

_____ , *Show Me No Mercy*
Abingdon, 1984. Novel.

*The Church's Ministry with Dis-
abled Persons.* Presbyterian
Publishing House. Survey your
congregation on disabilities,
attitudes; accessibility data

Wilke, Harold H. *Creating the Caring Congregation.* Abingdon,
1980.

The Exceptional Parent
605 Commonwealth Ave.
Boston, MA 02215

Eight issues/year; $3.50/issue or
$16/year
Feature articles: Traveling, instructions for respite care, hospitalization, tube feeding, continuous education programs
Departments: letters, resources,
children's page ("If I Ran the Hospital"), family life, news, editorial,
book reviews
They also offer books on parenting

March of Dimes
1275 Mamaroneck Ave.
White Plains, NY 10605

300 chapters; these do fundraising,
public education, helping high-risk
pregnancies
Prevention of birth defects, public health education, prenatal
health care
Catalog of Public Health Education materials includes *Your Special Child;* also *Families With
Special Needs Children* kit
(teacher book, 10 student, 2 tapes,
filmstrip)

Parents of Down Syndrome Children (PODS)
c/o Montgomery County ARC
11600 Nebel St.
Rockville, MD 20852

Publication, *Caring for Babies with Down Syndrome*

Books

Bartel, D., and A. Neufeldt. *Supportive Care in the Congregation* Mennonite Central Committee.

Cook, Ellen, ed. *Sharing the Journey*. William Brown, 1986.

Ikeler, Bernard. *Parenting Your Disabled Child*. Westminster, 1986.

Kingsley, M.L., and D. Heffelbower. *After We're Gone: Estate and Life Planning for a Disabled Person's Family*. Mennonite Central Committee.

Ministering to the Family of the Handicapped/A Handbook for Pastors. Grace Community Church, 1986.

Murphy, Judith K. *Sharing Care: The Christian Ministry of Respite Care*. Pilgrim Press, 1986.

Perske, Robert. *Hope for the Families*. Abingdon, 1981.

Wheeler, Bonnie G. *Challenged Parenting*. Regal, 1982.

Sports, Camping, Travel

American Camping Association
Bradford Woods
5000 State Rd. 67
N. Martinsville, IN 46151-7902

Parent's Guide to Accredited Camps lists camps for various kinds of disabilities

Canine Companions for Independence
P.O. Box 446
Santa Rosa, CA 95402-0446

Trains specially bred dogs to help people with disabilities other than blindness

Christian Berets
1325 Yosemite Blvd.
Modesto, CA 95354
Don Crooker, Executive Director

Summer camp program, field trips, other needs of handicapped people

Closing the Gap
P.O. Box 68
Henderson, MN 56044

Provides information on computer technology available for disabled people through publications, workshops, and an annual conference
  Publications: *Closing the Gap,* bimonthly, reviews, $26/yr U.S.; *Closing the Gap Resource Directory,* updated each year, $12.95

Crossroads (Queensland) Fellowship With Handicapped Persons
1st Floor – Wesley House,
140 Ann St.
Brisbane 4000, Australia

National Handicapped Sports and Recreation Association
1145 19th St. NW, Suite 717
Washington, DC 20036

Mostly skiing, but also fitness programs for paraplegics and quadriplegics; aerobics, strength, flexibility, weight, nutrition; exercise aerobics videotapes are available

National Wheelchair Athletic Association
3617 Betty Dr., Suite S
Colorado Springs, CO 80917-5993

Quarterly newsletter, rulebooks, local and regional games

Special Olympics International
1350 New York Ave NW, Suite 500
Washington, DC 20005

100,000 athletes, 600,000 volunteers, now in 73 countries
Publications: books and videos, 23 Sports Skills program books, newsletter

Travel Information Services
c/o Moss Rehabilitation Hospital
12th St. and Tabor Rd.
Philadelphia, PA 19141

Resource and Information Center for Disabled Individuals; for $5 (make check payable to Moss Rehabilitation Hospital), will provide an information package on three U.S. cities on travel accessibility: information on buses, trains, air travel, car rentals, hotels equipped for handicapped people; send one month ahead, no road maps

U.S. Association for Blind Athletes
33 North Institute St.
Brown Hall, Suite 015
Colorado Springs, CO 80903

Publications: rulebook for blind athletes; bimonthly newsletter, *SportsScoop*

Book

Miller, Earl H. *Camping with Persons with Handicapping Conditions* Pilgrim Press, 1982.

Sources of Additional Information

American Association on Mental Retardation
Religion Division
2533 Empire Forest Dr.
Tucker, GA 30084
(404) 621-0849

For $10, offers list from AAMR exhibit of religious materials

Bethesda Lutheran Home
700 Hoffman Dr.
Watertown, WI 53094
Resource and Outreach Service
(800) 458-0349; (414) 261-3050 x284 in WI

National Christian resource center on mentally retarded persons; database and library; information and referral

Directory for Exceptional Children
Porter Sargent Publishers
11 Beacon St.
Boston, MA 02108

Episcopal Awareness Center on Handicaps
4805 Manion St.
Annandale, VA 22003

Provides information on services required by handicapped people
Religious programs, leader training, referral, information, lending of materials; books, manuals, films

MORES – Ministry with Handicapped People
The University of Dayton
300 College Park
Dayton, OH 45469-0001

Resource book $8

National Catholic Office for Persons with Disabilities
401 Michigan NE, Room 11
P.O. Box 29113
Washington, DC 20017

Opening Doors is a two-volume pastoral manual and resource file designed to help foster participation of people with disabilities in churches

Publishers

National Information Center for Handicapped Children and Youth
Box 1492
Washington, DC 20013

(Formerly called *Closer Look*)
Personal responses to specific questions, referrals, information packets, technical assistance
Publications: general resources, fact sheets, legal information, careers in special education, resources for teachers

National Information System for Health Related Services

(800) 922-1107; directory of state services

People-to-People Committee for the Handicapped
P.O. Box 18131
Washington, DC 20036

Offers a Directory of Organizations Interested in the Handicapped

Abingdon Press
201 8th Ave. South
Nashville TN 37202

Augsburg Publishing House
426 South Fifth St.
Box 1209
Minneapolis, MN 55440

Bible Club Movement, International
(Handi*Vangelism)
237 Fairfield Ave.
Upper Darby, PA 19082

Cokesbury Service Center
201 8th Ave. South
Nashville, TN 37202

Concordia Publishing House
3558 S. Jefferson Ave.
St. Louis, MO 63118

David C. Cook Publishing Co.
850 North Grove Ave.
Elgin, IL 60120

Discipleship Resources
(United Methodist Church)
P.O. Box 840
Nashville, TN 37202

Faith and Life Press
718 Main St., Box 347
Newton, KS 63114-0347

Grace Community Church
13248 Roscoe Blvd.
Sun Valley, CA 91352

Harold Shaw Publishers
P.O. Box 567
388 Gunderson Dr.
Wheaton, IL 60189

Herald Press
616 Walnut Ave.
Scottdale, PA 15683

**MORES—Ministry with
   Handicapped People**
The University of Dayton
300 College Park
Dayton, OH 45469-0001

**Nazarene Publishing House
(Beacon Hill Press)**
6401 The Paseo
Kansas City, MO 64131

Paulist Press
997 Macarthur Blvd.
Mahwah, NJ 07430

Pilgrim Press
United Church Board/Homeland
   Ministries
132 W. 31st St.
New York, NY 10001

Presbyterian Publishing House
341 Ponce de Leon Ave., NE
Atlanta, GA 30365

**Scripture Press
(Victor Books)**
1825 College Ave.
Wheaton, IL 60187

Southern Baptist Convention
Sunday School Board
Special Ministries Department
127 Ninth Ave. North
Nashville, TN 37234

Standard Publishing
8121 Hamilton Ave.
Cincinnati, OH 45231

Templegate Publishers
302 E. Adams St.
Springfield, IL 62701

Westminster Press
925 Chestnut St.
Philadelphia, PA 19107

Winston Press, Inc.
Harper Religious Books
Icehouse 1-401, 151 Union St.
San Francisco, CA 94111

Word Publishing
Box 1790
Waco, TX 76796

Evaluation

*A test for determining
the knowledge of students
with trainable mental retardation*

Basic Information

Name _____ Age _____

Address _____

_____ Birthday _____

Telephone _____ Grade level in school _____

Parents' names _____

_____

Siblings' names _____

_____

_____

Does the family attend church regularly? _____

SECTION ONE: General Information

You will need a Bible and five pictures: 1. Jesus with children (including a handicapped child); 2. the devil (red man, horns, pointed tail, etc.); 3. a happy face and a sad face; 4. boys fighting; 5. boys shaking hands (or being friendly).

Question/Task	Response Desired	Comments
Sing "Jesus Loves Me"	The child sings along, says or mouths some of the words, or otherwise shows familiarity with it.	

Show the picture of Jesus and the children. Say,

Most people are happy when they are with somebody they love. Who are these children with?	Jesus	
Why are they happy?	They are with Jesus.	

Show a picture of the devil and ask the following questions:

Who is this?	The devil, Satan	
Where does he live?	Hell or "down there"	

Where do angels live?	With God, in Heaven, or similar answer	

Where do good people go when they die?	Heaven or "up there"	

Where do bad people go?	Hell or "down there"	

Show the pictures of the boys fighting and the boys shaking hands.

Which is the good thing to do?	Being friendly or shaking hands
Which boys have the happy faces?	The boys being friendly

Open a Bible between the two testaments.

What are the names of the two parts of the Bible?	Old Testament and New Testament
If no response, say, *These are called testaments. What kinds of testaments are they?*	First part is the Old Testament. Second part is the New Testament.
If no response, ask, *Which comes first, the Old or New Testament?*	Old Testament

SECTION TWO: God

Question/Task	Response Desired	Comments
Where does God live, in the sky or the ground?	In the sky	
Did God make me?	Yes	
Did He make clouds?	Yes	
Did He make worms?	Yes	
Does God listen to you?	Yes	

SECTION THREE: Jesus

You will need pictures or figures dressed like the good Samaritan, a priest, and a Levite, and three other sets of pictures: 1. A bedroom, hospital, and manger; 2. a mother and father, a mother and son, a pair of children, and a father and son; 3. Jesus as a boy, a child playing, a child working, a child being destructive.

Question/Task	Response Desired	Comments
Show pictures of a bedroom, hospital, and manger.		
Where was baby Jesus laid?	In a manger	
Show a picture of a mother and father, a mother and son, a pair of children, and a father and son.		
Which picture is like God and Jesus?	The father and son	
A new boy moved into town. Nobody wants to play with him. How would Jesus treat the new boy?	Jesus would show kindness to him.	
With figures dressed like the characters, tell the story of the good Samaritan.		
Which of the men would make Jesus happy?	The good Samaritan	
How should we act toward other people who need help?	Help them, be good to them	

Show pictures of Jesus as a boy. Tell that Jesus helped Joseph in the carpenter shop and played with other children. Show pictures of a child playing, a child working, and a child being destructive.

Which would Jesus not act like?

Jesus would not act like the destructive child.

Does Jesus want us to say and do bad things?

No

SECTION FOUR: The Bible

You will need four books: a telephone directory, a story book, a Bible, and a cookbook.

Question/Task	Response Desired	Comments
Show the four books.		
Which book is best?	The Bible	
Why?	Because it is God's Word. God gave it to us (or similar answers).	
Who gave us the Bible — Teacher, Mommy, Daddy, or God?	God	

SECTION FIVE: The Church
You will need six pictures: a church building, a house, a girl praying, a boy taking Communion, a boy playing ball, a girl singing.

Question/Task	Response Desired	Comments

Show a picture of a church building and a house.

Where do we usually go to worship with other people? — The church building

Show pictures of girl praying, boy taking Communion, a boy playing ball, a girl singing.

Which do we do in church? — All but play ball

Which day do we go to church — Tuesday, Sunday, or Monday? — Sunday.

SECTION SIX: Christian Activities
You will need some coins and three pictures: a woman talking on a telephone, a thief, and a person praying.

Question/Task	Response Desired	Comments

Show a picture of a person praying and a lady talking on the telephone.

How is praying like talking on the telephone?	We talk to God by praying. The lady talks to someone else by talking on the telephone.

Show the coins.

If a person gave you this money, would you keep it or give it to somebody who really needs it?	Give it to someone who needs it

If you found money on a table and knew whose it was, what would you do?	Give it to the owner

Show a picture of a thief and a picture of someone praying.

Which one is doing wrong?	The thief

Jesus is God's Son, and He died. Why did He die?	For us

If you saw a friend fall off his bicycle, what would you do?	Help him

Conclusions

Concepts the child needs to understand

1. _____

2. _____

3. _____

4. _____

5. _____

Other Comments

Dates the test was administered   First time/Retests

Section One
Section Two
Section Three
Section Four
Section Five
Section Six

Index

abortion 72f, 179

abstract principles 20, 28, 37-41, 109

acceptance 133f, 139, 143, 149, 167f, 178f, 186f, 191f, 194

accepting Christ 51, 61, 134f, 168

accessibility 80-2, 145-8, 168, 179, 187; audit for 82, 297; criteria for 147f; and hearing impairment 85f, 147; and learning disability 120; and mental retardation 148; and mobility impairment 14, 80-2, 146, 147, 186f; and visual impairment 147

adapting children's curriculum 50f, 194f

adaptive behavior 32, 33

adolescents, with learning disability 110-2; with mental retardation 33, 50, 197

adults, with behavior disorder 117-26, 156f; with hearing impairment 84f; with learning disability 107, 111f; with mental retardation 19-30, 33, 50, 151-4;

with mobility impairment 72-82, 186; with visual impairment 102, 104

aggression 24-6, 118

Alzheimer's disease 20, 23

American Association on Mental Retardation, 32, 302

American Sign Language 85f, 92

anxiety 44, 118

apostles 131f

architectural barriers 80-2, 146f, 168, 187

art activities 54, 64, 104

assistance 27, 34f, 73-6, 140, 156f, 158, 181-3

association 37, 44, 45

Association for Retarded Citizens 32, 193, 275, 276

attention-getting behavior 42, 156f

attention span 35f, 39, 42, 46, 52, 113, 118, 124f, 171, 195

attitude, barriers of, 133f, 136, 142-6, 148, 158, 180f; of children 101, 103, 106, 192f; of congregation 14, 133-5, 137, 139, 158,

313